Marketing Research

MARKETING RESEARCH

Richa Arora
Nitin R. Mahankale
both Faculty, Symbiosis Centre for Management Studies
Symbiosis International University
Pune (Maharashtra)

PHI Learning Private Limited
Delhi-110092
2013

₹ 250.00

MARKETING RESEARCH
Richa Arora and Nitin R. Mahankale

ISBN-978-81-203-4669-7

Published by Asoke K. Ghosh, PHI Learning Private Limited, Rimjhim House, 111, Patparganj Industrial Estate, Delhi-110092 and Printed by Raj Press, New Delhi-110012.

To

My Parents, Mr. Naresh Mehta and Mrs. Santosh Mehta

with Love and Respect

Richa Arora

To

All My Students

Nitin R. Mahankale

Contents

Preface

The increasing importance of **research** has inevitably been reflected in the popularity of courses dealing with financial theory, financial markets and financial instruments, at both the undergraduate and postgraduate levels. Indeed, these days virtually all MBA programmes have Marketing related core or elective courses.

So the motivation behind writing this book was to provide the necessary skills and knowledge for conducting or commissioning market research.

We have written this book with two audiences in our minds. First, it is aimed at undergraduate (BBA/BBM) as well as postgraduate students of business management (MBA/PGDBM) pursuing courses in marketing research. Second, it is aimed at practitioners who wish to know more about marketing research, or those who need a practical, yet theoretically sound reference. If you search for marketing research books on Google or Amazon.com, you will find that there is no shortage of such books. However, this book differs in many important ways.

We have designed this text as a bridge between the theory of conducting quantitative research and its execution, using market research process as a framework. The initial chapters (Chapters 1–3) give the definition, and discuss the characteristics, the types, scope of, and stages in marketing research as well as the organization of marketing research in India, and research plan(s)—its need, functions, and types as also its structure and funding. Chapters 4–6 clearly analyze research designs and their classification, and descriptive and experimental research, as well as uses and methods of, and latest techniques in quality research. While Chapters 7 and 8 are devoted to a discussion on marketing research process, attitude measurement and its various aspects as also different types of sampling methods and sample size determination, Chapters 9 and 10 cover methods and techniques of data collection and data processing analysis. Chapters 11 and 12 deal with statistical techniques such as measures of central tendency, measures of dispersion, correlation, regression analysis and time series analysis, as well as statistical packages. Finally, the concluding chapters (Chapters 13 and 14) give a detailed discussion on report writing and illustrations on consumer research, demand forecasting, and sales promotion campaign.

The distinguishing features of the book are:

- Indepth treatment of identifying, gathering, analyzing and interpreting primary and secondary data.
- Continuing examples across chapters that illustrate the links between various research concepts.
- **Caselets** have been given at the end of the book to illustrate the concepts discussed.
- The book is concise, focusing on the most important aspects that a market researcher or manager interpreting market research should know.
- Many chapters provide links to further reading and other websites to enable readers to delve deeper into the subject.

This book is intended as a text for undergraduate and postgraduate students of Management and budding managers who wish to know about using the results of marketing research in order to maximize economic performance of their business organizations. It would be equally useful to postgraduate students of commerce and professionals engaged in marketing research who have to **implement** their marketing research results.

We would welcome any constructive suggestions for improving the contents of the book.

Richa Arora
Nitin R. Mahankale

Acknowledgements

First and foremost, the first author would like to express her gratitude to God Almighty for all the blessings He has given her. She wishes to thank her parents, and her in-laws Mr. O.P. Arora and Mrs. Shashi Arora, for the love, encouragement and the support they have provided.

Above all, she wants to thank her husband, Mukul and her daughter, Vanshika for their support, encouragement and for their patience during the long hours she was away from them for completing this book.

The editorial and production team of PHI Learning has been unstinting in their support. We are especially grateful to Mr. K.C. Devasia, Executive Editor for his fine editing and very valuable suggestion for enhancing the quality of the book.

Richa Arora

Nitin R. Mahankale

1 Marketing Research An Overview

- Characteristics of Marketing Research
- Marketing Research—Meaning and importance
- The Functions of Marketing Research
- Types of Marketing Research
- Stages in Marketing Research Process
- Scope of Marketing Research Function
- Marketing Research—Limitations
- Discussion Questions

After going through this chapter, you will be able to:

- Define Marketing Research.
- Clearly spell out the functions of marketing research.
- Explain the types of marketing research.
- Discuss the classification of the marketing problem.
- Enumerate the critical factors in organizing a good marketing research study.
- Cite some of the possible application areas of marketing research.
- Discuss the scope of the marketing research function.
- Narrate the limitations of marketing research.

INTRODUCTION

The principal task of marketing management is to fulfill the aspirations of the consumers. It is imperative therefore to understand what the consumers want; how they make various choices; or what their sources of information and influence process are. Thus, marketing research is the function that provides the necessary information about the consumer to the marketer. In the process, an organization can identify new opportunities in the market; evaluate and monitor marketing actions and, in general, evolve a better marketing progamme to serve the interests of the consumer. Thus, marketing research acts as the link between the consumer and the marketer.

Market research is a systematic, objective collection and analysis of data about a particular target market, competition and/or environment. It always incorporates some form of data collection—whether it be secondary research (often referred to as desk research) or primary market research, which is collected directly from a respondent. The purpose of any market research project is to achieve an increased understanding of the subject matter. With markets throughout the world becoming increasingly more competitive, market research is now on the agenda of many organizations, whether they are large or small. Market research is quantitative or qualitative, or a combination of both. Both qualitative and quantitative market research method provide different insights into customer behaviour. Normally, research results are more useful when the two methods are combined.

Market research is an essential part of any business which wants to offer products or services that are focused and well targeted.

Business decisions based on good intelligence and good market research can minimize risk and pay dividends and, by making it part and parcel of the business process and having it throughout the lifecycle of a product or service, market research can bring the following benefits:

1. Market research will help you *communicate better*. Your current customers' experiences are a valuable information source, not only will they allow you to gauge how well you currently meet their expectations, they can also tell you where you are getting things right and, more importantly, where you are going wrong.
2. By asking the customer, you not only show them that you care, but *you also take the guess work out of customer services.*
3. Market research helps you *identify opportunities*. If you are planning to operate a new service and want to know the preconceived attitudes people have, then market research can help, not only in evaluating the potential for a new idea but also by identify the areas where a marketing message needs to be honed.
4. Market research will *minimize risk*. Market research can help shape a new product or service, identifying what is needed and ensuring that the development of a product is highly focused towards demand.

Market research creates benchmarks and helps you measure your progress—unless you measure you may not be able to gauge how well your business is performing. Early research may highlight glaring holes in your service or shortfalls in your product; regular market research will show if improvements are being made and, if positive, will help motivate a team.

"Marketing is the process of planning and executing the conception, pricing, promotion and distribution of ideas, goods and services to create exchanges that satisfy individual and organizational objectives". The marketing concept requires that customer satisfaction rather than profit maximization be the goal of an organization. In other words, the organization should be consumer oriented and should try to understand consumer's requirements and satisfy them quickly and efficiently, in ways that are beneficial to both the consumer and the organization.

This means that any research organization should try to obtain information on consumer needs and gather marketing intelligence to help satisfy these needs efficiently. Marketing research is a critical part of such a marketing intelligence system; it helps improve management decision making by providing relevant, accurate and timely (RAT) information. Every decision poses unique needs for information, and relevant strategies can be developed based on the information gathered through marketing research.

Definition of Marketing Research

The American Marketing Association officially defines marketing research as:

> Marketing research is the function that links the consumer and public to the marketer through information—information used to identify and define marketing opportunities and problems; generate, refine and evaluate marketing actions; monitor marketing performance and improve understanding of marketing as a process. Marketing research specifies the information required to address these issues, designs the method for collecting information, manages and implements the data collection process, analyses and communicates the findings and their implications.

This definition highlights the role of marketing research as an aid to decision making. An important feature is the inclusion of the specification and interpretation of needed information. Too often, marketing research is considered narrowly as gathering and analyzing of data for someone to use. Firms can achieve and sustain a competitive advantage through the creative use of marketing information. Hence, marketing research is defined as information input to decisions, not simply the evaluation of decisions that have been made. Market research alone, however, does not guarantee success; the intelligent use of market research is necessary for business achievement. A competitive edge is more the result of how information is used than of who does or does not have the information.

Characteristics of Marketing Research

Marketing research is systematic

Systematic planning is required at all the stages of the marketing research process. The procedures followed at each stage are methodologically sound, well documented and, as far as possible, planned in advance. Marketing research uses the scientific method in in so far as data that is collected and analyzed to test prior notions or hypotheses in concerned.

Marketing research is objective

It attempts to provide accurate information that reflects a true state of affairs. It should be conducted impartially. While research is always influenced by the researcher's research philosophy, it should be free from the personal or political biases of the researcher or the management. Research, which is motivated by personal or political gain, involves a breach of professional standards. Such research is deliberately biased that it results in predetermined findings. The motto of every researcher should be: "Find it and tell it like it is." The objective nature of marketing research underscores the importance of ethical considerations which are discussed part of this chapter.

Marketing research involves the identification, collection, analysis and dissemination of information

Each phase of this process is important. We identify or define the marketing research problem or opportunity and then determine what information is all about.

Marketing Research—Meaning and importance

Operationally speaking, marketing research is defined as the objective and formal process of collecting information; analyzing the results, and communicating the findings and their implications in terms of marketing actions. However, some further comments about this definition are essential. Marketing research is a systematic collection and analysis of information that is ultimately used in evolving some marketing decisions. All stages of a research study must be carried out in a logical manner. For instance, one should start with a concise statement of the issues to be investigated; indicate the information required to study those select problems; define the methods to be adopted to collect those data; specify the relevant technique to be employed for analyzing the data; and finally state the research findings and their specific implications for marketing decisions making.

Note that this definition indicates that marketing research should be conducted for specific issues. Secondly, it must ensure objectivity in every step. Finally, study findings must help the manager in decision making. In other words, marketing research must not be mere collection of statistical information; one must justify the choice of methodology of data collection and analysis. The researcher must not be too much preoccupied with techniques, but instead convey the meaning of the results in the marketing language even when some advanced or sophisticated tool is being used. Likewise, marketing manager(s) should also provide a clear, detailed scenario of the problems faced by the company before the marketing researchers (s). They must allow adequate time and budget for conducting the study. They must not use marketing research as a firefighting device or to justify some preconceived action(s).

Marketing research is the function that links the consumer with the organization through information. It involves systematic and objective search for an analysis of information that can be used for evolving some marketing decisions.

Any research study must clearly state the issues being investigated. It must apply systematic and formal procedure in collection and analysis of information. Such research must communicate the study findings in a manner that could help in arriving at some marketing decisions.

A research study will fail to serve its purpose if the marketing researcher merely collects some statistical facts or is preoccupied with techniques or uses data of questionable validity or communicates the findings in too much vague or technical language.

Likewise, a research study will suffer if the marketing manager does not offer a full perspective of the research problem; or allows inadequate time; or uses research as a firefighting device or does not really appreciate the value of research. The problem must be clearly defined and the reasons for undertaking the research from the point of view of marketing decision making should be clearly justified.

In order to carry out effective research programme:

1. Prepare a list of objectives to be examined
2. Avoid:
   - Vague terms of reference
   - Trivial research projects
   - Research where underlying purpose is unknown or with held.
3. Ensure concurrence about the terms of references (especially research objectives; plan of data collection, time and budget) among all concerned.

The Functions of Marketing Research

Marketing decisions involve issues that range from fundamental shifts in the positioning of a business or the decision to enter a new market to narrow tactical questions of how best to stock a grocery shelf. The context for these decisions is the market planning process, which proceeds sequentially through four stages:

1. Situation analysis
2. Strategy development

3. Marketing programme development
4. Implementation.

The evaluation of past strategic decisions serves as an input to the situation assessment and thus it is a never-ending process.

Situation Analysis

Situation analysis is a marketing term and involves evaluating the situation and trends in a particular company's market. Situation analysis is often called the three c's, which refers to the three major elements that must be studied:

- Customers
- Costs
- Competition

The number of c's is sometimes extended to four, five or even six, with "Collaboration", Company, and Competitive advantage being added.

Effective marketing strategies are built on an in-depth understanding of the market environment of the business and the specific characteristics of the market. The microenvironment includes political and regulatory trends, economic and social trends, and technological trends. Marketing researchers tend to focus on those trends that affect the demand for products and services.

Strategy Development

A strategy is an organization's plan to achieve its mission–which is the purpose for the organization's existence. The development process involves three conceptual ways in which firms achieve their mission:

- Differentiation
- Cost leadership
- Response

Effective strategies are also developed through proper evaluation of a SWOT analysis to gain competitive advantage. During the strategy development stage, the management decides on answers to three critical questions. Marketing research provides significant help in finding answers to these questions.

What business should we be in? Specifically, what products or services should we offer? What technologies will we utilize? Which market segments should we emphasize? What channels should we use to reach the market? These questions are compelling in markets that are mature and saturated, including not only most packaged goods but also household appliances, automobiles and services such as banking and air travel. Research supports this search for niches with large-scale quantitative market studies that describe buying behaviours, consumer beliefs and attitudes and exposure to communication media. Large samples are needed to delineate the segments, indicate their size and determine what the people in each segment seek in a product.

How can we compete? The management team has to decide why the business is better than the competition in serving the needs of the target segment and what should be done to keep it in front. Competitive superiority is revealed in the market as either differentiation along attributes that are important to target customers or the lowest delivered cost position.

Marketing research is essential for getting answers to three key questions about differentiation: What are the attributes of the product or services that create value for the customer? Which attributes are most important? How does the company compare with the competitors? An understanding of competitive advantage also requires detailed knowledge of the capabilities, strategies and intentions of present and prospective competitors. Marketing research contributes here in two ways: identifying the competitive set and collecting detailed information about each competitor.

What are the objectives for the business? An objective is a desired performance result that can be quantified and monitored. There are usually objectives of revenue growth, market share and profitability. Increasingly, firms are adopting objectives for service levels and customer satisfaction. Marketing research is needed to establish both the market share and the level of customer satisfaction.

Market Programme Development

Programmes embrace specific tasks such as developing a new product or launching a new advertising campaign. An action programme usually focuses on a single objective in support of one element of the overall business strategy. This is where the bulk of ongoing marketing research is directed. Developing the marketing programme—representative decisions that draw on marketing research involves the following:

Segmentation decisions

- Which segment should be the targeted?
- What benefits are most important for each segment?
- When should geographic area be entered?

Product decisions

- What product features should be included?
- How should the price be positioned?
- What type of package is preferred by the customers?

Distribution decisions

- What type of retailer should be used?
- What should be the mark-up policy?
- Should a few outlets or many outlets be employed?

Advertising and promotion decisions

- What appeals should be used in advertising?
- In which medium should the advertising be placed?
- What should be the budget?
- What sales promotion should be used and when should it be scheduled?

Personal selling decisions

- What customer types have the most potential?
- How many sales people are needed?

Price decisions

- What price level should be changed?
- What sales should be offered during the year?
- What response should be made to a competitor's price?

Branding decisions

- What should be the name, symbol, logo and slogan that will be associated with the product?
- What is the position that the brand should adopt vis-à-vis the competition?
- How can brand loyalty be increased?

Customer satisfaction decisions

- How should customer satisfaction be measured?
- How often should it be measured?
- How should customer complaints be handled?

Implementation

Implementation: Implementation is the carrying out, execution, or practice of a plan, a method, or any design for doing something. Hence, implementation is the action that must follow any preliminary thinking in order that something may actually happen. In the computer science context, implementation encompasses all the processes involved in getting new software or hardware operating properly in its environment, including installation, configuration, running, testing, standardizing or running an algorithm as a program and making the necessary changes. Many implementations may require some preconditions or general standards. For example, web browsers contain implementations of World Wide Web Consortium-recommended specifications, and software development tools contain implementations of programming languages. Policies entail theories which form the basis of all programs. These programs with command actions create the preliminary conditions. Implementation is the ability to build ensuing links in the fundamental chain so as to obtain the preferred result.

The process of implementation of the policy is vital to the success of any programmes. Different sectors will have different types of key areas for the chronology of the implementation process. The most carefully crafted policy that is widely accepted by those who are affected by it can fall flat because of improper implementation.

In the IT industry, the components that are sold are often not understood by the customer and hence an effective sales implementation would involve steering and channelizing the technical know-how of the product to the client. This guidance has to be undertaken right from the time of the purchase covering all the phases of life cycle of the product, i.e. from IT planning to software implementation to training and after-sales services. These life cycle spans of implementation require the expertise of professionals like project managers, business analysts, technical analysts, data scientists, social media architects, and cloud architects who will do requirements analysis, scope analysis, customization, systems integration, user policies, user training, and delivery and cloud integration.

In the political scenario, the legislators or the central or the state government formulates the policies and issues policy documents related to different sectors and thrust areas. The execution of these policies is called implementation. The public servants and bureaucrats work for the implementation of these policies within the parameters of administration, rules and adjudication. The implementation process itself is dynamic because it has to focus on the changes in socio-economic conditions, public opinion, public need, priority areas, the intent of the government, and so on.

The beginning of the implementation phase is signalled by a decision to proceed with a new programme or strategy and by the related commitments to objectives, budgets and time tables. At this point, the focus of marketing research shifts to such questions as:

1. Did the elements of the marketing programme achieve their objectives?
2. How did sales compare with the objectives?
3. In what areas were the sales disappointing? Why?
4. Were the advertising objectives met? Did the product achieve its distribution objectives?
5. Are any supermarkets discounting the product?
6. Should the marketing programme be continued, revised or expanded?
7. Are customers satisfied with the product?
8. Should the product be changed on more features added?
9. Should the advertising budget be changed?
10. Is the price appropriate?

For research to be effective at this stage, it is important that specific measurable objectives be set for all elements of the marketing programme. There should be sales goals by geographic area; distribution goals, perhaps in terms of the number of stores carrying the product; and advertising goals such as achieving certain levels of awareness. The role of marketing research is to provide measures against these objectives and to provide more focused studies to determine why results are below or above expectations.

TYPES OF MARKETING RESEARCH

Types of Research

Research can be classified according to its purpose and the end results expected out of it. It is done according to the objective or the intent and has different methodologies. According to the intent, research may be classified in the following manner:

1. Basic research: This is experimental and theoretical work undertaken to acquire new knowledge without looking for long-term benefits other than the advancement of knowledge. Clinical trials are research studies undertaken to determine better ways to prevent, screen for diagnose or treating diseases.

2. Epidemiological research: It is concerned with the description of health and welfare in populations through the collection of data related to health and the frequency, distribution and determinants of disease in populations, with the aim of improving health.

3. Evaluation research: Such research is conducted to measure the effectiveness or performance of a programme, concept or campaign in achieving its objectives. Literature review is a critical examination, summarization, interpretation or evaluation of existing literature in order to establish current knowledge on a subject.

4. Qualitative research: This type of research is undertaken to gain insights into attitudes, beliefs, motivations and behaviours of individuals to explore a social or a human problem and include methods such as focus groups, in-depth interviews, observation research, and case studies.

5. Quantitative research: This is concerned with the measurement of attitudes, behaviours and perceptions and includes interviewing methods such as telephone, intercept and door-to-door interviews as well as self-completion methods, e.g. mailouts and online surveys. Pure research or basic research is done for increasing and advancing knowledge. There is no direct benefit as it is a research for the sake of research. Generally, it is the source of most new theories, principles and ideas. Such research is intended to add to the body of scientific knowledge as well as to discover new facts, and learn more accurately the characteristics of known events without any particular thought as to immediate practical utility. It lays the foundation for applied research and offers solutions to many practical problems. Example: Einstein's Theory of Relativity, Newton's contribution, and Galileo's contribution. In other words, basic research lays down the foundation for the applied research that follows. It looks into many alternatives and probes into every alternative and then hits on the most suitable solution.

6. Applied research: It is designed to solve practical problems of the modern world, rather than to acquire knowledge for knowledge's sake. The goal of applied research is to find a solution to the real problems faced by businessmen everyday. It targets the immediate problem at hand and works on finding the solution and is directed primarily towards a specific, practical aim or objective, e.g. the marketing research budget in every corporation is for supporting activities and aimed at achieving specific answers for specific short-term or long-term problems.

7. Exploratory research: It is most commonly unstructured, informal research which is undertaken to gain background information about the general nature of the research. In strict all research is exploratory. This genre of research simply allows the marketer to gain greater understanding of something which is not known. For example, just because we know that 3G phones exist, it doesn't necessarily mean that we understand how they work. This kind of research is used principally to gain a deeper understanding of something. It is used to obtain deep insights into the behaviour of a few consumers. Common exploratory research methods include depth interviews, projective techniques, and focus groups.

8. Descriptive research: Descriptive research as the words suggest, works on collecting the data and then detailing and describing it analytically. It is done when a researcher wants more information and better understanding of an identified variable, e.g. a company making 2G phones wants to find out about the technology behind 3G because of the inclination of consumers towards advanced technology. It involves gathering data that describe events and then organizes, tabulates, depicts, and describes the data and deduces the various characteristics of a consumer group, community or institution.

9. Diagnostic study: 'Diagnostics refers' to the investigation and identification of a problem. An example of a diagnostic test is an emissions test on a car. It answers the whys and whats of a problem and then works on the alternative solutions.

10. Evaluation research: Evaluation is the systematic assessment of the worth or merit of some object. The generic goal of most evaluations is to provide useful feedback to a variety of audiences including sponsors, donors, client-groups, administrators, staff, and other relevant constituencies. Most often, feedback is perceived as "useful" if it aids in decision-making, but the relationship between an evaluation and its impact is not a simple one—studies that seem critical sometimes fail to influence short-term decisions, and studies that initially seem to have no influence can have a delayed impact when more congenial conditions arise. The major goal of evaluation should be to influence decision-making or policy formulation through the provision of empirically-driven feedback.

11. Action research: Action research is "learning by doing". A group of people identify a problem, do something to resolve it, see how successful their efforts were, and if not satisfied, try again. While this is the essence of the approach, there are other key attributes of action research that differentiate it from common problem-solving activities that we engage in everyday. There is a dual commitment in action research to study a system and simultaneously to pool in resources with members of the system in changing it in what is together regarded as a desirable direction. Susman (1983) gives different phases for action research, which involve diagnosing a problem, considering alternative action planning, selecting a course of action, studying the consequences of that action and, finally, taking action on the course of action selected.

According to the methods of study, research may be classified into different categories. These are now discussed.

1. Experimental research: This is based on cause/effect relationships. It is where variables are manipulated in order to see how the manipulation affects the constant. This type of research is used casually and is not often used to predict anything huge. Consumers engage in experimental research continuously in that they try things (e.g. new products or services) and see what happens. Consumers are comparing past experiences with new experiences. It's a trial and error type of behaviour. This approach used by consumers is referred to as experimental research.

2. Analytical study: As a style of qualitative inquiry, analytical research may consist of a system of mathematical models or statistical techniques used with numerical data. So it may be referred to as statistical method. It aims at testing hypothesis and specifying and interpreting relationships. Analytical research attempts to establish the why or the how of things.

3. Historical research: It is the process of systematically examining past events to give an account of what has happened in the past with a view to communicating to the present and future generation of what happened in the past. The nature of historical research is descriptive. It is a painstakingly slow and deductive method to get an insight into the past. The foundations of historical research are based on an analysis of evidence collected from various sources rather than direct observations.

4. Survey research: A survey is a data collection tool used to gather information about individuals. A survey may focus on factual information about individuals, or it might aim to collect the opinions of the survey takers. A "survey" can be anything from a short paper-and-pencil feedback form to an intensive one-on-one in-depth interview. Survey research is a process of acquiring data from the public; the information is used to develop new products, improve services, and is used by various institutions.

STAGES IN MARKETING RESEARCH PROCESS

Marketing research exercise may take many forms but systematic inquiry is a feature common to all such forms. Being a systematic inquiry, it requires careful planning of the orderly investigation process. Though it is an oversimplification to assume that all research processes would necessarily follow a given sequence, marketing research often follows a generalized pattern which can be broken down and studied as sequential stages. Figure 1.1 gives the stages in the marketing research process.

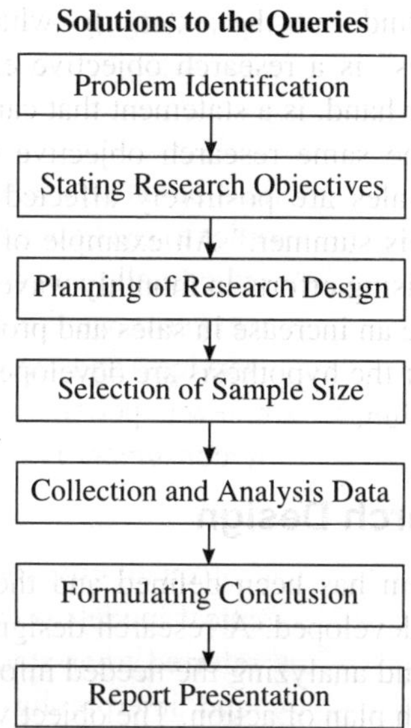

FIGURE 1.1 Stages in the marketing research process.

As shown in the figure, the research process begins with identification of the problem. The research task may clarify a problem or define an opportunity. The clear-cut statement of the problem may not be possible at the very outset of research process since often only the symptoms of the problem are apparent at that point. Thus, the problem statement may be made only in general terms to be made specific later after some exploratory research has been done to clarify the problem situation.

Defining the Problem

Clear problem definition is of crucial importance in marketing research since, in terms of both time and money, research is a costly process. Careful attention to problem definition allows the researcher to set the proper research objectives which in turn facilitate relevant and economic data collection. Problem definition in specific terms must precede the determination of the purpose of the research.

In order to define the problem more precisely, some sort of exploratory research may also be undertaken. The methods popularly in use are survey of secondary data, experience survey, or pilot studies.

Statement of Research Objectives

After clarifying and identifying the research problem with or without exploratory research, the researcher must make a formal statement of research objectives. Research objectives may be stated in qualitative or quantitative terms and expressed as research question statements or hypothesis. For example, the research objective "To find out the extent to which the sales promotion programmes affected sales" is a research objective expressed as a statement. A hypothesis, on the other hand, is a statement that can be refuted or supported by empirical findings. The same research objective could be stated as: "To test the hypothesis that sales are positively affected by the sales promotion programme undertaken this summer." An example of another hypothesis may be: "Concentrating advertising efforts in monthly waves (rather than advertising continuously) would cause an increase in sales and profits."

Once the objectives or the hypothesis are developed, the researcher is ready to choose the research design.

Planning the Research Design

Once the research problem has been defined and the objectives decided, the research design must be developed. A research design is a plan specifying the procedure for collecting and analyzing the needed information. It represents the framework for the research plan of action. The objectives of the study discussed in the preceding step are included in the research design to ensure that the data collected are relevant to the objectives. The researcher must, at this stage, also determine the type of sources of information needed, the data collection methods (surveys or interviews, for example), the sampling methodology, the timing, and the possible costs of research. The design chosen is from exploratory, descriptive, quasi-experimental or experimental design categories, which again include a number of alternative methods. You will study more about specific types of research designs and their suitability for particular kinds of research problem is entitled as "Research Design".

Planning the Sample

Although the sample plan is included in the research design, the actual sampling is a separate and important stage in the research process. Sampling involves procedures that use a small number of items or parts of the population to draw conclusion regarding the whole population. The first sampling question that needs to be asked is, who is to be sampled? This follows from the question. What is the target population? Defining the population may not be as simple as it looks.

For example, if you are interested in finding the association between savings and loans, you may survey the people who already have accounts, and the selected sample will not represent potential customers.

The next important issue is regarding the sample size. How large or how small should a sample be? Generally speaking, larger samples give more reliable information than smaller ones. However, if probability sampling is used, a small proportion of the population may give a reliable measure of the universe. The researcher is also required to know how to select the various units to make up the sample. There are two basic divisions of sampling methods—Probability and non-probability sampling.

Data Collection

The data collection process follows the formulation of research design including the sampling plan. Data which can be secondary or primary can be collected using a variety of tools. These tools are classified into two broad categories—Observation methods and Communication methods—both of which have their inherent advantages and disadvantages.

Data Processing and Analysis

Once the data has been collected, it has to be converted into a format which will suggest answers to the problem identified in the first step. Data processing begins with the editing of data and coding. Editing involves inspecting the data collection forms for omission, legibility and consistency in classification. Before tabulation, responses need to be classified into meaningful categories. The rules for categorizing, recording and transferring the data to data storage media are called **codes**. The coding process facilitates the manual or computer tabulation. If computer analysis is being used, the data can be key-punched and verified.

Analysis represents the application of logic to the understanding of data collected about the subject. In its simplest form, analysis may involve determination of consistent patterns and summarizing of appropriate details. The appropriate analytical techniques chosen would depend on informational requirements of the problem, characteristics of the research designs, and the nature of the data gathered.

Formulating Conclusion, Preparing and Presenting the Report

The final stage in the research process is that of interpreting the information and drawing conclusions for use in managerial decisions. The research report should effectively communicate the research findings and need not necessarily include complicated statements about the technical aspects of the study and research methods.

Often, the management is not interested in details of research design and statistical analysis, but in the concrete findings of the research. If executives are to act on these findings, they must be convinced of the value of the findings. Researchers, therefore, must make the presentation technically accurate, understandable and useful.

Frequently, the researchers are required to make both an oral and a written presentation. Since each project is different, the presentation in each case requires originality. However, the better the earlier steps in the research process taken, the more likely it is that a good presentation would result in. While the oral presentation depends a great deal on the personal style of the presenter and the management expectation, the written report, in order to be effective needs to include the following details:

- Title page
- Table of Contents
- Introduction
- Statement of Objectives
- Methodology
    - Research design
    - Data collection methods
    - Sampling
    - Field work
    - Analysis and interpretation
- Limitations
- Findings
- Conclusion and Recommendations
- Appendix
    - Copies of forms used
    - Tables not included in finding
- Bibliography, if needed

Scope of Marketing Research Function

In this section we will discuss the possible applications of marketing research in the corporate environment. Bulk of the research is done to measure consumer wants and needs. Also, marketing research is carried out to assess the impact of past marketing actions. Some research is done to understand the competitive, technological, social, economic, cultural, political or legal environments of the market.

Another way of looking at the function of marketing research is to look at the particular decision area where research results are used.

Sales Analysis

Much research is done in the following areas which are broadly referred as sales analysis:

- Measurement of market potential/demand projection
- Determination of market characteristics
- Market] share estimation
- Studies of business trends.

In fact, some of the more detailed studies to be carried out under the broad ambit of sales analysis could be as follows:

1. The types of consumers that constitute the potential market.
2. The size and location of the market.
3. The growth and concentration of the market over certain period of time.
4. The competitive picture for the product.
5. The major strategies of leading competitors with respect to price, offerings, distribution, etc.
6. The purchase habits of key market segments.
7. What is the pattern of pre-purchase deliberations made by the consumers?
8. Who are involved in the decision making?
9. What are the roles of different members in decision making?
10. How does the product fit into the consumers lifestyles? (Operation if it is an industrial product).
11. Do consumers prefer to buy some particular brands (i.e. assess the degree of brand loyalty)?

The above list is not exhaustive. Here, research is basically done with a view to know consumers' motivation, attitude, cognition, perceptions, etc. Thus, information will be collected in such a manner that they have some implications for various marketing decisions.

Sales Methods and Policies

Research is done to appraise the efficacy of present distribution system. Such studies are used in company polices that affect their selling activities. In the sales methods and policy area of marketing research, analysts examine firms' sales records and conduct a variety of sales-related activities which help in establishment of sales quotas, design of territory boundary, salaries and incentives to sales personnel, physical distribution and distribution cost analysis, etc. In addition, marketing research analysts are responsible for monitoring both in-house studies and off-site research, interpreting results, providing explanations of compiled data, and developing research tools. In order to find out consumer likes and dislikes, marketing research analysts collect data on brand names, trademarks, product design, and packaging for existing products, launching products, and in-process products.

Product Management

Product management aims at creating product strategy, marketing strategy, and product plans. Securing the buy-in from cross-functional team members in support of the product strategy (or overall corporate strategy) is critical. This refers to the activities of leading cross-functional teams including engineering, QA, UI design, marketing, sales and support to develop and launch the product on-time and on-budget. It includes securing resources, creating project timelines, tracking progress against timeline, identifying critical paths, getting additional resources when needed, and communicating status to the executive team. Companies do marketing research to form market segments through choice of alternative bases. Companies conduct a pre-production, a pre-launch research to assess or guess the acceptance of a new product, and a post-launch research to measure the actual acceptance of the product. Such studies help the companies to tactically capture the market. Simulated test marketing is used to reach a decision whether or not to launch a product. It's a kind of pre-test marketing based on consumer behaviour research. Here, consumers are exposed to stage advertising and purchase decisions to examine their response to a new product or service. Pricing studies, packaging research, design or physical characteristics are conducted to capture the market and prevail over it.

Advertising Research

Media research: Advertising is one of the most important and most expensive marketing functions, but a large share of advertising money is wasted every year. Media research allows companies and advertising agencies to assess many advertising innovative theories at various stages before production in order to identify a winning theory and prevent the investment of many man-hours and production resources in unproductive advertisements. Marketing research assesses the relative value of different media for particular products.

Copy research: Advertising agencies have been regularly engaged in activities where they test out alternative copy designs by obtaining the feedback from consumers. Studies on advertisement effectiveness show that advertising agencies regularly make use of marketing research studies to assess and monitor effectiveness of different advertising campaigns.

Corporate research: Corporate research is a full service marketing research firm in market analysis. These research activities pertain to different spheres of influence of a corporate-like productivity, employment and customer satisfaction. Corporate market research is result oriented and can be evaluated on quantitative terms.

Social values research: Social values method reveals the deepest drivers of people's beliefs and behaviours in the infrastructure of society. This powerful quantitative research tool uses a unique battery of questions to probe the mental postures that emphasize the attitude customers, employees, and citizens have when they live in a particular realm of knowledge with a dynamic set of specific eating habits, practising religious beliefs, etc.

Political research: Research on politics aims at understanding the impact of political parties and their work for the public.

Customer service research: Companies do customer service research to measure the customer's contentment level with the customer service department. Customer service research is done by observation, personal interviews, and online surveys and telephone surveys. It provides actionable information to help a company maintain good relationships with their existing customer base.

Syndicated Research

Syndicated research is a market research carried out by agencies and sold to several different companies. It is a single research study that is performed and conducted by a research company and sold to multiple client companies. It is used to pick up important baseline information about the market size and target market composition for companies. It can be customized based on household/consumer data that may be obtained through surveys, purchase and media panels or electronic scanner services. Surveys generate information rich in values, lifestyles, advertising evaluation, and even general information related to preference, purchase, consumption and other aspects of consumer behaviour. Panels target information on purchases or media consumption. Electronic scanner services provide scanner data (linked to panels or linked to panels and cable TV). The main advantage of this type of research is the lower cost. Examples include reports on the Information Technology industry written by the Gartner Group as well as reports giving customer satisfaction levels by J.D. Power. The main disadvantage of this type of research is the inability to formulate specific questions to address research objectives.

Marketing research: Marketing research is integral to the right kind of marketing and eventual success of business. Marketing efforts that are aimed at the wrong people or clients can be a waste of time and money and ultimately hinder a business's efforts to attract new customers. So marketing done without marketing research can result in big failures.

Marketing Research—Limitations

Accurate, uptodate information obtained by marketing research can be of enormous value to an organization in gaining and/or maintaining its competitive edge. However, there are a number of reasons why, in reality, these potential benefits may not be realized:

Budgetary constraints: Gathering and processing data can be very expensive. Many organizations may lack the expertise to conduct extensive surveys to gather primary data, whatever may be the potential benefits. Also, they may not be having the funds to pay specialist market research agencies to gather such data for them. In such cases, organizations may be forced to rely on data that is less than 'perfect' but can be accessed more cheaply, e.g., from secondary sources.

Time constraints: In a dynamic and changing market environment, the data collected becomes outdated very soon and the research findings based on them inappropriate. A research project takes several months in designing and execution and by the time the results are available to the management, they become dated. A research project should, therefore, be completed in such a way that its results are available at the time the marketing manager needs them for decision making

Reliability of the data: The value of any research findings depends critically on the accuracy of the data collected. Data quality can be compromised via a number of potential routes, e.g. leading questions, misleading samples' and prejudiced interviewers.

Research cost: Huge cost is involved in marketing research as collection and processing of data can be costly. Many firms do not have the know-how to carry out extensive surveys for collecting primary data, and might not also able to hire specialized market experts and research agencies to collect primary data. In that case, they go for obtaining secondary data which is cheaper to obtain.

Opinion or bias: The volunteers who give the information may affect the accuracy of the results because of some bias that they have, for example, the company may only survey one group of people who all respond that the product is not appealing or useful. On the other hand, another group of individuals may be more than ready to spend money on the product if it is accessible. One disadvantage of market research is only getting a certain group of target buyers' attitude rather than a broad sample.

Legal and ethical constraints: Researchers must ensure that the data they obtain is kept secure, and the privacy of the sources is not violated or compromised on ethical standards.

Lack of enough trained personnel: Another limitation of marketing research is the small number of trained research personnel.

SUMMARY

Marketing research serves marketing management by providing information, which is relevant to decision making. Marketing research does not itself make the decisions, nor does it guarantee success. Rather, it helps reduce the uncertainty surrounding the decisions to be made. It is important for a market research to be systematic, objective and analytical to ensure its effectiveness.

The process of marketing research includes various steps:

1. Problem recognition
2. Setting of objectives
3. Planning of research design
4. Data collection
5. Data processing and analysis
6. Tabulation of data

Marketing research is the function that links the consumer, customer and public to the marketer through information—information used to identify and define marketing opportunities and problems; generate, refine and evaluate marketing actions; monitor marketing performance; and improve understanding of marketing as a process. Marketing research specifies the information required to address these issues, designs the method for collecting information, manage and implements the data collection process, analyzes and communicates the findings and their implications. The market planning process proceeds sequentially through four stages:

1. Situation analysis
2. Strategy development
3. Marketing program development
4. Implementation

The manager or other individual initiating the research must provide guidance to the researcher in the form of a research brief. This document should state the purpose of the research, its objectives and the time by which it must be completed, the budget to which the researcher must work in developing the research design, and the timing and frequency of any interim reports, which the researcher is expected to make.

Having read, questioned and understood the research brief, the onus is then on the marketing researcher to respond by preparing the research design. The research design begins with an accurate and, as far as is possible, precise definition of the problem. This is followed by the generation of hypotheses. There will then be an intermediate stage whereby the hypotheses are restated in a testable form, i.e. the null form. This will probably be only done if it is intended that statistical analysis is to be undertaken. Where the research is qualitative in nature, it is still recommended that hypotheses should be developed. These should include alternative hypotheses, depending on what is already known about the research problem. One of three types of study might be undertaken, i.e. an exploratory study, a descriptive study, or a causal study. Before proceeding further, the researcher has to develop an analysis plan. It is only when the analysis plan has been considered that fieldwork, in the form of data collection, should be undertaken.

The final step in the research design is writing the report. Customer-oriented marketing researchers will have noted from the outset of the research which topics and issues are of particular importance to the person(s) who initiated the research and will weigh the content of their reports accordingly.

An information system is a continuing and interacting structure of people, equipment and procedures designed to gather, sort, analyze, evaluate and distribute pertinent, timely and accurate information to decision makers. A decision support system allows the manager to interact directly with the database to retrieve what is wanted and provides a modelling function to help make sense of what has been retrieved.

Marketing decisions involve issues that range from fundamental shifts in the positioning of a business or the decision to enter a new market to narrow tactical questions of how best to stock a grocery shelf. The context for these decisions is the market planning process, which proceeds sequentially through four stages: (i) situation analysis, (ii) strategy development, (iii) marketing programme development, and (iv) Implementation. This is a never-ending process; hence the evaluation of past strategic decisions serves as an input to the situation assessment.

DISCUSSION QUESTIONS

1. What is marketing research?
2. Briefly comment on the definition of marketing research.
3. Indicate whether marketing research is relevant to each of the following organizations and, if so, how each might benefit from it:
   (a) Your company
   (b) Central ministries in the Government of India
   (c) A retail shop
   (d) A bank
   (e) A services marketing company
4. What are the major weaknesses of marketing research?
5. Suggest some of the precautions to be adopted in the problem definition stage.
6. Suggest some possible areas of application of marketing research.

FURTHER READING

Boyd, H.W., Westfall, R. and Stasch, S.F. (1996): *Marketing Research: Text and cases*, Homewood (Illinois): Irwin, Richard.

Churchill, Gilbert A., Jr. (1976): *Basic Marketing Research*, Hinsdale (Illinois): Dryden Press.

Green, Paul E., Tull, Donald S., and Albaum, Gerald (2010): *Research for Marketing Decisions*, 5th ed., New Delhi: PHI Learning.

Jain, Arun K., Pinson, Christian R.A., and Rachford, Brian T. (1982): *Marketing Research: Applications and problems*, New York: Wiely.

Kinnear, Thomas C. and Taylor, James R. (1996): *Marketing Research: An applied approach*, Singapore: McGraw-Hill.

Majumdar, Ramanuj (1990): *Marketing Research: Text, applications and case studies*, New Delhi: Wiley Eastern.

Schoner, Bortrem and Uhl, K.P. (1969): *Marketing Research: Information systems and decision making*, New York: Wiley.

2 Organization of Marketing Research in India

Chapter Outline

- Growing Importance of Marketing Research in India
- Expenditure on Marketing Research in India and its Major Users
- Ways of Conducting Marketing Research in India
- Increased Demand for Outside Research Services
- Common Applications of Marketing Research
- Problems in Conducting Marketing Research in India
- Discussion Questions

Learning Objectives

After going through this chapter, you will be able to:

- Know as to why marketing research is becoming important in India.
- Describe arrangements that the Indian firms have for conducting marketing researches.
- Enumerate major applications of marketing research.
- Understand problems faced in doing marketing research in India.

INTRODUCTION

In Chapter 1, you have learnt the meaning, the nature and the importance of marketing research. You have also gained familiarity with steps involved in conducting marketing research. In this chapter, we shall discuss the role and organization of marketing research in India. More specifically, we shall explore as to why marketing research is becoming important in India and what organizational arrangements firms have for conducting researches. We will identify the major users and uses of marketing research in the country. We will also examine the problems which the researchers face while doing researches in India.

GROWING IMPORTANCE OF MARKETING RESEARCH IN INDIA

In the past, in India use of marketing research has been extremely poor. Only a few large firms, especially those having linkages with foreign firms, were making use of marketing research during the 1950s and 1960s. Even among such firms, only select ones were conducting researches on a regular basis and/or having a marketing research department within the organization. A number of reasons can be put forward to explain this phenomenon. The highly protected nature of the Indian market during the 50s and the 60s is amongst the most important reasons. A highly restrictive industrial licensing policy, coupled with a ban on capacity expansion, led to constant shortages of goods and services in the country. With demand always exceeding supply and a virtual absence of competition in the market, the firms were able to easily push to the consumers all their products. The focus of the firms at that time was primarily on procuring the licenses and raw materials. They hardly had any concern for product improvements or satisfaction of their customers' needs and wants. In a way, a sort of sellers' market prevailed at that time, and availability of an assured market to the producers did not provide any incentive to them to make use of marketing research for becoming more efficient, innovative and competitive in the market place.

Moreover, during those times the firms operated on small scales and, that too, within the peripheries of the local markets. Since they were very close to their customers and had personal knowledge about them, they did not feel the need for conducting any marketing research. Even those firms that were desirous of making use of marketing research could not do so because of the paucity of funds.

Lack of professional approach to management and decision making was another important reason for the neglect of marketing research among the business firms in India.

Of late, however, the situation has undergone considerable change. With successive deregulation of the economy in the ensuing period and abolition of the archaic industrial licensing system and other regulations, especially in the 1990s, the competition has hot up in the market. Many new firm—both Indian and foreign ones—have made a foray into the market. Scale wise also, firms have expanded their businesses and today they operate in the local as well as national and international markets. Due to fast changing technological environment, product life cycles have been shortened and many a new substitute has emerged. New methods of communications and distribution channels have radically transformed the Indian marketing scene, in many product categories; sellers' markets have paved way for buyers' markets. In the wake of these changes and growing customer sophistication, it is no longer possible for the firms to continue to base their marketing decisions solely on gut feelings and past experiences. Need for timely, accurate and relevant information about the markets and buying behaviour of the target market customers is fast becoming a *sine qua non* for improved decision making.

Expenditure on Marketing Research in India and its Major Users

Though no precise information is available, the guesstimate is that Indian firms do not spend much money on marketing research. Consulting and Research Enterprise (CORE), Hyderabad conducted a survey of the Indian firms in 1986 to ascertain their expenditure on marketing research and attitudes toward it. About 500 questionnaires were mailed out to the firms selling industrial goods, consumer products and services, out of which 130 responded. Despite an overall favourable attitude towards marketing research, the study found most of the firms spending less money on it. About 40% of the firms were found spending less than ₹ 1 lakh. Expenditure by the other 46% of the firms ranged between ₹ 1 lakh and ₹ 10 lakh. Only about 14% firms were spending more than ₹ 10 lakh, with highest figures being ₹ 1 crore.

The CORE study also attempted an analysis of the marketing research expenditure in relation to sales, and found that while 28% of the surveyed firms were spending 0.01% or even less of their sales volume on marketing research during the year 1985–86, 63% firms had their expenditure on marketing research in the range of 0.02%–0.4% of sales. Though the rest of the 9% of the surveyed firms were spending more than 0.4% on marketing research, it was only the firms producing consumer goods which had expenditure on marketing research in excess of 1% of their sales.

In the past, only big firms used to be major users of the marketing research. But of late, medium and small-size firms have also started showing interest in marketing research. Little wonder that even the marketing research agencies have started turning to them for securing research business from them. The number of the firms using marketing research on a regular basis is also on an increase.

Over time, a significant decline has occurred in the relative importance of the multinational firms. Two decades ago, multinational corporations were the major users of marketing research, and their share was as high as 67% of the total commercially available research in India. But their share has now started declining, and is expected to fall to 45% by the end of this century. In contrast, the Indian firms are fast emerging as the major users of the marketing research in the country.

Another noteworthy change is the increasing use of marketing research by industrial goods firms. Though even today consumer goods firms continue to dominate the scene, the share of industrial goods firms is likely to rise in future with increased competition in the industrial goods market.

WAYS OF CONDUCTING MARKETING RESEARCH IN INDIA

Broadly speaking, a firm can get the researches conducted in two ways: either through its own staff or by hiring the services of outside agencies. Some firms make use of both the alternatives. So far as in-house research is concerned, it can be conducted by the firm's sales and marketing staff, or else they can have specialized staff or department for conducting marketing research. Since the employment of specialized research staff or setting up of a separate research department entails huge expenditure, only large firms requiring researches on a frequent basis go in for this type of organizational arrangement. Small firms and organizations not so frequently requiring researches prefer using their sales or marketing staff for undertaking research studies. As and when the need arises, some of the sales and marketing persons are picked up and assigned the research tasks. These persons generally do not have specialized knowledge of marketing research and, moreover, perform side by side the routine sales, and the quality of the marketing research conducted by such persons remains doubtful.

The other important method of collecting information is the use of outside agencies or experts such as marketing research organizations, advertising agencies and consultants. Seeing the increased demand for research services, many marketing research organizations have come up in the country and help business firms through provision of customized as well as syndicated research services. When research is tailor-made to meet the information needs of one particular client, it is known as **customized research**. Since the benefit of such a research accrues to a single firm, that firm alone bears the entire research cost. Syndicated research, on the other hand, involves collection of a common pool of data for meeting the information needs of a number of firms. As the results of such a study are shared among several firms, it costs much less for a single firm. Quite often, these studies are undertaken on a regular basis by the research agencies and the information so collected is made available to the firms on a subscription basis.

Increased Demand for Outside Research Services

The demand for outside marketing research services has phenomenally increased during the 1980s and 1990s. This is evident from the increase in turnover of the marketing research agencies during this period. The value of marketing research conducted by the marketing research agencies was just ₹ 1 crore during the 1970s. It went up to ₹ 3 crore in 1983, and further up to ₹ 10.06 crore in 1988–89. Currently, the turnover of the research agencies is expected to be somewhere around ₹ 20–30 crore. Seeing the growth in demand for different kinds of outside marketing research services, a number of marketing research agencies and other organizations have mushroomed in the country to meet the information needs of the business firms. A list of some of these organizations is provided in Table 2.1.

TABLE 2.1 Major Organizations Offering Marketing Research Services in India

1	Operation Research Group (ORG)
2	Indian Marketing Research Bureau (IMRB)
3	Marketing and Research Group (MARG)
5	Marketing Operations Design and Enquiry Service (MODES)
6	Pathfinders
7	Advertising Consultants (India) Pvt. Ltd.
8	Concept Marketing and Advisory Pvt. Ltd.
9	Marketing and Business Associates (MBA)
10	Research Con sultants and Marketing Services Pvt. Ltd.
11	Consulting and Research Enterprise (CORE)
12	Marketing Research and Data Processing Consultancy Tata Consultancy Services
13	National Council of Applied Economic Research (NCAER)
14	Indian Institute of Public Opinion
15	Indian Institute of Foreign Trade (IIFT)
16	Feedback Marketing Services
17	Research Consultancy Group
18	C. Marck (India) Ltd.
19	Quantum Market research Pvt. Ltd.
20	Research International India
21	Indica Research

Source: Adapted from Sanjay K. Jain, "Marketing Research in India: A Perspective" *Management and Change*, Vol. 1, No. 1, April 1997, p. 82.

Notes:

1. It is only an illustrative rather than an exhaustive list of the organizations rendering marketing research services in India.
2. ORG and MARG have recently joined together and the new outfit is known as ORG-MARG.

Common Applications of Marketing Research

New product decisions constitute the most frequent usage of marketing research. The other important application areas include: estimation of market share, collection of competitive information, demand estimation, product modification decisions, measurement of customer satisfaction, product positioning, and diversification and market segmentation decisions. Only about one-third of the firms reported the use of marketing research for developing advertising theme/ message and arriving at pricing and customer service decisions. Application of marketing research for product elimination and evaluation of advertising effectiveness is prevalent only among 20% firms. Furthermore, 9% firms reported the incidence of marketing research for channel modification decisions.

The most common application areas of marketing research in India are listed now.

1. New product decisions
2. Estimating market share
3. Gathering competitive information
4. Demand estimation
5. Product modification decisions
6. Measuring consumer satisfaction
7. Product positioning decisions
8. Diversification decisions
9. Market segmentation decisions
10. Advertising theme/message decisions
11. Pricing decisions
12. Customer service decisions
13. Product elimination decisions
14. Evaluating advertising effectiveness
15. Channel modification decisions

Problems in Conducting Marketing Research in India

Due to the vast size of our country, heterogeneous population and infrastructural and attitudinal problems, it is not easy to conduct marketing research in India. Some of the major problems that you as a researcher would face in conducting marketing research in the country are discussed now.

India's large and heterogeneous population is a major stumbling block in conducting marketing research. Being a big and diverse country, national surveys require India to be divided into several hundred districts and interviewing several thousands of people. This calls for enormous time and money and a big fleet of field workers—well beyond the capacity of any small or medium-size company.

India is believed to have 1652 mother tongues (mostly dialects), of which 33 are spoken by people. There are 22 officially recognized languages. Any major survey in the country requires translation of the questionnaire in a minimum of five to six languages. Many a time, strict translation of certain technical words or phrases is not possible, thus giving rise to the problem of non-comparability of data across the regions.

Accessibility to people living in the hinterland of the country is another big problem. Of course, communication facilities with more and more people using cell phones. The postal system is also not up to the mark: Because of low literacy level, mail interviews are of limited application. Personal interviews seem to be the only viable alternative, but even these are beset with transport problems and lack of trained staff in small towns and rural areas.

Secondary data available in the country also suffer on account of poor coverage and redundancy of information. Data are at all not available for many a variable of interest to the researchers. Though census is conducted after every ten years in the country, it is after a considerable lapse of time that the full results are released. Even trade and industry associations lack complete and do not keep uptodate lists of the manufacturers and trades. The industry and firms' production and sales figures are also not complete, uptodate and reliable.

Use of random and other elaborate sampling techniques presupposes the existence of suitable sampling frames, i.e., list of the target market population from which the samples are drawn. Non-availability of such lists in the country complicates the research tasks and forces the researcher to use non-probability sampling methods, thus adversely affecting the reliability and validity of the survey results.

Attitudinal problems also restrict the use of marketing research in India. The study by Consulting and Research Enterprise (CORE) group, for instance, found that only two-third of the executives of the surveyed firms had the opinion that marketing research findings represent the real world, and marketing research data are reliable enough to be of use in decision making. In response to the question whether costs incurred on marketing research are low relative to the benefits that accrue from it, about 58% firms disagreed, implying low utility of marketing research. Further, only 57% of the executives refuted the statement that "gut feeling is more important than marketing research". The rest were either ambivalent or in agreement with the statement.

The managers also appeared quite concerned with the time involved in completing the marketing research studies. Only 42% of the respondents did not feel that "market research often takes too long to be of any real use". In terms of quality and sophistication too, marketing research in India, in the opinion of many executives, is far below the expectations.

Not only the business firms, but advertising agencies also do not hold favourable attitudes towards marketing research. Advertising executives view it as a hindrance to their creative work and hence do not like spending much money on it.

SUMMARY

Because of excessive regulations and lack of competition in the market in the past, not much need was felt for marketing research in India. However, with the dismantling of the licensing system and other regulatory measures during the last two decades or so, and increasing competition in the market, fast changing technology and growing consumer sophistication, it is no longer possible for the marketing managers to solely make decisions on the basis of mere gut feeling and past experiences. They have come to increasingly rely on the information collected through the process of marketing research. The Indian firms make use of both the in-house staff and outside research organizations, advertising agencies and consultants for getting researches conducted. Seeing the growth in demand for outside research services, a large number of marketing research organizations have come up in the country to provide both the customized and syndicated research services.

In view of the country's large size, heterogeneous population, language diversity, infrastructural bottlenecks, and lack of secondary data, it becomes an uphill task for the researcher to carry out researches in India. Unfavourable attitudes of the managers also come in a big way in the widespread acceptance of marketing research in India.

DISCUSSION QUESTIONS

1. What are the major reasons for growing importance of Marketing Research in India?
2. What are the different ways of conducting marketing research? Describe the scope for outsourcing of marketing research services in India.
3. Suggest some possible areas where marketing research would find increasing application in India.
4. Briefly comment on the problems faced by researchers in conducting marketing research in India.

FURTHER READING

Beri, G.C. (1993): *Marketing Research*, 2nd ed., New Delhi: Tata McGraw-Hill (pages 88–95—They provide an overview of the syndicated research services available in the country.)

Jain, Sanjay K. (1997): "Marketing Research Services Marketing", in Ravi Shankar (Ed.), *Services Marketing—The Indian experience*, New Delhi: South Asia Publications, pp. 392–415.

Jain, Sanjay K. (1997): "Marketing Research in India—A perspective", *Management and Change*, Vol. 1, pp. 71–100.

Rao, Sushila (1986): "Marketing Research in India—The state of the art", *Business India*, Nov. 17–30, pp. 111–115.

3

Research Plan

After going through this chapter, you will be able to:

- Know what is a research plan.
- Appreciate its need and purpose.
- Understand its functions.
- Know its different types and structure.
- Comprehend the tools and techniques used in a plan.
- Prepare a research plan.

INTRODUCTION

In the later chapter, we will discuss about Research Design and the importance of organization and planning in research. Research design involves formulating a strategy for your research. There are a number of factors involved while taking a decision in this regard. Once you have formulated a research design, the next step is to prepare a research plan. As with research design, research plan also gives your research a sound footing. This chapter is devoted to a detailed discussion of the different aspects of research plan.

DEFINITION

Research plan has been used synonymously with proposal and synopsis. This refers to a blueprint of your research. Both are used for documents that describe in detail:

- What type of research are you going to do?
- Why are you doing the research?
- How are you going to do it?
- What are the resources (time, money, infrastructure, etc.) needed for doing the job?
- Is there anything that you are not going to do?

A research proposal is thus a document to your plans and ideas of carrying out your research. You may be wondering, how it is different from research design. Research design is also a strategy of how you are you going to conduct your research. But it precedes research plan. Research design is a plan of the technical decisions regarding the what, why, and how of your research. Here we take decisions regarding the nature of investigation, data collection methods to be adopted, and number of contacts to be made with the subjects, and the period of reference with the subjects of study. Research plan can be formulated only when research design has been decided. In fact, research design helps to formulate research plan. It is the document that describes all the decisions that have been taken in the design stage plus the administrative decisions concerned with your research. It presents systematically everything, starting with the title of your project to the tentative structure of your thesis.

NEED AND PURPOSE

As already stated, we repeat that research is a systematic endeavour towards quest for new knowledge. There is a role for intuition also in research but a systematic step-by-step approach needs to be followed in research. Studying informally and casually may also yield new knowledge, but that is not research. In research, organized efforts need to be put right from thinking of a topic to the presentation of results. Research is a long journey from knowing and understanding the present state of knowledge in a particular field to exploring raw areas where additions and improvements can be done and finally making those improvements. It is a project that involves investment of considerable resources, and hence needs planning as a proposal.

The purpose of a research plan is to

- present for the researcher the proposed plan of action;
- present for the supervisor and other authorities also the plan of action for their approval.

The purpose of a research design is to provide information regarding:

- What is the study?
- Why is the study being carried out?
- Where will the study be carried out?
- How will the study be carried out?
- What will be the processes and tasks involved?
- What will be the data?
- How will the data be collected?
- What methods of sampling will be used?
- How will the analysis be done?

Functions of Research Plan

The functions of a research plan are to:

- give directions on what needs to be done, when and how and in what order;
- provide a route from stating the topic to finalizing the results;
- enable you to evaluate your progress during research;
- define your topic to limit its scope;
- prove to your supervisor that you have gone into the fine details of your topic; and
- enable you to conduct research.

Types of Research Plan

There are two types of research plans. Quantitative and qualitative proposals. Quantitative proposal is given for experimental and descriptive research, whereas qualitative proposal is given for descriptive and exploratory research. Though there is no hard line of demarcation, generally qualitative research doesn't have hypothesis and operationalisation of concepts. Operationalisation of concepts refers to giving operational definitions, finding out the independent and dependent variables, sample selection, and finalizing the measuring instruments, and their reliability and validity. Instead, the qualitative proposal will have research procedures which quantitative research doesn't have.

STRUCTURE

A research proposal has the following structure:

Title

The title of your study (dissertation or project) is the first part of your plan. You should ensure that the title is self-explanatory. It should convey what you intend to do. There should be no ambiguity. It should be clear, precise, and grammatically correct. It should not be broad or more specific than what you plan to study in the research. If you wish to study the impact of personality development programmes on the tackling of users by staff, then the topic could be: Handling of users by staff in libraries: Impact of personality development programmes.

Introduction

The introduction provides background information to the topic of your study. It includes a thorough review of what is available related to your area of study. Try to clarify the conceptual area zeroing down towards the topic. Introduction should cover the following aspects:

- An overview of the main area of study.
- A historical perspective (development, growth, etc.) pertinent to the area of study.
- Philosophical or ideological issues related to the topic.
- Trends in terms of prevalence, if appropriate.
- Major theories, if any.
- The main issues, problems and advances in the subject area under study.
- Important theoretical and practical issues relating to the central problem under study.
- The main findings related to the core issue(s).

Let us clarify this with the help of an example. If the topic of study is, "Impact of automation on the services of academic libraries in India", then the introduction should include:

- A brief discussion on the concept and history of automation.
- Attempts at automation of libraries in India.
- Trends of automation of academic libraries in India.
- Impact of automation on libraries and their services.

The Problem

Introduction and the problem could be visualized as occurring together in continuation as background to the study. The difference is that introduction is more general as compared to the problem. The problem starts where introduction ends.

It is continuation of introduction, focusing specifically on the topic. Why have you chosen the topic? Is there any need to conduct such studies? What is the rationale of your topic? What gaps in the existing knowledge does it intend to fill? The following issues are needed to be discussed in the problem:

- Identify the issues that are the basis of your study.
- Specify the various aspects of perspectives on these issues.
- Identify the main gaps in the existing body of knowledge.
- Raise some of the main research questions that you want to answer through your study.
- Identify what knowledge is available concerning your questions, specifying.
- Ascertain difference of opinion if differences exist in the literature regarding these questions.
- Develop a rationale for your study with particular reference to how your study will fill the identified gaps.

Let us discuss what needs to be discussed in the problem if the topic of research is: "Impact of automation on the services of academic libraries in India". It should include the following based on a review of literature:

- Categorize the different kinds of services and the impact of automation on them.
- Discuss the views and theories propounded by experts in this regard.
- Present case studies of attempts by professionals towards studying the impact of automation on services.
- Separate the impact on service providers and users.
- Bring to light issues that remain to be studied or point towards a need for more investigation.
- State the relevance of your study, why is it needed, how is it going to fill the gaps.
- If such studies have already been conducted, you could justify the need for your study if some aspects have not been studied, or some issues have cropped up from earlier studies, or your study is being conducted in a new environment or conditions, or it is a longitudinal study. These are studies conducted again on the same population after a gap of time to know the change in dependent variables over a period of time. It helps provide a pattern of change in the dependent variable.

Scope

After the problem has been stated, it is important to explain its scope also. In the scope one should indicate to what extent one intends to probe the topic. One should clarify the scope in relation to the subject content and the geographical area. There should also be a submission of the scope regarding the coverage of the time period. The scope must give an indication of the limitations of the topic.

Objectives

After stating the problem, the plan should state the objectives of your study. This is one of the most important parts of your plan. It helps the reader know what you intend to do. Anyone interested in your study gets to know the whole picture from just the objectives. You can very well judge the importance of objectives. Therefore, it is important that they are stated in a crisp language so that they are clear and unambiguous. Moreover, they should convey what is the intended outcome of your study. Where do you reach to when you start from here? For that you need to use action verbs like: to know, to find out, to evaluate, to automate, to design, etc.

Another thing to be borne in mind while stating objectives is that they should not be broad. One should be able to clearly make out the intentions of one's study that could help him/her or even you while evaluating. It is a pointer to measure how far you have succeeded in your project.

Let us discuss the same example again, "Impact of automation on the services of academic libraries in India". The objectives of the study could be stated as to study the impact of automation on:

- change in the form of services;
- any new services introduced;
- the service providers;
- the frequency of use of services; and
- ease of use of services.

Hypotheses

The next section of your plan should be devoted to hypotheses. Hypothesis is an assumption, presumption or, a supposition for further study.

It is an assumption of relationships between the dependent and independent variables. Hypotheses provide the researcher a line of action along which he/she moves to find out answers to the problem he/she is working on. It is not necessary that every research study has a hypothesis.

Though we have stated that hypotheses formulation involves guess, it does not mean there is no base to it. A thorough review of literature is needed to understand the concept and the relationships existing between the various variables. It is on the basis of this review and discussion with peers and others in the field that we propose a relationship between the variables. This is tested during the course of study. It is pertinent to recall what we have studied in the earlier chapters, that hypotheses, if proved true later, results in theories and finally into laws. There are two kinds of hypotheses: **null** and **alternative**. Hypothesis is stated as null hypothesis, which is a negative statement. We state the relations expected between the variables in a negative way, e.g., if we expect that automation has resulted in increased use of library services. We should frame the null hypothesis as:

HO = there is no increase in use of library services due to their automation. The alternative hypothesis would then be:

H1 = there is increase in use of library services due to library automation. Thus, if null hypothesis is proved to be false, the alternative hypothesis is proved to be true.

Review of Related Literature

After the hypotheses are stated, a brief review of literature is presented. It helps the researcher to know and assimilate what others have already done in the field. It gives him the direction of movement into his research. He comes to know the ripe areas for research. Whenever we plan to research, we have to start from somewhere, which we come to know by literature review. Literature review is conducted at two different stages of research work. The first stage involves a brief review of related literature. It is done again after the proposal is approved and the study is conducted. The second stage has a greater scope of review of literature; it covers all aspects, and the period of coverage depends on the subject and topic of study.

Research Design

The plan of research from the point of operationalisation of hypotheses to the analysis of data is presented as research design. The research design is the blueprint of your nature of investigation, data collection methods to be used, the number of contacts to be made with the subjects, and the reference period of study. Broadly, your nature of investigation can be exploratory, descriptive, or experimental. It depends on the topic you choose. A study can adopt more than one topic also. For example, any research starts with an exploratory investigation where you tend to explore your topic. It is a stage where you formulate your topic based on the review of literature and discussion with others in the field. The research here does not rigidly follow research methodology. The data collection methods also do not follow strictly probability sampling. As in social sciences, in library science also, descriptive methods of research are followed. These methods describe the situation of an object, phenomenon, or a process, or an event in the past or present. If they describe a situation in the future, it becomes experimental research. If your topic of research is: "Impact of automation on the services of academic libraries in India", it has to be descriptive research. Similarly, you have to describe the data collection design—whether it will be survey, or case study, or content analysis. It will be survey for the topic, ''Impact of automation on the services of academic libraries in India". A mention of the number of contacts to be made with the subjects and the period of reference also needs to be made here. In the research design, you should also clearly mention the population under study. Describe the data that you intend to collect in terms of the dependent and independent variables.

Then you also need to clarify whether you will collect data from the whole of the population or from only a sample. If it has to be a sample study, you need to specify what methods of sampling would be used: whether it would be probability sampling or non-probability sampling. Within probability and non-probability sampling also, state which type of sampling method would be used. The size of the sample should be mentioned here. Next, in the research design, the researcher should mention the techniques and tools of data collection. In the techniques, she should mention whether it would be observation, questioning, or interview, what tools of data collection would be used—questionnaire (mailed or self-administered), interview schedule, etc. The research design should also state when and where the data collection will be done.

After the data collection methods are discussed, the methods of its presentation and analysis should be described. Here, a mention should be made of the types of tables and graphs that you intend to use to present your data. Also explain how you would analyze your data. What statistics do you intend to use? If you plan to do the analysis using some software package like SPSS, MS-Access, or MS-Excel, etc., mention it in the design.

Tentative Chapterisation

The physical structure of the research report is also presented in the research plan as tentative chapterisation. What will be the chapters in your thesis are presented here. Normally, the final report also contains the chapters: Introduction, which comprises the preliminaries, the problem, scope, objectives, hypothesis, limitations, and operational definitions. The other chapters are review of literature, conceptual structure, research design, data collection, analysis of data, discussion, and conclusion.

Limitations

Every research study has its limitations. These could be from the point of view of the contents (coverage of the subject), geographical area, time period of study, etc. The researcher should earnestly admit the limitations in his/her study. This is no drawback for the study. The limitations vary according to the level of study and that of the researcher. If the limitations are presented, the evaluation of the thesis is done keeping these in view.

Operational Definitions

The research, like any other work, has to deal with vocabulary. We know the nature of any language is such that there is a lot of flexibility. The occurrence of synonyms, homonyms, and other such concepts may result in confusion. Thus, in the beginning itself, terms that are to be used are standardized in the form of operational definitions given in the research plan.

FUNDING

Research involves financial investment. The researcher can get support for this investment from different agencies. In India, these agencies are the University Grants Commission (UGC), Council of Scientific and Industrial Research (CSIR), Indian Council of Agricultural Research (ICAR), Indian Council of Medical Research (ICMR), Indian Council of Social Science Research (ICSSR), and other. Researchers in library and information science can get their research proposals funded from any of these agencies depending on their area of study.

Why should an agency fund for your research? It should fund for the following reasons:

- Such funding encourages you to do research.
- Makes you realize that research adds to the intellectual wealth of a nation.
- Makes the institution realize that your research topic lies within the scope of the institution and would be beneficial for it.

The research plan in the case of a research for funding should also submit a financial estimate. The financial estimate should be presented under different heads, i.e., the purpose for which you are asking for grants. These may be:

- Space/Rooms
- Equipment
- Books/Journals
- Stationery
- Travel
- Publishing.

The agency may provide grants for some or even all of these expenses. As far as publishing is concerned, this grant is provided after the completion of the project/ theses.

MONITORING

Like any other project, monitoring too is an important component of research. Research plan should also indicate your plans to monitor your research work. You need to apply time management and prepare a work plan to be submitted along with your research plan. The work plan should indicate when (month and year) you would

- start your research;
- review related literature;
- prepare data collection instruments;
- collect data;
- do coding of data;

- do statistical analysis of data;
- prepare draft of your report; and
- finally submit the report.

It is may not be always possible to follow the time schedule exactly as specified. Since it is only a plan, there may be some flexibility here and there. While planning it is important to make adjustments for any possible disturbances in the time schedule. Monitoring should be done regularly to avoid any delays in fulfilling the schedule. The researcher should be regular in her work and subdivide her plan into short time plans. She should translate the plan into tasks to be undertaken every day and should evaluate her day's work to diagnose the cause of delays and root out the cause of delay. In the case of academic research for the award of degrees, the progress report is to be submitted quarterly or half-yearly approved by the supervisor to be submitted to the authorities. Similarly, the progress report has also to be submitted to the funding authorities to prove accountability.

Ethics

The researcher should follow a *code of ethics* in research. We need not overemphasize that ethics is important in research as in any other activity. Following ethics in work implies doing the work in the right way. The right way implies that it is done in a way acceptable to the society. Ethics has been used interchangeably with morals though they are different. Ethics is concerned with what one *ought to do*.

To analyze and make it convenient to understand, Hart (2005) divides the ethical issues in research as those concerned with:

- research;
- researcher;
- subjects; and
- sponsoring body/university.

While doing the right things, the researcher should understand that the above four should not suffer through your decisions while doing research. Let us discuss by way of examples the areas where ethics has to be taken into consideration:
State the topic in an unambiguous way. It should not be the topic of some other study. The research should add to the repertoire of knowledge. Acknowledge the works of others that have been used in the research. Plagiarism should not be resorted to. Ask for financial grants only where required for research. In data collection, the anonymity of the subjects should be maintained. The privacy of subjects should also be maintained.

In case the subjects are animals or plants as in the case of sciences, their treatment should be ethical. Tampering of data to achieve results should not be done.

SUMMARY

In this chapter we have discussed the various aspects of research plan. We introduced the concept and discussed the need for, purpose and functions of research plan. The chapter gave comprehensive details on the structure of a plan. A step-by-step approach was followed to explain all parts of a plan. Adequate examples were given at all the stages to make all the steps clear. Research can be funded through various agencies, which was also described in the chapter. We also discussed heads under which the researcher can apply for funds. The researcher should take care that she follows ethics while conducting research. The specific areas have been stated for the help of the researcher. Ethics was discussed in this chapter so that the researcher gets conscious of it from the start of the research. We ended the chapter with some model plans given as examples.

DISCUSSION QUESTIONS

1. Discuss the areas where ethical considerations are important in a research plan.
2. Define hypothesis. Differentiate between null and alternative hypotheses.
3. Taking a hypothetical example, state the objectives of your study.
4. Describe what you would discuss in the introduction to the plan of your study.
5. Define research plan. How is it different from a research design?

FURTHER READING

Ackoff, Russell (1953): *The Design of Social Research*, Chicago: University of Chicago.

Adams, Gerald R. and Schvaneveldt, Jay D. (1985): *Understanding Research Methods*, New York: Longman.

Hart, Chris (2005): *Doing Your Masters Dissertation*, Delhi: Vistaar.

Kothari, C.R. (2004): *Research Methodology: Methods and techniques*, 2nd ed., New Delhi: New Age International.

Kumar, Krishan (1998): *Research Methods in Library Science*, 2nd ed., New Delhi: Har-Anand.

Neuman, W. Lawrence (1997): *Social Research Methods*, 3rd ed., Boston: Allyn and Bacon.

Kumar, Ranjit (1999): *Research Methodology: A step-by-step guide for beginners*, New Delhi: Sage Publications.

4 Research Design

- Research Design—Meaning and importance
- Classification of Research Designs
- Exploratory Research Design
- Descriptive Research Design
- Factors Influencing Validity of Experiments
- Discussion Questions

After going through this chapter, you will be able to:

- Explain the concept and importance of research design in the context of marketing research problems.
- Discuss the causality factor in the context of research design.
- Describe the various kinds of research designs and their applications for different research situations.

INTRODUCTION

In Chapters 2 and 3, you studied about the nature and importance of marketing research. In this chapter you will learn about the first phase in planning the research project, which is formulating a research design. Based on causality, research designs have been divided into four categories: exploratory, descriptive, quasi-experimental, and experimental designs. While exploratory and descriptive studies provide information on events and attributes from which inferences can be drawn, they can only offer tenuous conclusions. In order to draw conclusions, it is important to formulate quasi-experimental or experimental designs. This chapter describes different types of designs within the four categories mentioned above as well as the marketing situations where these designs could be most appropriately applied.

RESEARCH DESIGN—Meaning and importance

Research design is the specification of strategy, the plan, and the composition of investigating a research to be carried out. A research design is the determination of the general research plan taken up. It is the overall operational pattern or outline of the plan that specifies what kind of information is to be collected from which source and what methods are to be applied to collect that data within the budget and with accuracy.

To be effective, a research design should furnish at least the following details:

1. A statement of objectives of the study or the research output.
2. A statement of the data inputs required on the basis of which the research problem is to be solved.
3. The methods of analysis which will be used to treat and analyze the data inputs

Let us try to understand these through an example:

Example

A newly opened supermarket sells a broad line of merchandise ranging from provision to household appliances and kitchenware. The General Manager, Sales believes that the total profits of the supermarket can be enhanced by getting people to buy in larger quantities which could be achieved by offering attractive cash discount on bigger purchases, the other executives are doubtful about this. The hypothesis can be tested by carrying out a marketing research exercise.

1. The objective is to calculate the margin earned on sales when this discount is offered and compare it with the margin when discount is not being offered.

2. The data to be collected over a period of time
   (a) Sales in rupees to a selected sample of customers during the period when the discount is offered.
   (b) Sales in rupees to the same customer when the discount is not being offered.
   (c) The average order size in the two periods.
   (d) The average margins earned during the two periods.
   (e) The cost of promotional inputs regarding the discount.
3. The analysis of the data will be:
   (a) Sales in rupees in period 1 minus those in period 2.
   (b) Subtract cost of incentives.
   (c) Also subtract cost of promotional inputs.

Simply stated, it is the outline for the research study that guides the collection and examination and interpretation of data. Research design is important as it sets up a proper structure within which the research work will be conducted. It's actually like a sailor's compass which points to the direction in which the ship has to move. Research design too should indicate the direction of research. It brings in efficiency in investigation and builds confidence in the final outcome of the study. Research design gives proper direction and schedule to the whole research activity. It keeps sufficient check on the research work and ensures its completion within the stipulated time. It keeps the whole research project on the right track.

A sound research design leaves less room for errors in alignment with the research problem, information requirement, etc. It gives practical direction to the whole research work and makes it applicable to the marketing problems faced by the corporate. Finally, it makes the whole research process compact and result oriented. A researcher should move forward with his research project only after the research design is framed properly.

At the stage of analysis and interpretation also, the research design helps in providing direction to the computation and interpretation process to arrive at the solution and make recommendations. This is, however, not to suggest that a design is a rigid straitjacket to which the study must always conform. The research design only represents an expectation of likely results but, as the study proceeds, many unexpected results may come forth, which may necessitate framing of new hypothesis or at least modifying some. The research design is only a guiding and not a limiting framework for research study.

Researchers have developed different types of research designs to facilitate their study. Their research actions include organization of the variables, selection of samples, schedule for data collection, and methods for statistical examination.

Research designs can be classified in different ways. The decisive factor for the use of any particular research design depends on the need of the research work being undertaken. On the basis of experiment, the research designs can be classified into experimental and non-experimental research. In non-experimental design, the researcher studies existing trends without intrusion in the structure of these trends, whereas experimental design requires some kind of experiment with the intrusion of the researcher.

Classification of Research Designs

Research designs can also be classified according to their purpose or use. Fundamentally, it can be observed that research designs can be classified in many ways. However, one point may be noted that the source of classification of different types of research designs is causality. Let us get an idea by taking an example. Suppose the sales manager of a company manufacturing kitchen cabinets carried out a training programme for its salesmen operating in a state. Three months after the training programme, it was observed that there was an increase in sales in that state by 30%. The sales manager asserted the importance of training and emphasized that the sales teams across the country should be put under training for increasing sales. Now this theory or hypothesis assumed by the sales manager needs to be tested for its validity. The sales manager felt that the direct result of training would be increase in sales. But in a dynamic environment, the effect of one variable on the whole scenario is not possible in its entirety. There may be other reasons or other variables whose presence or absence goes unnoticed. The increase could be more because of demographic factors such as a large number of newly married couples buying their own houses. This leads to setting up of modern kitchens (modular kitchens) from a particular vendor, with nonavailability of competitor's product due to logistics problems, increased product penetration in the distribution channel, sudden trend of having modern classy homes, etc.

Therefore, it is vital that the sales manager should know the conditions under which proper causal statements can be made. To be able to make any causal statements, one should make sure whether the following conditions are met:

1. Evidence to assert the existence of a strong association between a causal variable and the eventual result of the effect variable.
2. The other condition for the causal relationship is that the causal variable must come first before the observed result of the effect variable.
3. A strong evidence to say that there were no causal factors which could have also given the observed result.

The first condition is that of concomitant variation. It is a method of scientific induction according to which a phenomenon varying in any way whenever another phenomenon varies in some particular way is a cause or effect of that phenomenon or is related to it through some fact of causation. So a concomitant variation is the extent to which a cause *X* and an effect *Y* occur or differ jointly. In the foregoing example, the sales training programme and increase in sales have to take place together for a conclusion based on causality. However, it is important to note that the presence of a strong relationship between two variables does not amount to a proof of a causal relationship. It is quite likely that the strong relationship between two variables may be the result of random variation, or both the variables may be influenced by an unconnected variable.

The second condition for causal relationship is the requirement that the causal action must come either earlier or concurrently with the effect factor. But again, it is not necessary that it is the outcome of such concurrent happening. The element of coincidence should not be completely disregarded in the whole scenario. Also, we must always consider the possibility that actually the effect of training was the reason of increased sales in our example.

The third condition for deducing causation is that there were no causal factors which could have also given the observed result. This means that all other possible factors influencing the result (in our case increase in sales of kitchen cabinet) is either absent or are kept constant.

Now we will examine some broad classifications: exploratory research designs and descriptive research designs.

EXPLORATORY RESEARCH DESIGN

The exploratory research design is meant to explore a problem or situation to provide insights into and understanding of such problem or situation. Such a design attempts to discover general information about a subject that is not well understood by the marketer. The exploratory research design, as the name suggests, means getting a feel of the situation and works on a discovery of ideas that may help in identifying areas of further rigorous study. For instance, a marketer has heard about cloud computing technology that is helping competitors but he is not familiar with the technology. So he will have to do research to learn more about it. When gaining insight (i.e., discovery) on an issue is the primary goal, exploratory research is used. The main aim of the exploratory research is to taper down the broad problem into a specific problem statement and generate possible hypotheses. It, therefore, gives useful direction for further research. The exploratory studies are mainly used for: formulating a problem or defining a problem more precisely, identifying the alternative courses of action, developing hypotheses, providing information to enable a more precise problem definition or hypothesis formulation and establishing research priorities, and separating key variables and associations for further assessment. The design of the exploratory studies is informal because it is for gaining insight and is necessarily not conclusive. The existence of a standard or structured design in terms of questionnaires is not possible because questions have to be conceptualized according to the kind of insight that is needed into the problem. Exploratory designs are based on convenience sampling of data. The most commonly methods used are:

- The existing database are surveyed.
- Veteran individuals are surveyed.
- Situations are examined on the basis of the circumstances of the cases.

Published facts or data present a very cost-effective basis of studying with the intention of creating the premise of hypothesis and narrowing down of the problem. Books, journals, newspapers and periodicals, information published by trade associations such as Chamber of Commerce, publications of the Government of India and ongoing or completed research activity of individuals and the company itself are the sources of data generation. This kind of survey gives a direction or channelizes the research process.

The survey conducted on veterans in their respective fields will give an insight into how to solve the problem. The information may or may not be collected scientifically but the information taken is definitely scientific as it is taken from people who know their respective fields. Again, the accuracy of the information is largely dependent on the type of response given to the respondent and the kind of questions that have been asked to elicit a favourable response.

When situations are analyzed on the basis of the circumstances in the case, then some extreme examples are taken and the deduction is based on the thorough analysis of the problem. The relationships between different variables are identified and the research subject is researched deeply so as to identify the problem in marketing and the overall understanding of the research problem. For example, a company is interested in finding out the various reasons for the unproductivity on productivity of its salesmen. As an exploratory study, it could methodically analyze the case of some of its best and some of its worst salesmen. This exercise may help in identifying possible relationships between demographic and/or individuality variables which may be affecting the productivity in sales.

Descriptive Research Design

Descriptive research design is a valid method for researching specific subjects and as a precursor to more quantitative studies. While there are some valid concerns about the statistical validity, as long as the limitations are understood by the researcher, this type of study is an invaluable scientific tool. It is used to describe methodically the facts and characteristics of a population or area of interest, accurately and precisely. It is a kind of introductory study design primarily used to aid accountability and deduction about a given population—its preferences and the association of two or more variables. Description or deduction could be quantitative or qualitative in nature. Descriptive designs only describe the occurrence under study attempting to establish a relationship between factors. For example, descriptive research design could be suited to measure the various characteristics of successful sales personnel, or appraise a training plan or a selling situation. Customer's behaviour can be checked on the introduction of a new sales programme by the help of this design. This research design cannot, however, assess or gauge the level of relationship between the different variables though it can ascertain or establish that a relationship exists between variables. Descriptive designs are intended to provide correct descriptions of variables pertinent to the problem under deliberation and are used for preliminary and explorative studies. The decision makers sometimes accept descriptive data which allows inference drawing about causality between variables. This is because the use of descriptive designs is more cost effective as compared to experimental designs.

Descriptive designs are commonly used research designs for conclusive studies also. They are used to describe the attributes of target groups of research to the marketer, e.g. consumption by the user, targeted beneficiary, and actual beneficiary of advertisement by the company, to assess the percentage of people in a given population who act in a certain way, for example, the proportion of consumers who are open for bargains or discount deals, to make specific predictions for specified future periods, to deduce whether certain variables are connected, for example, purchasing power and shopping place inclination. Descriptive study research designs are formal and less flexible than exploratory research designs.

Descriptive studies are generally characterized by two methods of study which are self-report observations. In a **self-report study**, information is collected from individuals by means of meeting, questionnaires, or standardized attitude scales. In an **observation study**, information is only obtained by questioning the individuals and by observing them. As the descriptive design is directed at collecting qualitative and quantitative data to facilitate explanation of variables, it involves formulation of a specific hypothesis and testing them through statistical inference of discipline designs. It includes case research designs, longitudinal and cross-sectional designs as well as focus group studies. We will look into the panel, cross-sectional and focus group designs.

Panel Research Design

Panel research design is also called *longitudinal research.* The elements of this panel may be retail outlets, consumers or just individuals. In a panel the same set of people are asked to respond periodically. Panel design involves the periodic information collection from a fixed panel or sample of respondents. So, basically in this research design, the respondents are regularly questioned for the information over a span of time, usually from retail outlets, dealers, consumers or just individuals. This continuous evaluation of variables helps in guessing the future actions of the respondent or the concerned. The longitudinal analysis involves continual measurements of the similar variables to aid a variety of deductions to be drawn about the behaviour of the respondents of the panel. The omnibus panel is also formulated where, though a fixed sample of respondents is maintained, the information accumulated from the sample affiliates may differ over time or differ between individuals, for example, at one time information on reactions with respect to a future packaging change may be necessary while at another time the information on attitudes with respect to a proposed packaging change may be sought; yet at another time the information may relate to respondent attitude to a pamphlet. Panel studies are increasingly being used by research agencies to facilitate frequent gauging of consumer attitudes, initial buyer profiles, brand loyalties in the market, and forecasting changes in market situation of different brands.

Cross-sectional Design

The cross-sectional design is meant for assessing the situation or occurrence in which the researcher or marketer is interested in, for example, how many people recalled advertisement out of the total population of viewers. So this way it provides a cross-section. The cross-sectional study is aimed at taking a single collection of the condition or the occurrence in which the researcher is interested. Cross-sectional designs give the representation of the condition at a given point of time. For instance, if the marketer is interested in knowing the market situation of the company in comparison with its competitors, a cross-sectional design can be used to gather this kind of data. The information gathered in this design consists of reactions from a sample which holds a large number of sources. It provides a "cross-section" of the whole condition. In some marketing situations, cross-sectional data provides good feedback. For example, an instant food manufacturing company has given exhibit racks for its sellers so that its product can be prominently exhibited. Before launching the next round of distribution of these racks, it wants to know the number of retailers who have actually used these racks and the type of retailing industry they belong to. The marketer was not seeking the existence of any casual relationship for the exhibit rack. He was seeking information on a single occurrence and the relation therein. Cross-sectional studies may find out relationships, which may be finally tested by using the experimental designs. Though the cross-sectional studies may have an informal design, sometimes, the design only includes the nature and the source of data, the analytical methods, and the nature of the likely results.

Focus Group

The focus group design is an informal research design in which a group of people come together and discuss at length about their experiences or opinion. Usually, such conversations are recorded and then analyzed later on. The discussion is guided by a moderator. The focus group is integrally an informal design consisting of combining a group of people to have a wide-ranging, free flowing discussion describing their experience or viewpoints. The standard modus operandi is to tape record the conversations and later draw inferences from them. The discussion in the focus group is piloted and manoeuvered by a moderator who has a fairly consistent way of creating a relaxed and affable ambience and starting the conversation and keeping it focused on the point. The intention of the focus group design is exploratory, looking for respondent's viewpoints of experiences on a particular topic. The objectives of the focus group study are clearly outlined, but the conversation is not structurised. In fact, an attempt is made to keep the discussion lucid and smooth. The success of the focus group design depends on a skilled and efficient moderator who can keep the conversation on to the desired course and draw out responses from all the members of the group.

Example: A well-known shampoo manufacturer wishes to modify the existing ad for his prominent brand of shampoo, so as to reinforce its image as an excellent shampoo, using a focus group of teenage girls, college students, housewives and corporate workers. An unrestrictive discussion about expectations from hair products in general and the shampoo in particular was generated and recorded to give important ideas and insights for the creative tactic to be used for the advertising theme. Focus groups act as first-rate tools for introductory research as they disclose problems and prospects which stem from the free flowing and candidly honest discussions by the consumers (when they are relaxed) about their problems, beliefs, expectations, likes and dislikes. They are easy to set up and interesting to analyze, and become very good sources of ideas for promotions, product development or repositioning, desirability of deals, dealer selection, and so on. The danger associated with focus group lies in the possibility that, once analyzed, the focus group data may be used for decisive reasons. The shortcoming of a focus group is its small size and the resulting conclusion that comes from a smaller group of people may be subject to a lot of factors including biases, personal opinions and preferences.

Factors Influencing Validity of Experiments

A well-designed and assembled experiment will be tough under probing, and will focus on conclusions, rather than latent experimental errors. A sound experimental design should follow the established technical modus operandi and generate good statistical data helpful in making sound decisions.

There are two important concepts of validity that are related to experimentation, namely, internal validity and external validity which are now briefly described.

Internal Validity

Internal validity is the assurance that we can place in the cause and effect relationship in a research. The integral question that a researcher needs to ask about his research observations is that whether there can be any alternative grounds, or reasons, that may describe his observations and result.

External Validity

External validity is at the foundation of every good experimental design. The decisive factor of external validity is the process of simplification, and whether results attained from a small sample group, often in laboratory environment, can be used to make predictions about the total populace.

An experiment should gratify both internal and external validity, it is not odd to find experiment meeting all the internal validity requirements and yet be invalid externally. It may be so because of the environment variations during different times and venues of testing. The results obtained for one time period may not be valid for a longer time span, and so on.

An experiment's validity is subject to many factors. Let's discuss some of them.

1. Past records: Past records tell about the occurrence of some incidences which are non-repetitive or non-recurring. Though they are peripheral to the experiment, somehow they occur simultaneously. Suppose we have to calculate the sales of a territory prior to and subsequent to the training of the sales personnel. The variation in the sales may point out to the management the effect of the training. Yet, an increase in sales cannot be totally the result of the training. A development in business circumstances prior to and after the training may have been the reason for increased sales. Hence, the longer the intervals amid observations, the bigger the possibility that past records will confound an experiment of this type and will considerably affect the results.

2. Completion: Completion is related to the modifications that happen with time in the individuals involved in the design. In the example training related job the increase in sales can be attributed to the better expertise of the sales personnel with the hands-on experience that they have acquired on the job. It may be noted that it is not only people that change over time, but also retail outlets, geographic regions, institutions, etc. The time-span covered during these experiments has a direct relationship with the completion effect.

3. Checking: In the course of an experiment, if the respondents are aware that their behaviour is under observation, their responses may become more orchestrated than genuine. In the example of training sales personnel, if the salespersons are aware that the effectiveness of their training is being checked, they may make an extraordinary effort to do well in their sales activity.

4. Selection bias: If groups are ascertained for research on the decision of the researcher, there is a likelihood of selection bias. The selection process should be random since it will result in a measureable random variation. On the other hand, if a non-random process is adopted, the results will be affected by a non-measurable error.

5. Test unit mortality: It is quite possible that some of the test units or respondents might drop out from the experiment while it is in the growth stage. Let's use the sales training example to explain this. If some of the sales persons who are going through training leave before the training is over, there is no way of knowing who was responsible for improving sales, who would have responded to training better than the others, and so on.

SUMMARY

This chapter on Research Design gives an overview of the research designs and their application in marketing research. After discussing the meaning and benefits of a research design, the discussion focuses on the four basic types of designs, namely, exploratory, descriptive, quasi-experimental and experimental. Causality, the relationship between data and conclusions, forms the basis of this classification. We also discussed about the nature of causality and the need to measure it. Besides covering the major design categories and their applications, we gave an outline of the specific subtypes within the major categories discussed, under the descriptive design, panel design, cross-sectional design and focus groups. The quasi-experimental designs discussed include after-only without control group, before-after without control group the static group comparison, longitudinal design, and multiple time series designs. Under the experimental design categories, the designs covered are after-only with one control group; before-after with one control, Solomon four-group design completely randomized design, randomized block design, and Latin square design. Finally, we dealt with issues of internal and external validity of the experimental validity of experiment.

DISCUSSION QUESTIONS

1. Explain the Solomon four-group design. How far does this design succeed in controlling different extraneous variables? Illustrate your answer with the help of a suitable example from marketing.
2. Explain the various extraneous variables which if not controlled in an experiment may contaminate the effect of the independent variable.
3. What design would you use to:
   (a) Test whether the coloured newspaper advertisement is more effective than the existing black and white advertisement?
   (b) Know which of the several promotional techniques is most efficient in selling a particular product?
   (c) Determine whether additional shelf space allocated to a product would increase the sales of that product in the supermarket?
   (d) Determine the type of customers who would be the first adopters of a newly introduced brand. Justify your answer.
4. What are the marketing research situations suitable for
   (a) Focus group study
   (b) Panel research design
   (c) Cross-sectional design
   (d) Quasi-experimental design
5. Distinguish between exploratory and descriptive research designs.

FURTHER READING

Body, H.W., Westfall, R. and Stasch, S.F. (1996): *Marketing Research: Text and cases*, Homewood (Illinois): Richard D. Irwin.

Freund, John E. and Williams, Frank J. (1979): *Elementary Business Statistics—The modern approach*, Englewood Cliffs (New Jersey): Prentice Hall International Edition.

Green, Paul E., Tull, Donald S. and Albaum, Gerald (2010): *Research for Marketing Decisions*, 5th ed., New Delhi: PHI Learning.

Kinnear, Thomas C. and Taylor, James R. (1995): *Marketing Research—An applied approach*, New York: McGraw-Hill International Edition.

5 Descriptive and Experimental Research

- Descriptive Research
- Experimental Research
- Discussion Questions

After going through this chapter, you will be able to:

- Describe the steps involved in descriptive research.
- Explain the characteristics and features of types of descriptive research such as survey research, documentary analysis, co relational studies and causal-comparative studies.
- Describe the steps involved in experimental research.
- Identify and explain a few designs for experimental studies.

INTRODUCTION

As you studied in the earlier chapters, a research method is a particular way of studying a problem. The features of the research problem and also the field of inquiry determine the method. In this chapter, we shall discuss in detail Descriptive Method and Experimental Method of Research.

DESCRIPTIVE RESEARCH

Descriptive research studies are designed to obtain information about the current status of a given phenomenon. They are concerned with the existing conditions or relationships, prevailing practices, current beliefs, points of view or attitudes, processes that are going on and their effects, and the developing trends. In short, they determine the nature of a situation as it exists at the time of study. The aim of descriptive research is to describe "what exists" with respect to variables or conditions in a situation.

The descriptive research method is appropriate in behavioural sciences. Many types of behaviour that interest the researcher cannot be arranged in a realistic setting. For example, it would be unthinkable to prescribe cigarette smoking for the purpose of studying its possible relationship to throat or lung cancer, or deliberately arrange accidents, in order to evaluate the effectiveness of seat-belts or helmets in preventing serious injuries.

Although some experimental studies of human behaviour can be appropriately carried out, both in the laboratory and in the field, the prevailing method used in social sciences is descriptive. Under the conditions that naturally occur at home, inside the classroom, on the playground or within the community, human behaviour can be systematically examined and analyzed. This analysis may lead to the modification of factors or influences that determine the nature of human interaction. It is through this modification of factors that social institutions may become more effective influences in promoting human welfare.

Descriptive Research: Main Steps

In descriptive studies, we do not present private convictions and data based on casual or cursory observations. In descriptive study, we:

(a) examine the problematic situation;
(b) define our problem and state our hypothesis;
(c) list the assumption upon which our hypothesis and procedures are based;
(d) select appropriate subjects and source material;
(e) select or construct technique for collecting data;
(f) validate the data gathering techniques;
(g) make objective and discriminating observations; and
(h) describe, analyze and interpret data in clear and precise terms.

We, as researchers, collect evidence on the basis of some hypotheses, tabulate and summarize the data carefully, and then analyze the results thoroughly in an endeavour to draw meaningful generalization that will advance knowledge.

Collection of Data

When presenting a descriptive research report, you must identify not only the kind of data obtained but also the exact nature of its population. The units that constitute a population may be people, items, events or objects. After identifying the population, you must decide whether to collect data from (a) the total population or (b) a representative sample of the population.

Total population: Obtaining information from every unit of a small population is not difficult in most instances, but the findings are not applicable to any population other than the group studied. After collecting information from every student in one particular institute of any university, you may draw generalizations about the average age or the kind of profession of students in the institute; but you cannot claim that these generalizations will hold true for students in any other institute. Similarly, after studying the attitude of teachers of one institute of the university, the university researcher cannot claim that the findings will hold true for teachers in other institutes of the university.

Sample: Obtaining information from a large population, such as all teachers in the state, is often impractical, impossible or exorbitantly costly. Contacting, observing, measuring or interviewing every unit in the group may need so much time that the data becomes obsolete before the study is complete. To overcome these difficulties, investigators often collect information from a few carefully selected units drawn from a population. While carrying out the research on Study Habits of postgraduate students of a University, the researcher cannot collect data from all the 50,000 (approximate number) postgraduate learners. She will have to select a representative sample of the population. However, the sample will have to be selected from different categories of the population, viz., male/female, employed/unemployed, and so on. If these sample units represent accurately the characteristics of the population, generalizations based on the data obtained from them may be applied to the entire group. But selecting a representative sample is a difficult task. So care must be taken before selecting or finding out the representative sample.

Descriptive data may be expressed qualitatively (in verbal symbols) as well as quantitatively in mathematical symbols. A study may consist almost exclusively of one form or may contain both forms. Qualitative data may predominate in studies that examine the general nature of a phenomenon. Qualitative studies give social scientists useful information, but verbal symbols lack precision as words do not hold the same meaning for all people, at all times, and in all contexts. However, qualitative studies need not be looked down upon; for, they help workers identify the significant factors to measure. Until these general explorations are made, measurement cannot be utilized fruitfully.

Types of Descriptive Research

In this section, we shall discuss various types of descriptive research. These are (i) survey studies, (ii) analysis of documents, (iii) correlational studies, and (iv) causal-comparative investigation. There is nothing sacrosanct about such a categorization, but it helps us understand the phenomenon (research) more clearly.

(i) Survey studies: Quite often, descriptive research itself is termed survey research, but it is better to think of it as a category under descriptive research. 'Survey' is probably the most widely used method for obtaining descriptive and evaluative information in social research. When trying to solve problems, non-governmental, governmental, industrial and political organizations often conduct surveys. Detailed descriptions of existing phenomena are collected with the aim of employing the data to justify current conditions or practices or to make more intelligent plans for improving them. The objective may not only be to ascertain status, but also to determine the adequacy of status by comparing it with selected or established standards. Researchers who wish to improve existing status of health of children may survey how others have solved similar problems. At times, we need to collect all three types of information:

- Data concerning existing status, e.g., to find out the study habits of postgraduate students of a university.
- Comparison of status and standards, e.g., to compare the achievement level of distance education students and conventional education students.
- Means of improving status, e.g., to find out measures to improve student support services in distance education programmes.

On the other hand, we can also limit our studies to one or two of these types.

Surveys may be broad or narrow in scope. They may be confined to a small geographical area or whole state or even the country. The scope and the depth of the survey depend primarily on the nature of the problem. The steps involved in the case of surveys are presented as follows:

1. Selection of topic involves the determination of what topic is to be investigated and what population is to be studied. At this stage, one also decides the methods and procedures that will be used to collect the data.
2. Sampling involves decision making about which people from the population are to be included in the survey. If one is to generalize from the sample to the population, it is essential that the sample selected be representative.
3. Construction of a tool for data collection involves writing the questions and planning the format of the instrument to be used. Among the data collection techniques used in surveys are personal interviews, questionnaires, rating scales, etc.
4. Collection of data includes pre-testing the instrument to determine whether it will obtain the desired data, interviewing subjects or

distributing questionnaires to them, and verifying the accuracy of the data gathered.

5. Processing and analysis of the data includes tabulating the data, computer processing and analysis of the data, interpreting the results, and reporting the findings.

(ii) Analysis of documents: From documents and records, we can unearth pertinent data. Documentary analysis, which is sometimes referred to as 'content', 'activity', or 'informational' analysis is very much like historical research. Both methods of investigation require that researchers examine existing records: historical research is primarily concerned with the more distant past, but descriptive research is concerned chiefly with the present.

A wide variety of documentary surveys are made. Some scholars analyze judicial decisions, state laws and rulings. Researchers may also collect data describing existing NGO's practices, processes and conditions from administrative records, committee reports and minutes of meetings, budget and financial records, etc. Documentary research produces valuable information, but the method has certain limitations, and investigators may draw faulty conclusions from the data.

Some documentary researches are of little value because the investigators fail to analyze the representative sample of source materials. Many studies do not provide information concerning the adequacy of the sample size or the conformity of the universe of the sample to the universe. If an analysis is made of newspaper editorials concerning the problems of agricultural labour, for example, the researcher must judge for himself/herself whether the newspapers selected represent the opinion of the different social, religious, economic or political groups from all the parts of the country. Very often, the write-ups are not representative in nature.

Documentary research in not without other pitfalls as well. Data do not become true reflections of reality through the magic of publication. In using documentary sources, one must bear in mind the fact that data appearing in print may not necessarily be trustworthy. One must subject each documentary source material to the same rigorous external and internal criticism that a historian does. Moreover, the categories used in the available statistical material do not always coincide precisely with the variables which the researcher wants to investigate. Sometimes the definitions of categories are ambiguous, and they may change from one year to another. The boundaries of some units of analysis, e.g., villages, districts, age cohort, etc. can also change; different agencies collecting similar data do not always use exactly the same classificatory system. The data collected always reflect the orientation, concerns, self-interests, and the levels of accuracy preferred by the producers of the records, which may not be an accurate reflection of reality or behavior.

(iii) Correlational studies: Human behaviour at both individual and the social levels is characterized by great complexity. However, given the present state of social research, we understand too little of this complexity. One approach to a fuller understanding of human behaviour is to begin by testing out simple relationships between those factors and elements which are supposed to have some bearing on the phenomenon in question. The value of correlational research is that it is able to achieve this end. We know that one of the primary purposes of science, as conceived traditionally, is to discover relationships among phenomena with a view ultimately to predicting and, in some situations, controlling their occurrence.

Much of social sciences research is concerned at our present stage of development with the first step in this sequence, i.e., establishing interrelationships among variables. Correlational studies are concerned with determining the extent of relationship existing between variables. They enable us to measure the extent to which variations in one variable are associated with variations in another. We may wish to know, for example, how delinquency is related to social and class background, or whether a relationship exists between the number of years spent in full-time education and subsequent annual income, or whether there is a link between personality and achievement.

Correlational studies are generally intended to answer three questions. They are:

1. Is there a relationship between two variables (or two sets of data)? If the answer to this question is 'yes', then other questions follow:
2. What is the direction of the relationship?
3. What is the magnitude of the relationship? The magnitude of the relationship is determined by the coefficient of correlation.

For instance, on the basis of her experience, a researcher may hypothesize that there is a relationship between performance in an intelligence test and a test of achievement in arithmetic. The correlational technique will help her test her hypothesis about the relationship. Pearson's product moment, one of the best known measures of association, is a statistical value of the coefficient of correlation ranging from –1.0 to +1.0, through zero and expresses the relationship in quantitative form.

Where the two variables fluctuate in the same direction, i.e., as one increases so does the other, a positive relationship is said to exist. A negative correlation or relationship, on the other hand, is to be found when an increase in one variable is accompanied by a decrease in the other variable. The values near zero indicate a weak relationship between the variables, whereas values closer to either +1.0 or – 1.0 indicate a stronger relationship in either direction. Thus, the coefficient of correlation tells us something about the relationship between two variables. However, other measures exist which allow us to specify relationship when more than two variables are involved. These are known as **measures of multiple correlation** and **partial correlation**.

One danger in interpreting correlations is to assume that because two variables are related in a predictable fashion to one another with a high degree of probability, they are also in a causal relationship. This is not necessarily the case. For one thing, there is never more than a probable relationship between variables. For another, it is quite possible for two variables to be related to one another with a high degree of probability but with a third variable accounting for the nature of relationship. Correlation must not be interpreted to mean that one variable is causing the scores in other variable to be what they are. For example, it may be found that there is a negative correlation between measures of anxiety and measures of intelligence. It should not be interpreted that there is a causative relationship between anxiety and intelligence, that is, that pupils are anxious because they are unintelligent or that pupils appear unintelligent because they are anxious. It might be that there are other underlying characteristics of individuals that tend to make some appear unintelligent and anxious, and others, intelligent and not anxious.

Interpretation of such a correlation is difficult without experimental confirmation. For example, the relationship between anxiety measures and intelligence measures could be investigated experimentally by deliberately inducting anxiety in a testing situation and determining the effect on intelligence test scores.

Characteristics of correlational studies

Correlational studies can be broadly classified either as relational studies or as prediction studies. As a method, the former is particularly useful in exploratory studies in fields where little or no previous research has been undertaken. It is often a shot in the dark aimed at verifying hunches which a researcher has about a presumed relationship between some characteristics or variables. Take, for example, a complex notion like teacher effectiveness. This is dependent on a number of complex factors operating singly or in combination. Factors such as intelligence, motivation, person, perception, and verbal skills come to mind as possibly having an effect on teacher outcomes. A review of the literature of research will confirm or reject these possibilities. Once an appropriate number of such possibilities has been identified in this way, suitable measures may be chosen or developed to assess them. They are given to a representative sample, and the scores obtained are correlated with the complex factor that is being investigated, namely, teacher effectiveness. As it is an exploratory undertaking, the analysis will consist of correlation coefficients only. The investigation and its outcomes may then be used as a basis for further research or as sources of additional hypotheses.

In contrast to exploratory research studies, prediction studies are usually undertaken in an area having a firmer and securer knowledge base. Prediction through the use of correlational technique is based on the assumption that at least some of the factors that will lead to the behaviour to be predicted are present and measurable at the time the prediction is made. For example, since we know that IQ and General Achievement (GA) are positively correlated, we can predict with some degree of accuracy that an individual with a high IQ will probably have a high GA. To be valuable for prediction, the extent of correlation between two variables must be substantial; of course, the higher the correlation, the more accurate the prediction.

(iv) Causal-comparative investigation: There is, at times the need to discover how and why a particular phenomenon occurs, and not confine our investigation to what a phenomenon is like. In this instance, the investigator tries to compare the similarities and differences among phenomena to find out what factors or circumstances seem to accompany or contribute to the occurrence of certain events, conditions or practices. Unlike a scientist working in a laboratory, a social researcher cannot always select, control and manipulate factors that are necessary to study cause-effect relations. An investigator cannot, for example, manipulate domestic background, social class, intelligence, etc. in situations that do not allow researchers manipulate the independent variable and establish the controls that are required in 'true experiments', they may conduct a causal-comparative study.

In a causal-comparative investigation, a researcher studies a real-life situation in which subjects have experienced what she wants to investigate. For example, if an investigator wants to study emotional instability, she does not place children in a situation where all factors are kept constant except one variable which is manipulated to determine what causes a particular type of emotional disturbance. Rather, she chooses children who, according to a selected criterion, are 'disturbed' and compares them with emotionally stable children. After searching for factors or conditions which seem to be associated with one group and not the other, she may present a possible explanation of the underlying causes of the emotional problem.

Limitations

1. Lack of control is a serious limitation and weakness of causal-comparative method of investigation.
2. It is usually difficult to identify the relevant factors causing a particular condition or phenomenon. For instance, the fact that students like a teacher depends on a number of factors and a researcher may not be able to identify all the factors. She may only be able to identify good teaching and mastery of subject matter as some of the factors affecting students' liking for a teacher.
3. The joint method of agreement and disagreement requires that a single factor must be the cause for the occurrence or non-occurrence of the phenomenon. But in the case of social phenomena, with which a researcher is usually concerned, this condition does not come invariably. In fact, these situations/events usually have multiple rather than single causes. Further, a phenomenon may result not only from multiple causes but also from one cause in one instance and from another cause in another instance.
4. When a relationship between variables is established, it is difficult to distinguish between the cause and the effect.

5. The classification of subjects into dichotomous groups for the purpose of comparison also presents problems.
6. In comparative studies of natural situations, the researcher does not have the same control over the selection of subjects as she has in experimental studies. It is difficult to identify existing groups of subjects who are alike in all respects except for their exposure to one variable.

Though causal-comparative studies have many limitations, and they do not often produce precise and reliable knowledge that can be gained through rigorous experimental studies, they provide the means of tackling problems that cannot be probed in laboratory situations. Besides, they yield valuable information and clues about the nature of phenomena and are well suited to many types of field studies seeking to establish causal relationships

Experimental Research

Experimental research studies are designed for establishing causal relationships. This method begins with a question about the relationship between two or more variables. At the same time, the researcher advances one or more hypotheses stating the nature of the expected relationship. The experiment is the event planned and carried out by the researcher to gather evidence relevant to the hypotheses.

In its simplest form, an experiment has three characteristics:

1. An independent variable is manipulated.
2. All other variables except the independent variable are held constant.
3. The effect of the manipulation of the independent variable on the dependent variable is observed.

The independent variable and the dependent variable(s) are important in an experiment. The independent variable is manipulated or changed by the experimenter. The variable on which the effects of changes are observed is called the **dependent variable**, which is observed but not manipulated by the experimenter. The dependent variable is so named because its value is hypothesized to depend on, and vary with, the value of the independent variable. For example, to examine the effect of training for empowerment on decision making, an investigator would manipulate training, the independent variable, by using different training methods in order to ascertain their effect on decision making, the dependent variable.

Three Characteristics of Experimental Research

There are three essential ingredients in the conduct of an experiment: control, manipulation and observation. We discuss each of them now:

(i) Control: Control is the first essential ingredient of experimental method. Without control, it is impossible to evaluate unambiguously the effects of an independent variable. Basically, the experimental method rests on two assumptions regarding variables:

1. If two situations are equal in every respect except for a variable that is added to or deleted from one of the situations, any difference appearing between the two situations can be attributed to that variable. This statement is called the **Law of the Single Variable**.
2. If two situations are not equal, and it can be demonstrated that none of the variables is significant in producing the phenomenon under investigation, or if significant variables are made equal, then any difference occurring between the two situations after the introduction of a new variable to one of them can be attributed to the new variable. This statement is called the **Law of the Only Significant Variable**.

The main purpose of 'control' in an experiment is to arrange a situation in which the effect of variables can be measured. The conditions to be fulfilled under the first law can be obtained more easily in physical sciences. A high degree of control is much easier to achieve in a laboratory setting than in a situation outside the laboratory. In the laboratory, there is only limited number of variables which can be manipulated easily. However, as social research is concerned with human beings, there are always many variables present in a situation. To attempt to reduce social problems to the operation of a single variable is not only unrealistic but perhaps impossible as well. Fortunately, we do not require such rigorous control to be introduced in social settings, for many factors involved in such a setting may be quite insignificant and irrelevant for our study. To that extent, in social research, the law of the single significant variable is more appropriate. For example, if we were to study the effect of two methods of teaching alphabets to two groups of adult learners, we are likely to select the two groups which are identical in every respect except in the way they are taught alphabets. But it is impossible to have two groups that are identical in every respect. So, the endeavour of the researcher should be towards obtaining two groups that are as similar as possible, at least in those factors that are thought to have an effect on learning alphabets. These could be general intelligence, motivation, reading ability, etc. Other variables that are not likely to affect achievement in learning alphabets can be ignored. Thus, in experimental studies in social research we need procedures that permit us to use to compare groups on the basis of significant variables. *Control* is used to indicate an experimenter's 'procedures' for eliminating the differential effects of all variables extraneous to the purpose of the study. (An 'extraneous' variable is one that is not related to the purpose of the study but may affect the dependent variable.) The experimenter exercises controls, for instance, when the groups are made comparable on extraneous variables that are related to the dependent variable. If a variable is known to be unrelated to the dependent variable, it cannot influence the dependent variable and we do not need to control it for its effects.

(ii) Manipulation: Manipulation of a variable is another distinguishing characteristic of experimental research. It refers to a deliberate operation performed by the researcher. In contrast to the descriptive research in which the researcher simply observes conditions as they occur naturally, the researcher in the experimental research actually sets the stage for the occurrence of the factors whose performance is to be studied under conditions where all other factors are controlled or eliminated. In social research and other behavioural sciences, the manipulation of a variable takes a characteristic form in which the experimenter imposes a predetermined set of varied conditions on the subjects.

This set of varied conditions is referred to as the *independent variable*, the *experimental variable*, or the *treatment variable*. Then, different conditions are designed to represent two or more values of the independent variable; these may be differences in degree or differences in kind. That is, the independent variable may give two or more values and the difference in the values may be of quantitative or qualitative nature. Methods of teaching, attitudes, socio-economic status, personality characteristics, types of motivation, etc. are some common examples of the independent variable in social research. For example, if the researcher compares two methods of teaching, then the method of teaching is the independent variable and can be manipulated by the teacher. We may manipulate a single variable or a number of variables simultaneously.

(iii) Observation: In experimentation, we are interested in the effect of the manipulation of the independent variable on a dependent variable. Observations are made with respect to some characteristics of the behaviour of the subjects employed in the research. These observations, which are quantitative in nature, may constitute the dependent variable. This needs some explanation. The dependent variable in social research is often changing of some attitude, such as attitude towards learning. We are often interested in explaining or predicting attitude. Since attitude cannot be measured directly, we can only estimate it through measures like scores in a scale. Therefore, strictly speaking, the dependent variable is scores or observations rather than change in attitude.

Steps Involved in Experimental Research

There are number of steps involved in experimental research. Here, we shall talk about four steps to reach the stage of the 'actual experiment'. Brief explanations are needed for steps 3 and 4 only. The steps are:

1. Surveying the literature related to the problem
2. Identifying and defining the problem
3. Formulating hypotheses is an important step in experimental research. Hypothesis suggest that an antecedent condition or phenomenon (independent variable) is related to the occurrence of another condition, phenomenon, event, or effect (dependent variable). To test a hypothesis, the experimenter attempts to control all the conditions except the

independent variable which she manipulates. Then she observes the effect on the dependent variable presumably because of the exposure to the independent variable.

4. Constructing an experimental plan is the next step in experimental research. This refers to the conceptual framework within which the experiment is conducted. This would involve:
   (a) Selecting a research design
   (b) Selecting a sample of subjects to represent a given population
   (c) Assign subjects to groups, and assign experimental treatments to the groups (subject implies the respondent or the living organism that is studied)
   (d) Selecting or constructing and validating instruments to measure the outcomes of the experiment
   (e) Stating the procedures for collecting the data and possibly conducting a pilot or "trial run" to perfect the instruments or design
   (f) Stating the statistical or null hypothesis.

The above steps bring the researcher to the stage when she actually conducts the experiment, applies statistical measures to the data obtained, and then tests the significance of the results. In the ensuing section, we take up the various designs involved in the experimental method.

Designs of Experimental Study

A research design is very important for the researcher. A well-developed design provides the structure and strategy to control the investigation and extract dependable answers to the questions raised by the problem or hypothesis. It is the nature of the problem that determines the appropriateness of the design.

Before we discuss the experimental designs, we will explain the notations:

X = independent variable, which is manipulated by the researcher. It is also referred to as the *experimental variable* or the *treatment variable.*

Y = measure of the dependent variable. Y_1 represents the dependent variable before the manipulation of the independent variable X (It is usually a pre-test of some type administered before the experimental treatment.) Y_2 represents dependent variable after the manipulation of the independent variable X.
It is usually a post-test administered to subjects after the experimental treatment.)

S = subject or respondent used in the experiment.

E group = experimental group—the group that is given the independent variable treatment.

C group = control group—the group that does not receive the experimental treatment.

R = random assignment of subjects to the experimental groups and the random assignment of treatments to the groups.

There exist a large number of experimental designs. Various authors have classified experimental design into certain categories. Most common categorization comprises:

- Pre-experimental design
- True experimental design
- Quasi experimental design

Some authors like Donald Ary et al. (1985) have added more categories such as

- Factorial design
- Time series

Various designs under the above-mentioned categories are given in Table 5.1:

TABLE 5.1 Designs under Different Categories

Pre-experimental	True experimental	Quasi-experimental	Factorial design	Time series design
• One group pre-test post-test design	• Randomized 'subjects' post-test only control group design	Non-randomized control group, Pre-test post-test design	Simple factorial design	One group time series design
Static group comparison	Randomized matched subjects, post-test only control group design	Counter-balanced design		Control group time series design
	Randomized subjects pre-test post-test control group design			
	Solomon four group design			

However, in this section, we shall discuss only a few most frequently used designs, from each of the five categories.

Pre-experimental design: The two designs classified as pre-experimental designs offer minimal control of extraneous variables. Still they are used quite often in social research. These designs help illustrate the advantages of more rigorously controlled designs that are presented later.

Design 1: One group pre-test post-test design

When this design is employed, the dependent variable is measured before the independent variable or treatment is applied or withdrawn, and then measured yet again. The one group design usually involves three steps:

1. Administering a pre-test measuring the dependent variable
2. Applying the experimental treatment X to the subjects
3. Administering a post-test again measuring the dependent variable.

Differences attributed to application of experimental treatment are then determined by comparing the pre-test and post-test scores.

Design 1: One Group Pre-test Post-test Design

Pre-test	Independent variable	Post-test
Y_1	X	Y_2

To illustrate the use of this design, let us assume that we want to evaluate the effectiveness of a particular self-instructional material in rural development for postgraduate students. How should we go about this task?

At the beginning of the academic year, the students are given a standardized test that measures the objectives of the course quite satisfactorily, following which the distance learning teacher introduces the self-instructional material. At the end of the year, the students are administered the standardized test a second time. Comparing the scores of the two tests would reveal what difference the exposure to the SIM has made.

However, using only one group, as in Design 1, gives the superficial control. The major limitation of the one-group design is that, since no control group is used, the experimenter cannot assume that the change between the pre-test and the post-test scores is brought about by experimental treatment alone. It is quite possible that some extraneous variables account for all or part of the change. For example, students experience changes with the passage of time; they grow mentally as well as physically, or they may acquire additional learning experiences that would affect the dependent variable. This extraneous variable can be thought of as maturation, i.e., with the passage of time students attain maturity and, this in turn, may effect achievement level.

Another type of extraneous variable that can operate between the pre-test and the post-test scores and which cannot be controlled is **history**. History as a source of extraneous variances refers to the specific events that can occur between the pre-test and post-test other than the experimental treatment. In the example cited above, not receiving material regularly or illness just before the test could decrease achievement scores. Similarly, a crucial research finding in history could increase widespread interest and hence affect the test scores. In fact, history and maturation become increasingly influential sources of extraneous variance when the time interval between Y_1 and Y_2 is long.

Another shortcoming of Design 1 is that it offers no way of assessing the effect of the pre-test Y_1 itself. We know that "practice effect" exists when subjects take a test a second time or take an alternative form of the test. In other words, subjects do better the second time even without any instruction or relevant discussion during the interval. This is true not only for achievement and intelligence tests but also for personality tests. In the case of personality tests, a tendency towards better adjustment is generally observed.

To sum up, Design 1 has little to recommend it; without a control group to make a comparison possible, the results obtained in a one group design are basically uninterruptable. The results of the experiment would have been dependable if there could be a comparable group, i.e. control group to which SIM had not been given.

Design 2: Static group comparison

Design 2 utilizes two or more groups, only one of which is exposed to experimental treatment. The groups are assumed to be equivalent in all relevant aspects; they differ only in their exposure to *X*.

This design is often used in social research, for example, achievement of adult learners taught by a new method is compared with that of similar class taught by a traditional method.

Design 2 has a control group or groups, which permit(s) the comparison that is required for scientific respectability. If the experimental group is superior on the Y_2 measure, the researcher then has more confidence in her conclusion that the difference is due to experimental treatment. However, there is a basic flaw in this design. Since neither randomization nor even matching is used to assign subjects to the experimental and control groups, we cannot be sure that the groups are equivalent prior to the experimental and control groups. They may differ on certain relevant variables, and it may be that these differences rather than *X* are responsible for the observed change.

Because we cannot be sure that the groups are equal with regard to all the factors that may influence the dependent variable, this design is considered to be lacking in the necessary control and must be classified as pre-experimental.

Design 2: Static Group Comparison

Group test	Independent variable	Post-test
E	*X*	Y_2
C	—	Y_2

True experimental designs: The following two designs belong to the 'true experimental' design because of the control that they provide, i.e.

1. Random assignment of subjects to the groups.
2. Random assignment of treatment to the groups.
3. Post-testing all the groups.

Design 3: Randomized subjects, post-test only control group design

This particular design requires two groups to which subjects are randomly assigned and each group is assigned to a different condition. No pre-test is used; randomization controls all the possible extraneous variables. This does not mean that randomization procedures (like drawing names out of a hat, or flipping a coin) remove the extraneous variables, such as the IQ or age, which may affect the dependent variable, or control their presence. These extraneous variables still affect the inquiry; but, now, it is the laws of chance rather than the personal feature of E that operate. In fact, the larger the number of subjects used, the more equivalent or similar the groups will tend to be. Suppose a researcher wants to study the effect of instructional material on achievement in a course during a contact programme. She may randomly assign the students to the groups and provide treatment to one of the groups. The assigning of the treatment will be random. At the end of the contact programme, she may test both the groups.

After the subjects are assigned to the groups, only the experimental group is exposed to the experimental treatment. Otherwise, in all other respects, the two groups remain similar. Members of both groups are then measured on dependent variable Y_2. Scores are then compared to determine the effect of X.

Design 3: Randomized Subjects, Post-test only Control Group Design

Group test	Independent variable	Post-test
(R) E	X	Y_2
(R) C	—	Y_2

The main advantage of Design 3 is randomization, which assures statistical equivalence of the groups prior to the introduction of independent variable. Design 3 provides controls for the main effects of history, maturation and pre-testing; because no pre-test is used, there can be no interaction effect of pre-test and X (treatment).

Design 4: Randomized matched subjects, post-test only control group design

This design is similar to Design 3 except that it uses a matching technique, rather than random assignment, to obtain equivalent groups. Subjects are matched on one or more variables that can be measured conveniently, such as IQ or reading scores.

The matching variables used are generally those that have a significant correlation with the dependent variable. On the basis of these variables, subjects are paired so that opposite members/scores are as close as possible; and then, one member of each pair is randomly assigned to one treatment and the other to the second treatment.

Design 4: Randomized Matched Subjects, Post test only Control Group Design

Group test	Independent variable	Post-test
(R) E	X	Y_2
(R) C	–	Y_2

Matching is most useful in studies where small samples are to be used and where Design 3 is not appropriate. Also, the matched subjects' design serves to reduce the extent to which experimental differences can be accounted for by initial differences between groups. However, for matching to really become a means of control, the matching of all the potential subjects must be complete, and assignment of the members of each pair to the groups must be determined randomly. If one or more subjects should be excluded because an appropriate match could not be found, this would bias the sample. When using Design 4, it is essential to match every subject, even if only approximately, before random assignment is effected.

Quasi-experimental design: One of the quasi-experimental designs is Non-randomized control group, pre-test post-test design. You would notice that Randomized control group pre-test post-test design is a true experimental design which we have presented before. The only difference on the quasi-experimental design is that the groups are not randomized. Hence they are unlikely to be comparable. In fact, it is on this ground that the design becomes quasi-experimental and not true experimental. Since the rest of the design related characteristics remain common with the randomized control group pre-test post-test design of the true experimental design category, we do not need to provide any further details on this design.

Group test	Pre-test	Independent variable	Post-test
(R) E	Y_1	X	Y_2
(R) C	Y_1	—	Y_2

Factorial designs: A factorial design is one where two or more variables are manipulated simultaneously in order to study the independent effect of each variable on the dependent variable as well as the effects due to interaction among the several variables. Factorial designs are of two types. In the first type, one of the independent variables may be experimentally manipulated. The researcher is primarily interested in the effect of a single independent variable but she must take other variables into consideration which may influence the dependent variables. In the second type of design, all the independent variables may be experimentally manipulated. Factorial designs have been developed at varying levels of complexity, the simplest factorial design is the 2 by 2 (2 × 2) Design. The two independent variables have two values.

Level 1 subjects receive Treatment A and others Treatment B. Some level 2 subjects receive Treatment A and others Treatment B.

Attribute variable X_2	Experimental variable X_1	Variable X_2
	Treatment A	Treatment B
Level 1	Cell 1	Cell 3
Level 2	Cell 2	Cell 4

The strength of the factorial design is that it can achieve in one experiment which might otherwise require two or more separate studies.

Time series design: We have already discussed pre-test post-test designs. They generate one time data on the dependent variable before and after the experimental treatment. There are instances where it becomes necessary to compare changes in the trend of a particular phenomenon or process or product. For example, let us assume that learners behaviour to attitudes, achievements, etc. changes over a period of time. If a specific treatment is introduced in an institution to study the change in attitude or achievement, it is useful to study the trend through measurement at certain intervals before the introduction of the treatment. Instead of one time pre-test, the test is repeated three or four times before the treatment is administered. This generates data on the trend of behaviour. Similarly, after the treatment is administered, instead of one time post-test, the post-test is administered several times at intervals. This provides data to derive the trend in the change in behaviour. Since both pre-tests and post-tests are used over a time series design, the effect of the treatment on the dependent variable is tested by comparing the trends. This can be represented in the following form:

$Y_1 \quad Y_2 \quad Y_3 \quad Y_4 \quad Y \quad Y_5 \quad Y_6 \quad Y_7 \quad Y_8$

What we have described above is one group time series design. If you add a control group and repeat the same time series measurement without the treatment of the control groups, it becomes control group time series design. Similarly, control group time series design is represented as:

Group									
E	Y_1	Y_2	Y_3	Y_4	X	Y_5	Y_6	Y_7	Y_8
C	Y_1	Y_2	Y_3	Y_4	X	Y_5	Y_6	Y_7	Y_8

SUMMARY

In this chapter, we studied two important research methods, namely, Descriptive Method and Experimental Method. Descriptive research describes what the condition is and involves the description, recording, analysis and interpretation of conditions that exist. We also studied various types of descriptive research, for example, survey, documentary analysis, correlational and causal comparative studies. Finally, we discussed about experimental research which describes what will happen when certain variables are carefully controlled or manipulated.

DISCUSSION QUESTIONS

1. Draw and compare the figures representing pre-test post-test experimental design and one group time series design.

2. Explain briefly the significance of control, manipulation, and observation in an experimental study.
3. Explain briefly the purpose of correlational studies. List the weaknesses of causal-comparative studies.
4. List the steps involved in survey studies. Describe briefly in about 30 words the objectives of documentary analysis.

FURTHER READING

Ackoff, R.L. (1953): *The Design of Social Research*, Chicago: University of Chicago Press.

Ary, D., Jacobs, Lucy, C. and Razavich, A. (1972): *Introduction to Research in Education*, 3rd ed., Holt (New York): Rinehart & Winston.

Bailey, Kenneth D. (1978): *Methods of Social Research*, London: The Free Press.

Baker, L. Therese (1988): *Doing Social Research*, New York: McGraw-Hill.

Black, James A. and Champion, Dean J. (1976): *Methods and Issues in Social Research*, New York: Wiley.

Campbell, D.T. and Stanley. J.C. (1963): *Experimental and Quasi Experimental Designs for Research*, Boston: Houghton Mifflin.

Chapin, F.S. (1974): *Experimental Design in Sociological Research*, New York: Harper.

6 Qualitative Research

After going through this chapter, you will be able to:

- Differentiate between qualitative research and quantitative research.
- Identify possible applications of qualitative research in the area of marketing.
- Understand various methods of conducting qualitative research.

Introduction to Qualitative Research

Figure 6.1 shows different ways by which information regarding customers can be acquired.

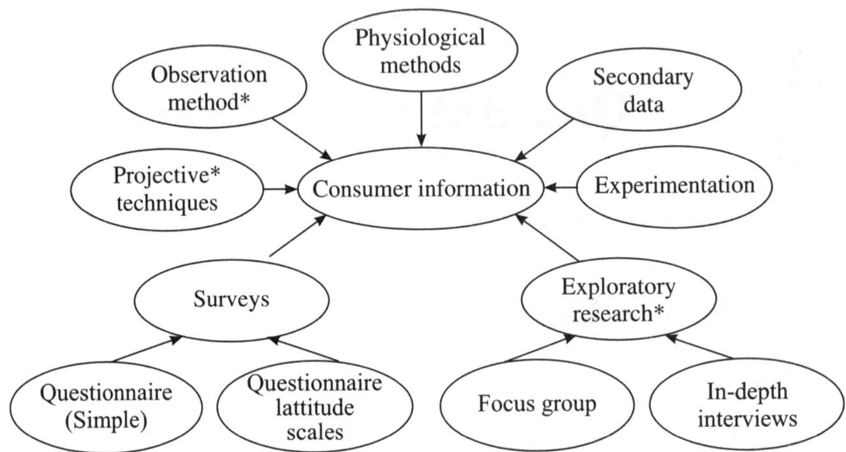

FIGURE 6.1 Different ways of acquiring information on customers.

*Some of the methods that listed fall into the category of quantitative research and some others under the method of qualitative research.

What is Qualitative Research?

We may say that qualitative research:

1. Is used to understand the behavioural pattern of the target groups; hence, its nature is basically problem solving.
2. Involves a target group of small numbers who are tested for the first time.
3. Is impressionistic rather than definitive.
4. Is used to make theoretical suggestions for advanced research.
5. Is used understand the pattern on which a customer buys and purchases in the dynamic market.
6. Gives a delicate understanding of the functioning of the product in the dynamic market.
7. Gives a hypothetical base and not solid technical principles so that it helps in eliciting conclusions rather than being conclusive itself.
8. Is used normally along with quantitative research in a market research project.
9. Though useful to study consumer behaviour, any attempt to generalize the findings for the entire population is very risky, as the findings are based on a very small sample size.

10. Is highly personal because of a small target group and highly skilled people are required to conduct interviews and analyze the data.

Figure 6.2 elucidates the significance of qualitative and quantitative research:

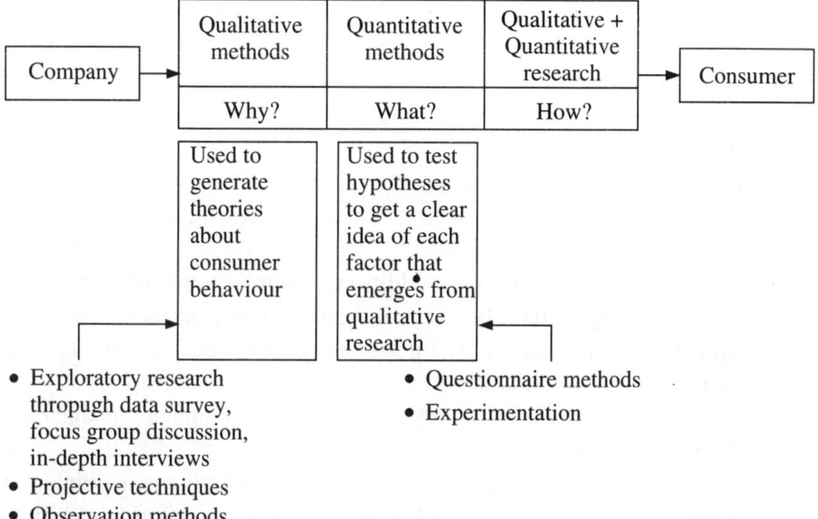

FIGURE 6.2 Significance of qualitative and quantitative research.

Difference between Qualitative Research and Quantitative Research

Qualitative research	Quantitative research
Exploratory or diagnostic in nature—used to understand behaviour and generate hypotheses.	Once a hypothesis has been generated, it is used to test out the hypothesis.
No calculation of sample size possible—size of the sample depends on data available to conduct research, as well as the cost, and variation in the population.	Generally, a probabilistic approach is used to calculate sample size, using the sample size formula.
Sample selected is such that it represents different sections of the population.	Random selection of respondents to be part of research work—may or may not represent different population segments, depending on the sampling method employed.
It is dangerous to generalize conclusions for the entire population.	Conclusions are generalized to the universe, of which the sample purports to be representative.

USES OF QUALITATIVE RESEARCH

1. **Qualitative research is used:** In concept generation and evaluation, e.g., when a fresh product has to be developed, a qualitative research needs to be conducted among the consumers to recognize the latest needs or demands of the consumer. Therefore, every time when you go to the market place, you will find newer models of the same product with addition/deletion of features, new and better external appearance, and better finished product.
2. To describe the difficulty areas more fully—Marketing research starts with qualitative research which is authenticated by additional quantitative research.
3. To put together a premise for additional examination/and quantification.
4. To collect large quantity of data about attitude, outlooks, etc. as data input for making questions for survey, outlook scales. This is utilized for multivariate examination
5. To conduct post-research study, i.e., to work on some points that emerge from a major study.
6. Because in the perception of the consumer, marketing research has to be flexible and dynamic, and not limited always by question-based surveys.
7. It is better to use quantitative approach in studies of allocation control, sales, and cost policy. The choice of the right approach depends on the purpose of the study area, and the kind of policies and decisions to be taken from the recommendations and conclusions reached upon by the research work.

METHODS OF CONDUCTING QUALITATIVE RESEARCH

There are several methods of conducting qualitative research, which are now described.

Individual 'Depth' or 'Intensive' Interviews

The in-depth interviews may be classified as:

- Non-directive interview
- Semi-structured or focused interview.

In a non-directive interview, the respondent is given maximum freedom to respond in a manner that he wishes to, within a reasonable limit of relevancy to the topic under discussion. However, the interviewer retains the initiative in the interview process; else the focus of the interview would be lost. Thus, with this technique, the respondent is given a chance to freely express his ideas and thoughts, which act as an important feedback to the company on its products/ service.

In a semi-structured or focused interview, the initiative is retained by the interviewer, and the interview has to cover specific list of points which have been decided in advance. There is also a tighter control over the interview, in order to maximize data collection and also collect data relevant to the topic under consideration. The interviewer is also determined as to which questions are to be asked. The best example to highlight this interview process is the chat shows that take place on television. Even though the participants are given maximum freedom with respect to their answers, the initiative is retained by the interviewer, and he has decided in advance the questions that he would be asking in the course of the interview.

In-depth interviews are appropriate in the following situations:

1. When detailed probing of an individual's behaviour, attitude, and needs are required.
2. When the subject matter is of a highly confidential nature (e.g., how do you plan your investments: required for annual tax planning).
3. When the subject matter is an emotionally charged one or of an embarrassing nature (e.g., how do you spend when you go on a date).
4. When a step-by-step understanding is required of complicated decision making. *Example:* (a) How does a family plan its holiday—selection of vacation site, mode of travel and stay (b) How does a family decide when purchasing a house—which is normally a lifetime decision.
5. When interviews are conducted with highly qualified professionals (e.g., surgeons—on the usage/problems with various medical equipment), a normal questionnaire would not suffice for getting information, and a detailed probing is required, which would come out only through an in-depth interview.
6. When a respondent may not be able to express his true feelings in a group discussion: Very often in a group discussion, a few aggressive people tend to dominate the discussion, hardly giving an opportunity to others in the group to express their views. To avoid such a situation, a researcher may decide to conduct an in-depth interview instead of a group discussion. Also, when the topic of the group discussion is of a personal nature and socially embarrassing, people in the group would tend to conform to the views of the overall group, rather than express their own individual ideas.

Limitations of in-depth interview

1. Lack of availability of skilled interviewer (A skilled interviewer is very critical in drawing out the respondent's true feelings.)
2. Interviewer not familiar with non-verbal communication. For, in an interview, there is not only verbal communication, but also non-verbal

communication, and the interviewer should also keep track of the respondent's voice tone, facial expressions, and movement of hands (gestures).
3. The sample size cannot be large, as conducting in-depth interviews takes a longer time.
4. Analysis and interpretation of data is a highly subjective process, thus generalization to the entire population cannot be done.
5. In-depth interviews act as a source of generation of hypothesis, and development of questionnaire for further research work.

Focus Group Discussion

There are broadly two ways in which a group discussion can be conducted:

1. Brain-storming

Here, there is no moderator for the group, and the group freely expresses its ideas on the given topic. The ideas could be absolutely abstract, but then this would help in generating new product ideas and also better ways of conducting a particular business. In this, tape-recorder is used to record the group discussion, video-taping of proceedings is also done in order to record the facial expressions of the participants, as also the intensity of their feelings.

2. Focussed group discussion

In such a method, the group is given a topic and asked to discuss the topic. A moderator would also be involved in order to ensure that the group 'discussion remains relevant and does not go off the track. The moderator could stop the, discussion between time intervals to find out what conclusions are being drawn by the group after each time interval.

Size and composition of a group discussion panel: It is not possible to prescribe the exact number of people needed for a Group Discussion. How big or small the group is depends on (a) the subject matter under discussion, and (b) the type of participants. Normally, eight or twelve individuals in a group discussion panel is an ideal number. However, for highly professional and articulate people, five or six participants in the group would be ideal, as the participants would be able to contribute more to the topic under discussion.

The group members should be such that they reflect the characteristics of a particular market segment under study. The sampling plan is drawn up first, which then helps in deciding the composition of the group discussion panel members.

The role of the moderator in a group discussion is to establish a rapport with the group members. He/she also informs the members of the rules to be followed in the group discussion. The moderator acts as a stimulus to provoke heated discussion in, the group, so that all underlying ideas, feelings and emotions emerge. The moderator also intervenes after time intervals, to assess the extent of agreement/disagreement with the ideas that are emerging.

Application areas of group discussion: The following are the situations where a group discussion could be used:

1. For development of new product ideas, abstract concepts.
2. For product positioning ideas—how does a consumer perceive a particular product/service/idea?
3. For determining hidden feelings/attitudes of the consumer.
4. For establishing consumer vocabulary, as a preliminary step when developing questionnaires. When conducting survey research, it is not always possible to think of all the questions associated with product/brands. The group discussion helps in developing suitable questions.
5. For advertising and communication research, what to say to the consumer, how to say it, what should be the focus of the message, etc.

Advantages of a group discussion

1. In a Group Discussion setting, the interaction among members acts as a stimulant to generate new ideas, which may never be possible in an in-depth individual interview situation.
2. The Group Discussion setting leads to spontaneity in conversation which cannot come in individual interview situation.
3. The group setting is emotionally provocative. The conversation may set off the thinking process, and one would recall older memories and conversations that may be relevant to the discussion on hand.

Disadvantages of group discussion

1. Qualified and trained personnel are required to conduct Group Discussion.
2. Analysis and interpretation are highly subjective.
3. A few members in a group could dominate the entire discussion.

Projective Techniques

When a researcher is conducting an in-depth interview, or conducting a survey through the questionnaire method, he might face problems in the form of language barriers with the respondent, or illiterate respondent (especially in social research and rural research), or social barriers (the respondent is embarrassed to talk about a topic) or psychological barriers (recall of event or feelings at that moment of interview is not there or trying to avoid certain questions or "can't say" answer). In order to overcome such barriers faced during an interview process, the researcher may replace the questionnaire with the projective techniques.

The basic concept behind projective techniques is that in certain situations, it is impossible to obtain correct information about what a person thinks or feels by asking him to describe his/her feelings—but this information can be obtained by making the respondent to project his feelings on to some other person or object.

The following are the different types of projective techniques:

Word association test: In this method, the respondent is presented with a list of stimulus words, and for each word, is asked to respond with what he thinks about the word. The respondent is not given time to think of the responses. The idea is that the first thought responses are likely to reveal the true feelings of the respondent about the stimulus.

Example: Suppose a company wishes to understand what a person thinks about leisure time:

Stimulus word	**Response by Respondent**
• Train	
• Books	
• Television	
• Swimming	
• Automobile	
• House	

The first responses to these words would give a fair idea as to how the respondent would like to spend his leisure time.

The analysis of the word association test is done as follows:

- Determine the frequency with which the various responses emerge.
- Created category of attitudes (e.g., favourable/neutral/unfavourable) and words.

Example: If a researcher wants to study the perception of students regarding MBA course, the categories that could emerge are:

Practical	impractical
Interesting	boring
Easy	difficult
Job oriented	theoretical

The words that emerge from word association tests can be useful in developing semantic differential scale, Likert scale—adjectives that describe products/ services.

Sentence completion test: This is an extension of the word association test. In this method, the respondent is asked to finish an incomplete sentence with the first thought that comes to his mind. The idea is that the respondent projects his own feelings into the sentence.

Examples

I like to drive motor bikes because ....

Most people smoke because ....

I smoke because ....

Cars are ....

As with the word 'association', the frequency of responses is taken into consideration while analyzing the results of the sentence association test.

Fantasy situation: Here, the respondents are asked to imagine that they are converted into a product itself, e.g., car, on box of chocolate. This leads to the respondent imagining himself to be product itself and gives human characteristics to the product. This method is used for developing brand perception and brand personality.

Cartoon completion: In this method the respondent is shown a cartoon that is similar to a comic strip, with 'balloons' indicating speech. Usually, two people are shown talking to each other about a particular product/service/situation, but only one balloon contains the speech.

The situation that is shown in the cartoon is obviously of special interest to the researcher, and is part of the research project under hand. The respondent has to fill the other 'balloon' with his answer to what the other person is saying.

With this, one tries to measure one's attitude towards a product or service. Analysis and interpretation of these results are highly subjective.

Picture interpretation (Thematic Apperception Test): Thematic Apperception Test (TAT), along with the Rorschach Inkblot Test, is probably the most widely known and used projective technique in Clinical Psychology. The same basic technique used above is applied for marketing research applications. Here, the respondent is shown a picture—either a line drawing, illustration or photograph which is rather ambiguous—and is asked to describe what is going on or tell a story about what is illustrated. For example, a retail outlet, e.g. a gift shop, is interested in knowing what a shopper thinks while buying a gift, how does he look at the various display items, and what he expects during the shopping experience. For such a research project, a researcher might show the photograph of a person entering the gift shop to the respondent, and ask him to develop a story on what he thinks could be happening inside the shop. Normally, a respondent would project his own feelings while developing the story from the photograph. This gives an idea to the researcher as to what the respondent expects on entering the gift shop. The major drawback with this method is that there is a great deal of subjectivity in interpretation of the responses to these projective tests. These projective techniques are used in exploratory research, whose output acts as input for developing hypothesis and full-fledged quantitative research.

Observation Method

The Observation Method is another very powerful tool for getting information about the consumer. This method is used for recording behaviour of people, objects, and events. Informal observations are extensively used for observing customer buying patterns, impact of competitive advertisement on buying, product availability, etc.

The observation method is always used in conjunction with other research techniques. The inherent danger in this method is that one could draw wrong conclusions as the method is highly subjective, and a lot depends on the observer's perception of a situation.

Advantages

1. The observation method does not rely on the willingness of the respondent to cooperate and provide information.
2. Behaviour patterns, which a respondent is not aware of, can be recorded by observation only, e.g., the facial expression of a consumer while examining a new product displayed in a store.

Disadvantages

1. By observation method one cannot observe a consumer's beliefs, feelings, awareness, etc. (other research techniques such as focus groups, in-depth interviews are required).
2. The observed behaviour pattern must be of short duration, should occur frequently, in order to qualify for observation, and act as input to other research techniques.

Classification

(a) Natural vs. *Contrived observation*

Natural observation is recording of consumer behaviour as it takes place, e.g., the shopping process. Contrived observation is one in which an artificial environment is created and then consumer behaviour is observed, e.g., simulated test marketing.

(b) Disguised vs. *Undisguised observation*

Disguised refers to whether or not the consumer is aware of being observed, e.g. two-way mirrors, hidden cameras in shops, observers dressed as sales clerks, and so on.

(c) Structured vs. *Unstructured observation*

In a structured observation, the decision problem is clearly defined. Information needs are clearly defined, and so this reduces observer bias and increases the reliability of observed data. In an unstructured observation, the problem is yet to be defined and formulated, and is ideal for exploratory research.

(d) Human vs. *Mechanical observation*

By replacing humans with mechanical devices, the accuracy of observation increases, observer bias is reduced and lower costs are incurred. Special mechanical devices used for observation could be video cameras (shopping behaviour), Audimeter/Peoplemeter (TRP ratings), Eye-cameras, etc.

LATEST TECHNIQUES IN QUALITATIVE RESEARCH

Qualitative Research is taking more and more inputs from psychology to develop latest techniques in Qualitative Research. Some of the latest techniques used are as follows:

1. Imagery technique: This technique is used to determine the images of two competing brands, as an example, readers were asked to describe two competing magazines.

Magazine 1 was described as young, attractive, bubbling teenager.

Magazine 2 was described as older, less interesting, introvert lady. This information helped the owner of the magazine to reposition magazine 2.

2. Synectics: This technique gives the researcher an insight into the intuitive or emotional impressions of the consumer for either a brand or advertising campaign, by unleashing the creative side of the consumer. The respondents are asked to go through a series of games designed to lower their inhibitions which help in unleashing the child present in every adult. The basic idea is that creativity works at child level. With this exercise, the researcher can get original ideas for use in developing advertising campaign, as also the consumer's real feelings about products.

Neuro-linguistic Programming

Neuro-linguistic programming provides an insight into the, *non-verbal impact* of an advertisement on the target consumer. This is done by analyzing as to which of the five senses (smell, taste, touch, sight, and sound) a consumer uses to remember an ad. As an example, the Airtel promotional campaign was evaluated using a form of neuro-linguistic technique and it was able to reveal a strong sensory effect of music. The fundamental idea behind this method is that much of the recording of experience goes on 'below the surface' and outside conscious awareness. For purposes of marketing, there is a codification of the sensory modalities into visual, auditory and kinesthetic (touch, taste and smell). The shorthand version is called VAK segmentation. Humans are emotional creatures, and a person would buy on emotion and justify the purchase on lace

Thus, to decode the sentiments surrounding the product purchase and experience, researchers use the NLP technique. NLP techniques are modelled on techniques used in other fields of psychology (Erieksonian Hypnosis and Classical Conditioning), and hence only persons trained in the field of psychology can use this technique.

SUMMARY

In this chapter, we have discussed the various methods by which information about consumers can be obtained are broadly classified into two categories—qualitative research and quantitative research. Qualitative research may be used to generate hypothesis for further research, is exploratory in nature, and involves a small number of people who are not sampled on probabilistic basis. Qualitative research can provide leads and insights which would be extremely helpful in conducting quantitative research. We also dealt with various methods of conducting qualitative research. These are indepth interviews, focus groups, observation and projective techniques like word association test, sentence completion test, cartoons, thematic apperception test. Finally, we saw how qualitative research is increasingly using inputs from psychology and some of the latest techniques being used include imagery, synectics and neuro-linguistic programming.

DISCUSSION QUESTIONS

1. Highlight the main differences between qualitative and quantitative research.
2. With the help of examples, discuss the areas where qualitative research can be used in marketing.
3. What are the various methods of conducting qualitative research? Discuss the advantages and disadvantages of each of these methods.
4. Observe a few shoppers of chocolates in your neighbourhood store. What insights could you gain from these observations on purchase of chocolates? Submit a report based on your observations.
5. Select any product and brand of your interest. Administer each of the following techniques to five fellow colleagues to develop an idea of their feelings towards the brand: (a) Word Association Test, (b) Sentence Completion Test, (c) Cartoon, (d) Thematic Apperception Test, and submit the report.
6. Conduct a focus group interview with six people in your organization on the purchase and consumption of fast food and Packaged fruit juices. Prepare a report based on your findings.
7. Conduct a depth interview with one person to find out her feelings on the purchase and consumption of packaged fruit juices and ice-creams. Prepare a report based on your findings.

FURTHER READING

Parasuraman, A. (2006): *Marketing Research*, Reading (Mass.): Addison-Wesley.

Tull, D. and Hawkins, D. (1993): *Marketing Research—Measurement and method*, New York: Macmillan.

7 Marketing Research Process Scaling and Attitude Measurement

- Stages of Marketing Research Process
- Meaning of Research Problem
- Choosing the Problem
- Review of Literature
- Formulating the Problem
- The Concept of Measurement
- Components of Measurement
- Components of Measurement Accuracy
- Measurement Accuracy and Measurement Development
- Direct Response Attitude Scales
- Data Interpretation
- Report Writing
- Discussion Questions

After going through this chapter, you will be able to:

- Identify marketing research process.
- Discuss the nature, source and methods of data collection.
- Know about outline sampling and questionnaire preparation.
- Speak about presentation, analysis and interpretation of data.
- Explain the research report contents and techniques.
- Describe research proposal contents and preparation

INTRODUCTION

We have already pointed out that the decision-maker should clearly communicate the purpose of the research to the marketing researcher. However, it is often the case that the objectives are not fully explained to the individual carrying out the study. Decision-makers seldom work out their objectives fully or, if they have, they are not willing to fully disclose them. In theory, responsibility for ensuring that the research proceeds along clearly defined lines rests with the decision-maker. In many instances, the researcher has to take the initiative.

In situations in which the researcher senses that the decision-maker is either unwilling or unable to fully articulate the objectives then he will have to pursue an indirect line of questioning. One approach is to take the problem statement supplied by the decision-maker and to break this down into key components and/or terms and to explore these with the decision-maker. For example, the decision-maker could be asked what he has in mind when he uses the term 'market potential'. This is a legitimate question since the researcher is charged with the responsibility of developing a research design which will provide the right kind of information. Another approach is to focus the discussions with the person commissioning the research on the decisions, which would be made given alternative findings, which the study might come up with. This process frequently proves to be of great value to the decision-maker in that it helps him think through the objectives and perhaps select the most important of the objectives.

STAGES OF MARKETING RESEARCH PROCESS

Step 1: Defining the problem: For any research to be conducted, the problem area which needs to be delved into should be defined. The aim of the research, proper information about the background of the research area, the kind of information needed, and the use of the information so obtained should be identified by the researcher. All this requires dialogues and discussions with the policy makers, professionals of the same field, collecting secondary data, and analyzing it and using data collected from focus groups for some qualitative research. Only after the problem has been specifically identified, the research programme can be designed and accomplished properly.

Step 2: Formulation of a stratagem to deal with the problem: This would involve working out a strategy to work out a solution for the research problem. It may involve making an objective, chalking out the hypothetical structure, investigative models, and research questionnaires, and identifying the dynamics that may influence the research design. This procedure is carried out by taking inputs from professional and technical experts, by referring to case studies and replicating models and doing qualitative research based on realistic and practical deliberations.

Step 3: Research design development: *Research design.* Research design is the specification of strategy, the plan, and the composition of investigating a research to be carried out. A research design is the determination of the general research plan that is taken up. It is the overall operational pattern or outline of the plan that specifies what kind of information is to be collected from which source and what methods are to be applied to collect that data within the budget and with accuracy. Simply stated, it is the outline for the research study which guides the collection and examination and interpretation of data. Research design is important as it sets up a proper structure within which the research work will be conducted. The question of how the data should be collected from the respondents has to be answered. It is imperative to design a set of questions and a sampling plan to choose respondents for the research.

More formally, formulating the research design involves the following steps:

1. Secondary data analysis
2. Qualitative research
3. Methods of collecting quantitative data (survey, observation and experimentation)
4. Definition of the information needed
5. Measurement and scaling procedures
6. Questionnaire design
7. Sampling process and sample size
8. Plan of data analysis

Step 4: Collection of data: Collection of data needs research associates who work at different levels and in different areas, for instance, moving for personal interviews—in person, by mails on telephones, or through questionnaires. The right selection, training, direction and assessment of the research associates or basic workforce help minimize data collection errors.

Step 5: Data grounding and study: Data research includes editing, coding, recording and substantiating of data. The survey results are scrutinized and edited, if required. Numbers are allocated to characterize every reaction to all the questions. The data from the questionnaires are recorded in the computer. Authentication ensures that the data from the original questionnaires have been accurately transcribed, while data analysis, guided by the plan of data analysis, gives meaning to the data that have been collected. Univariate techniques are used for analyzing data when there is a single dimension of each component in the sample or if there is several capacities of each element, and each RCH variable is analyzed in separation. On the other hand, multivariate techniques are used for analyzing data when there are two or more dimensions of each element and the variables are analyzed concurrently.

Step 6: Report preparation and presentation: The whole project should be accounted for in a report, which deals with the particular research questions identified, the approach explained, the research design, data compilation and data analysis and presents the results and major findings. The conclusions should be presented in an intelligible and lucid form so that they can be readily used in the policy-making process. In addition, a presentation should be made to show using tables, figures and graphs to enhance clarity and impact. For these reasons, interviews with these proficient are more useful in accomplishing marketing research for manufacturing firms and for goods of a technological nature, where it is comparatively easy to recognize and approach the experts. This process is also helpful in circumstances where not much information is available from other sources, as in the case of some new products.

Meaning of Research Problem

A research problem is the situation that causes the researcher to feel apprehensive, confused and ill at ease. It is the demarcation of a problem area within a certain context involving the who or what, the where, the when and the why of the problem situation.

There are many problem situations that may give rise to research. Three sources usually contribute to problem identification. One's *own experience* or the *experience of others* may be a source of problem supply. A second source could be *scientific literature*. You may read about certain findings and notice that a certain field was not covered. This could lead to a research problem. *Theories* could be a third source. Shortcomings in theories could be researched.

Research can thus be carried out for (a) clarifying or substantiating an existing theory; (b) clarifying contradictory findings; (c) correcting a faulty methodology; (d) correcting the inadequate or unsuitable use of statistical techniques; and (e) reconciling conflicting opinions or solving existing practical problems.

Research really begins when the researcher experiences some difficulty, i.e., a problem demanding a solution within the subject is of his discipline. This general area of interest, however, defines only the range of subject matter within which the researcher would see and pose a specific problem for research. Personal values play an important role in the selection of a topic for research. Social conditions do often shape the preference of investigators in a subtle and imperceptible way.

The formulation of the topic into a research problem is, really speaking, the first step in a scientific enquiry. A problem, in simple words, is some difficulty experienced by the researcher in a theoretical or practical situation. Solving this difficulty is the task of research.

The analysis by R.L. Ackoff, the American management guru, gives considerable guidance in identifying a problem for research. He visualizes five components of a problem:

(i) *Research-consumer:* There must be an individual or a group that experiences some difficulty.

(ii) *Research-consumer's objectives:* The research-consumer must have available, alternative means for achieving the objectives he desires.

(iii) *Alternative means to meet the objectives:* The research-consumer must have available, alternative means for achieving the objectives he desires.

(iv) *Doubt in regard to selection of alternatives:* The existence of alternative courses of action in not enough; in order to experience a problem, the research-consumer must have some doubt as to which alternative to select.

(v) *There must be one or more environments to which the difficulty or problem pertains:* A change in environment may produce or eliminate a problem. A research-consumer may have doubts as to which will be the most efficient means in one environment but would have no such doubt in another.

Choosing the Problem

The selection of a problem is the first step in research. The term 'problem' means a question or issue to be examined. The selection of a problem for research is not an easy task; the word 'problem' itself is a problem. It is least amenable to formal methodological treatment. Vision, an imaginative insight, plays an important role in this process. A person with a critical, curious and imaginative mind who is sensitive to practical problems could easily identify problems for study.

The sources from which we can identify research problems or develop problems awareness are:

- Review of literature
- Academic experience
- Daily experience
- Exposure to field situations
- Consultations
- Brainstorming
- Research
- Intuition.

Review of Literature

Frequently, an exploratory study is concerned with an area of subject matter in which explicit hypotheses have not yet been formulated. The researcher's task then is to review the available material with an eye on the possibilities of developing hypotheses from it. In some areas of the subject matter, hypotheses may have been stated by previous research workers. The researcher has to take stock of the various hypotheses with a view to evaluating their usefulness for further research and to consider whether they suggest any new hypothesis. Sociological journals, economic reviews, the bulletin of abstracts of current social sciences research, directory of doctoral dissertations accepted by universities and other periodicals provide a rich source of valuable information. In addition to these general sources, some governmental agencies and voluntary organizations publish listings of summaries of research in their special fields of service. Professional organizations, research groups and voluntary organizations are a constant source of information about unpublished works in their special fields.

Formulating the Problem

The selection of one appropriate researchable problem out of the identified problems requires evaluation of those alternatives against certain criteria, which may be grouped into the following:

Internal Criteria

Internal criteria consists of the following:

(i) Researcher's interest: The problem should interest the researcher and be a challenge to him. Without interest and curiosity, he may not develop sustained perseverance. Even a small difficulty may become an excuse for discontinuing the study. Interest in a problem depends on the researcher's educational background, experience, outlook and sensitivity.

(ii) Researcher's competence: A mere interest in a problem will not do. The researcher must be competent to plan and carry out a study of the problem. He must have the ability to grasp and deal with internal problems. He must possess adequate knowledge of the subject matter, relevant methodology, and statistical procedures.

(iii) Researcher's own resource: In the case of a research to be done by a researcher on his own, consideration of his own financial resource is important. If it is beyond his means, he will not be able to complete the work unless he gets some external financial support. Time resource is more important than finance. Research is a time-consuming process; hence, it should be properly utilized.

External Criteria

(i) Researchability of the problem: The problem should be researchable, i.e., it should be amenable for finding answers to the questions involved in it through scientific method. To be researchable, a question must be one for which observation or other data collection in the real world can provide the answer.

(ii) Importance and urgency: Problems requiring investigation are unlimited, but available research efforts are very much limited.

Therefore, in selecting problems for research, their relative importance and significance should be considered. An important and urgent problem should be given priority over an unimportant one.

(iii) Novelty of the problem: The problem must have novelty. There is no use wasting one's time and energy on a problem already studied thoroughly by others. This does not mean that replication is always needless. Sometimes in social sciences, it is appropriate to replicate (repeat) a study in order to verify the validity of its findings to a different situation.

(iv) Feasibility: A problem may be a new one and also important, but if research on it is not feasible, it cannot be selected. Hence, feasibility is a very important consideration.

(v) Facilities: Research requires certain facilities such as well-equipped library facility, suitable and competent guidance, and data analysis facility. Therefore, the availability of the facilities relevant to the problem must be considered.

(vi) Usefulness and social relevance: The study of the problem should make significant contribution to the concerned body of knowledge or to the solution of some significant practical problem. It should be socially relevant. This consideration is particularly important in the case of higher level academic research and sponsored research.

(vii) Research personnel: Research undertaken by faculty and by research organizations requires the services of investigators and research officers. However, in India and other developing countries, research has not yet become a remunerative profession. Talented persons are not therefore attracted to research projects.

Each identified problem must be evaluated in terms of the above internal and external criteria and the most appropriate one may be selected by a research scholar.

The Concept of Measurement

Measurement can be defined as a standardized process of assigning numbers or other symbols to certain characteristics of the objects of interest, according to some pre-specified rules. Measurement often deals with numbers because mathematical and statistical analyses can be performed only on numbers and they can be communicated throughout the world in the same form without any translation problems. For a measurement process to be standardized process assignment, two characteristics are necessary. First, there must be one-to-one correspondence between the symbol and the characteristic in the object that is being measured. Second, the rules for assignment must be invariant over time and the objects being measured.

Levels of Measurement

The level of measurement refers to the relationship among the values that are assigned to the attributes for a variable. What does that mean? Begin with the idea of the variable, in this example, "party affiliation". That variable has a number of attributes. Let's assume that in this particular election context the only relevant attributes are "Secular", "Democratic" and "Independent". For purposes of analyzing the results of this variable, we arbitrarily assign the values 1, 2 and 3 to the three attributes. The level of measurement describes the relationship between these three values. In this case, we are simply using the numbers as shorter placeholders for the lengthier text terms. We don't assume that higher values mean "more" of something and lower numbers signify "less". We don't assume the value of '2' means that members of Party A are twice those of Party B. We don't assume that members Party B are in the first place or have the highest priority just because they have the value of 1. In this case, we only use the values as a shorter name for the attribute. Here, we would describe the level of measurement as 'nominal'. Figure 7.1 gives the level of measurement.

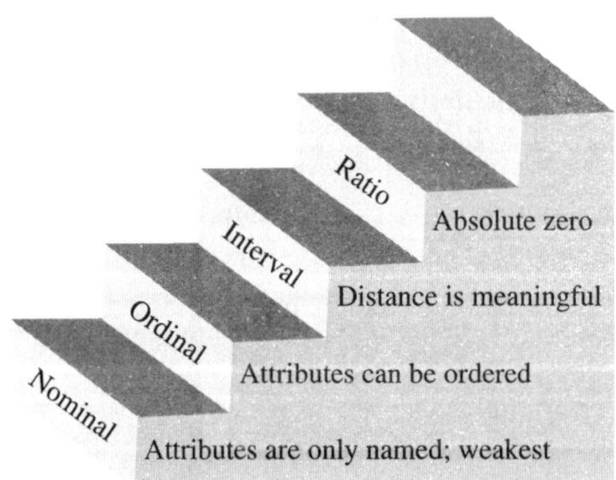

FIGURE 7.1 Level of measurement.

Why is Level of Measurement Important?

First, knowing the level of measurement helps you decide how to interpret the data from that variable. When you know that a measure is nominal (like the one just described), also you know that the numerical values are just short codes for the longer names. *Second*, knowing the level of measurement helps you decide what statistical analysis is appropriate on the values that were assigned. If a measure is nominal, then you know that you would never average the data values or do a t-test on the data.

There are typically four levels of measurement that are defined:

- Nominal
- Ordinal
- Interval
- Ratio

In nominal measurement, the numerical values just "name" the attribute uniquely. No ordering of the cases is implied. For example, jersey numbers in football or basketball are measures at the nominal level. A player with No. 30 is not more of anything than a player with No. 15 and is certainly not twice whatever No. 15 is. (In fact in Soccer, No. 10 jersey is normally worn by the best player.)

In ordinal measurement, the attributes can be rank-ordered. Here, distances between attributes do not have any meaning. For example, on a survey you might code Educational Attainment as 0 = less than H.S.; 1 = some H.S.; 2 = H.S. degree; 3 = some college; 4 = college degree; 5 = postgraduation. In this measure, higher numbers mean *more* education. However, is distance from 0 to 1 same as 3 to 4? Of course not. The interval between values is not interpretable in an ordinal measure.

In interval measurement, the distance between attributes *does* have meaning. For example, when we measure temperature (in Fahrenheit), the distance from 30–40 is the same as distance from 70–80. The interval between values is interpretable. Because of this, it makes sense to compute an average of an interval variable, where it doesn't make sense to do so for ordinal scales. However, note that in interval measurement ratios don't make any sense – 80 degrees is not twice as hot as 40 degrees (although the attribute value is twice as large).

Finally, **in ratio measurement**, there is always an absolute zero that is meaningful. This means that you can construct a meaningful fraction (or ratio) with a ratio variable. Weight is a ratio variable. In applied social research, most "count" variables are ratio, for example, the number of clients in the past six months. Why? Because you can have zero clients and because it is meaningful to say that "...we had twice as many clients in the past six months as we did in the previous six months".

It's important to recognize that there is a hierarchy implied in the level of measurement idea. At lower levels of measurement, assumptions tend to be less restrictive and data analyses tend to be less sensitive. At each level up the hierarchy, the current level includes all of the qualities of the one below it and adds something new. In general, it is desirable to have a higher level of measurement (e.g., interval or ratio) rather than a lower one (nominal or ordinal).

Components of Measurement

In the component of measurement, the researcher makes the assignment of numbers according to the system which should always be in accordance with the properties of the various components being calculated by the researcher during the measurement process. This can be further elaborated by the help of the simple rule mentioned below: a train route is given a number code to differentiate it from other routes and from other trains as well. Here, the only property is identity and any assessment of numbers is meaningless.

Nominal Scale

In a nominal scale, objects are assigned to mutually exclusive, labelled categories, but there are no essential associations among the classes, i.e. no ordering or spacing is implied. If one train is allocated, the same number code as another train, then both these trains are identical according to the number codes, i.e. they are identical with respect to a nominal variable. Otherwise, both the trains are different.

Nominally scaled variables may be gender, geographic locations, pin codes and marital status. The researcher can only carry out arithmetic operation which can be done by counting of each category performed on such a scale. Thus, during the research, the researcher can calculate the number of FMCG dealers in any state such as Maharashtra or the number of soaps being used by a consumer on an hourly, daily or monthly basis.

Ordinal Scale

An ordinal scale is found by grading or ranking items or things by sequencing them with regard to some common variable. The question is simply whether each object has more or less of this variable than some other object. The scale enables the researcher by providing the information as to how much variation there is between the objects. Because we do not know the amount of difference between objects, the allowable arithmetic operations are restricted to statistics such as the median or mode but not median. For example, suppose a sample of 1,000 consumers ranked five brands of frozen mixed vegetables according to quality. The results for Birds-eye brand were as follows:

Quality Brands Number of Respondents Giving Rankings to Birds-Eye	
Highest	150
Second	300
Third	250
Fourth	200
Lowest	100
Total	**1,000**

The second quality category is mode; the third category is the median. However, it is not possible to compute a mean ranking because the differences between ordinal scaled values are not necessarily the same. The finishing order in a horse race per class standing illustrates this type of scale. Similarly, brands of frozen vegetables can be ranked according to quality, from the highest to the lowest.

Interval Scale

In an interval scale, the numbers used to rank the objects also represent equal increments of the attribute being measured. This means that differences can be compared. The difference between 1 and 2 is the same as between 2 and 3, but is only half the difference between 2 and 4. The location of the zero point is not fixed since zero does not denote the absence of the attribute. Fahrenheit and Celsius temperatures are measured with different interval scales and have different zero points.

Interval scales have very desirable properties because virtually the entire range of statistical operations can be employed to analyze the resulting number, including addition and subtraction. Consequently, it is possible to compute an arithmetic mean from interval-scale measures.

Ratio Scale

A ratio scale is a special kind of interval scale that has a meaningful zero point. With such a scale—of weight, market share or dollars in savings accounts, for example, it is possible to say how many times greater or smaller one object is than another. This is the only type of scale that permits us to make comparisons of absolute magnitude. For example, we can say that an annual income of ₹80, 000 is twice the income of ₹40, 000.

There have been some contemporary efforts to adapt ratio scales to the measurement of social opinion. Some researchers have attempted to use magnitude estimation scales to overcome the loss of information that results when categories arbitrarily constrain the range of opinion. Magnitude scaling of attitudes has been calibrated through numeric estimation.

Components of Measurement Accuracy

Attitude measures used in marketing must be both accurate and useful. Aspects that contribute accuracy are validity, reliability and sensitivity. There are now briefly discussed.

Validity

An attitude measure has validity if it measures what it is supposed to measure. If this is the case, then differences in attitude scores will reflect differences among the objects or individuals on the characteristic being measured. How a researcher is to know whether measured differences in the attitudes of managers, consumer activists and consumers toward marketing practices, regulations and the contribution of the consumer movement are true. There have been three basic approaches to this question of validity assessment.

Consensus validity is invoked when the argument is made that the measurement so self-evidently reflects or represents the various aspects of the phenomenon that there can be little quarrel with it. For instance, buyer's recognition of advertisements is usually accepted at face value as an indication of past ad exposure.

Criterion validity is more defensible, for it is based on empirical evidence that the attitude measure correlates with other criteria variables. If the two variables are measured at the same time, concurrent validity is established. Better yet, if the attitude measures can predict some future event, then predictive validity is established.

Reliability

Reliability has to do with quality of measurement. In its everyday sense, reliability is the 'consistency' or 'repeatability' of measures. Before we can define reliability precisely, we have to lay the groundwork. First, you have to learn about the foundation of reliability, the true score theory of measurement. Along with that, you need to understand the different types of measurement errors because errors in measures play a key role in degrading reliability. With this foundation, we can consider the basic theory of reliability, including a precise definition of reliability. Then we will find out that we cannot calculate reliability—we can only estimate it. Because of this, there are different types of reliability that each has multiple ways to estimate reliability for that type. In the end, it's important to integrate the idea of reliability with the other major criterion for the quality of measurement—validity—and develop an understanding of the relationships between reliability and validity in measurement.

The total error of a measurement consists of systematic error component and a random error component. Random error is manifested by lack of consistency (unreliability) in repeated or equivalent measures of the same object or person. As a result, any measurement can be expressed as a function of several components:

Observed Score = True Score + Systematic Error + Random Error

If the measure is to be valid, it has to be reliable. A measure is highly reliable if random error is zero and still has a substantial systematic error that distorts the validity. In brief, reliability is a necessary but not a sufficient condition for validity. The basic methods for establishing reliability can be classified according to whether they measure stability of results over time or internal consistency of items in an attitude. Stability over time is assessed by repeating the measurement with the same instrument and the same respondents at two points of time and correlating the results.

Sensitivity

The third characteristic of a good attitude measure is sensitivity or the ability to discriminate among meaningful differences in attitudes. Sensitivity is achieved by increasing the number of scale categories; however, the more categories there are, the lower the reliability will be.

Generalization

'Generalization' refers to the ease of scale administration and interpretation in different research settings and situations. Thus the generalization of a multiple-item scale is determined by whether it can be applied in a wide variety of data collection modes, whether it can be used to obtain data from a wide variety of individuals and under what conditions it can be interpreted.

Relevancy

Relevancy of a scale refers to how meaningful it is to apply the scale to measure a construct. Mathematically, it is represented as the product of reliability and validity. Relevance = reliability + validity. If reliability and validity are evaluated by means of correlated coefficients, the implications are: The relevance of a scale can vary from 0 (no relevance) to 1 (complete relevance). If either reliability or validity is low, the scale will possess little relevance. Both reliability and validity are necessary for scale relevance.

Measurement Accuracy and Measurement Development

Questionnaire Designing

Questionnaire construction is properly regarded as an imperfect art. There are no established procedures that will lead consistently to a good questionnaire. A good questionnaire accomplishes the objectives of the research. Surveys should be custom built to the specification of given research purposes and they are much more than a collection of unambiguous questions. A number of constraints are imposed on the development of an appropriate questionnaire. For example, the number, form and ordering of the specific questions are partly determined by the data collection method.

The following is a sequence of logical steps that every researcher must follow to develop a good questionnaire:

1. Plan what to measure.
2. Formulate questions to obtain the needed answers.

3. Decide on the order and wording of questions and on the layout of the questionnaire.
4. Using a small sample, test the questionnaire for omissions and ambiguity.
5. Correct the problems and pre-test again.

Plan What to Measure

The most difficult step is specifying exactly what information is to be collected from each respondent. Poor judgment and lack of thought at this stage may mean that the results are not relevant to the research purpose or that they are incomplete. When a questionnaire that is incomplete in important aspects is sent into the field, the error is irreversible. To avoid this situation, the following considerations must be ensured:

- Clear research objectives which describe, as fully as possible, the kind of information the decision-maker needs, the hypotheses, and the scope of the research.
- Exploratory research which will suggest further relevant variables and help the researcher absorb the vocabulary and point of view of the typical respondent.
- Experience with similar studies.
- Pre-testing of preliminary versions of the questionnaire.

Format the Questions

Before specific questions are phrased, a decision has to be made as to the degree of freedom to be given to respondents in answering the question. The alternatives are:

1. Open-ended questions with no classification, where the interviewer tries to record the response verbatim.
2. Open-ended, where the interviewer uses preceded classifications to record the response.
3. The closed or structured format in which a question or supplementary card presents the responses that the respondent may consider.

Question Wordings

The wording of particular questions can have a large impact on how a respondent interprets them. Even small changes in wording can shift respondent's answers but it is difficult to know in advance whether or not a wording change will have such an effect. The following guidelines are of greatest value in critically evaluating and improving an existing question:

1. Is the vocabulary simple, direct and familiar to all respondents?
2. Do any words have vague or ambiguous meaning?

3. Are any questions double-barrelled?
4. Are any questions leading or loaded?
5. Are the instructions potentially confusing?
6. Is the question applicable to all respondents?
7. Split-ballot technique: Whenever there is doubt as to the appropriate wording, it is **desirable** to test several alternatives.
8. Are the questions of an appropriate length?

Sequence and Layout Design

The order or sequence of questions will be determined initially by the need to gain and maintain the respondent's cooperation and make the questionnaire as easy as possible for the interviewer to administer. Once these considerations are satisfied, attention must be given to the problem of order bias—the possibility that prior questions will influence answers to subsequent questions. The basic guidelines for sequencing a questionnaire are straightforward:

1. Open the interview with an easy and non-threatening question.
2. The questionnaire should flow smoothly and logically from one topic to the next.
3. For most topics it is better to proceed from broad, general questions to the more specific.
4. Sensitive or difficult questions dealing with income status, ability and so forth should not be placed at the beginning of the questionnaire.

Pre-test Design

Effective pre-testing demands that the researcher be open to criticism and willing to pursue the deficiencies. There are some very specific reasons for pre-test questions. Four common tests for specific questions are as follows:

(i) Variation: Testing items for an acceptable level of variation in the target population is one of the most common goals of pre-testing.

(ii) Meaning: The intended meaning of the question for the investigators may not be the meaning the respondents interpret it to be.

(iii) Task difficulty: A meaningful and clear question can still be difficult to answer if the question requires that a respondent makes connections or puts together information in unfamiliar ways.

(iv) Respondent interest and attention: Excessive repetition within a question or use of the same format within a question can reduce the amount of attention paid to questions by respondents.

Direct Response Attitude Scales

There are many ways to present a respondent with a continuum of numbered categories that represent the range of possible attitude judgments. They can be generally classified as **single item scales** and **multiple item scales**.

Single Item Scales

Single item scales are those that have only one item to measure a construct. Under the single item scales, the itemized category scale is the most widely used by marketing researchers. In some situations, comparative scales, rank order scales or constant-sum scales have advantages.

Itemized Scale

There are four categories from which respondents can choose to indicate their overall level of satisfaction with their present health insurance plan:

1. Very satisfied
2. Quite satisfied
3. Somewhat satisfied
4. Not at all satisfied

This satisfaction scale has the following characteristics:

- All categories are labelled.
- The respondent is forced to make a choice; there is no provision for neutral opinion or "don't know" response.
- There are more favourable than unfavourable categories; so the scale is unbalanced.
- There is no explicit comparison of the respondents' present plan with other health insurance plan.

Comparative Scales

Another version of the preceding scale would label the categories "excellent", "Very good", "fair", and "poor", thereby eliminating the implicit comparisons. The problem with a comparative scale is that the reference point is unclear and different respondents may use different reference points or standards.

Rank Order Scale

Rank order scale requires the respondent to arrange a set of objects with regard to a common criterion: advertisements in terms of interest, product features in terms of importance or new-product concepts with regard to willingness to buy in the future. The result is an ordinal scale with the inherent limitations of weak scale properties. Ranking is widely used in surveys, however, because it corresponds to the choice process occurring in shopping environment where a buyer makes direct comparison between competing alternatives (brands, flavours, product variations, and so on).

Q-Sort Scale

When the number of objects or characteristics that are to be rated or ranked is very large, it becomes rather tedious for the respondents to rank order or to do pair-wise comparisons. If the respondent is forced to rank ordering or a pair-wise comparison, problems and biases creep into the study. To deal with such situations, the Q-sort scaling process is used. In Q-sort scale, the respondents are asked to sort the various characteristics or objects that are being compared into various groups, such that the distribution of the number of objects or characteristics in each group follows a normal distribution. For example, let us take the case of a toy manufacturing company such as Toys 'R' developing a new product. After a marathon brainstorming session, the new product team has come up with 100 different products, each with minor variations in features and wants to test and find out from consumers, which feature combination is most preferred and will generate maximum sales. The best scaling procedure that can be used in this context is Q-sort scaling.

Constant Sum Scales

Constant sum scales require respondents to allocate a fixed number of rating points (usually 100) among several objects to reflect the relative preference of each object. It is widely used to measure the relative importance of attributes.

Pictorial Scales

In the pictorial scales, the various categories of the scale are depicted pictorially. The respondents are shown a concept or read an attitudinal statement and are asked to indicate their degree of agreement or interest by indicating the corresponding position on the pictorial scale.

Paired Comparison Scales

The brands to be rated are presented two at a time, so each brand in the category is compared once to every other brand. In each pair the respondent is asked to divide 10 points among the brands on the basis of how much they like one compared to the other. The score is then totalled for each brand. Although this scale performs well on the criteria, it is cumbersome to administer. Another possible limitation is that the frame of reference is always the other brands in the set being tested. These brands may change over time.

Derived Attitude Scales

Attitudes towards complex objects such as health plans, automobiles, credit instruments or transportation modes have many facets. Thus, it is often unrealistic to attempt to capture the full picture with one overall attitude-scale questions. For example, the public appears to support the general idea of income tax reforms but opposes the elimination of the most popular tax loopholes. The most frequently employed of these methods are Likert, Thurstone and semantic-differential scales; these now discussed.

Likert Scales

Likert scale requires a respondent to indicate a degree of agreement or disagreement with a variety of statements related to the attitudes or objects. They are also called **summated scales**, because the scores on the individual term are summed to produce a total score for the respondent. A Likert scale usually consists of two parts—the item part and the evaluative part. The item part is essentially a statement about a certain product, event or attitude. The evaluative part is a list of response categories ranking from "strongly agree" to "strongly disagree". An important assumption of this scaling method is that each of the items (statements) measures some aspects of a single common factor; otherwise, the items cannot be legitimately summed. In other words, the resulting scale is one dimensional.

Thurstone Scales

The procedure of Thurstone scale is also known as the **method of equal appearing** intervals since the objective is to obtain a one-dimensional scale with interval properties. The first step is to develop a large number of statements or adjectives reflecting all degrees of favourableness toward the attitude objects. Then a group of judges is given this set of items and asked to classify them according to their favourableness or unfavourableness.

Semantic Differential Scales

Semantic differential scales are used widely to describe the set of beliefs that comprise a person's image of an organization or brand. The procedure is also an insightful procedure for comparing the images of competing brands, stores or services. Respondents are asked to rate each attitude object in turn on a number of five- or seven point rating scales, bounded at each end by polar adjectives or phrases.

Observation and Psychological Measures

Observation methods are limited to providing information on current behaviour. Too often, this limitation becomes an excuse for not considering observational methods. Because many researchers do not use these methods, they may not appreciate their considerable benefits. Nevertheless, there are strong arguments for considering the observation of ongoing behaviour as an integral part of the research design.

Data Interpretation

Classification of data

Data are facts and other relevant materials, past and present, serving as bases for study and analyses. The data needed for a social science research may be broadly classified into:

- Data pertaining to human beings
- Data relating to organization
- Data pertaining to territorial areas

Personal data or data related to human beings consists of: Demographic and socio-economic characteristics of individuals: Age, sex, race, social class, religion, marital status, education, occupation, income, family size, location of the household, lifestyle, etc.

Behavioural Variables

Behavioural variables include attitudes, opinions, awareness, knowledge, practice, intentions, etc. Organizational data consist of data relating to an organization's origin, ownership, objectives, resources, functions, performance and growth. Territorial data are related to geophysical characteristics, resource endowment, population, occupational pattern, infrastructure, degree of development, etc. of spatial divisions like villages, cities, taluks, districts, state and the nation. Data form the basis for testing the hypothesis formulated in a study. Data also provide the facts and figures required for constructing measurement scales and tables.

The Sources of Data

The sources of data may be classified into:

- Primary sources
- Secondary sources.

Primary sources of data: Primary data are first-hand information collected through various methods such as observation, interviewing, mailing, etc. Primary data are directly collected by the researcher from her original sources.

Primary sources are original sources from which the researcher directly collects data that have not been previously collected, e.g. collection of data directly by the researcher on brand awareness, brand preference, brand loyalty and other aspects of consumer behaviour from a sample of consumers by interviewing them. Primary data are first hand information collected through various methods such as observation, interviewing, mailing, etc.

Primary data collection is necessary when a researcher cannot find the data needed in secondary sources. Market researchers are interested in primary data about demographic/socioeconomic characteristics, attitudes/opinions/interests, awareness/knowledge, intentions, motivation and behaviour. Three basic means of obtaining primary data are observation, surveys and experiments. The choice will be influenced by the nature of the problem and by the availability of time and money.

Secondary sources of data: The secondary sources of data consist of readily available compendia and already compiled statistical statements and reports. Secondary sources are not limited in time and space. That is, the researcher using them need not have been present when and where they were gathered. Secondary data, if available, can be secured quickly and cheaply. Wider geographical area and longer reference period may be covered without much cost. Thus, the use of secondary data extends the researcher's space and time reach. The use of secondary data broadens the data base from which scientific generalizations can be made. The use of a secondary data has its own limitations. The most important limitation is the available data may not meet our specific needs. The secondary data are not up-to-date and become obsolete when they appear in print because of time lag in producing them.

Secondary data is information gathered for purposes other than the completion of a research project. A variety of secondary information sources is available to the researcher gathering data on an industry, potential product applications, and the market place. Secondary data is also used to gain initial insight into the research problem.

Secondary data is classified in terms of its source—either internal or external. Internal or in-house data, is secondary information acquired within the organization where research is being carried out. External secondary data is obtained from outside sources.

The two major advantages of using secondary data in market research are time and cost savings.

Methods of Data Collection

There are various methods of data collection. A 'Method' is different from a 'Tool'. Whereas a method refers to the way or mode of gathering data, a tool is an instrument used for the method. For example, a schedule is used for interviewing. The important methods are

- Observation
- Interviewing
- Mail survey

- Experimentation
- Simulation and projective technique.

Importance of Data

The search for answers to research questions is called collection of data. Data are facts and other relevant materials, past and present, serving as bases for study and analyses. The data needed for a social science research may be broadly classified into the following:

- Data pertaining to human beings
- Data relating to organization
- Data pertaining to territorial areas

Meaning of Data Processing

Data in the real world often comes with a large quantum and in a variety of formats that any meaningful interpretation of data cannot be achieved straightaway. Social science researches, to be very specific, draw conclusions using both primary and secondary data. To arrive at a meaningful interpretation on the research hypothesis, the researcher has to prepare his data for this purpose. This preparation involves the identification of data structures, the coding of data, and the grouping of data for preliminary research interpretation. This data preparation for research analysis is termed as **processing of data**. Further selection of tools for analysis would to a large extent, depend on the results of this data processing.

Data processing is an intermediary stage of work between data collection and data interpretation. The data gathered in the form of questionnaires/ interview schedules/field notes/data sheets is mostly in the form of a large volume of research variables. The research variables recognized is the result of the preliminary research plan, which also sets out the data processing methods beforehand. Processing of data requires advanced planning, and this planning, may cover such aspects as identification of variables, hypothetical relationship among the variables, and tentative research hypothesis.

The various steps in data processing may be stated as:

1. Identifying the data structures
2. Editing the data
3. Coding and classifying the data

Editing: Editing is a process of checking to detect and correct errors and omissions. Data editing happens at two stages—one at the time of recording of the data and the other at the time of analysis of data.

Coding: The edited data are subject to codification and classification. The coding process assigns numerals or other symbols to the several responses of the data set. It is therefore a prerequisite to prepare a coding scheme for the data set. The recording of the data is done on the basis of this coding scheme.

The responses collected in a data sheet varies. Sometimes the responses could be the choice among a multiple response, sometimes the response could be in terms of values, and sometimes the response could be alphanumeric. At the recording stage itself, if some codification were done to the responses collected, it would be useful in the data analysis. When codification is done, it is imperative to keep a log of the codes allotted to the observations. This code sheet will help in the identification of variables/observations and the basis for such codification.

Classification: When open-ended responses are received, classification is necessary to code the responses. For instance, the income of the respondent could be an open-ended question. From all responses, a suitable classification can be arrived at. A classification method should meet certain requirements or should be guided by certain rules. First, classification should be linked to the theory and the aim of the particular study. The objectives of the study will determine the dimensions chosen for coding. The categorization should meet the information required to test the hypothesis or investigate the questions.

Transcription of data: When the observations collected by the researcher are not very large, the simple inferences, which can be drawn from the observations, can be transferred to a data sheet, which is a summary of all responses on all observations from a research instrument. The main aim of transcription is to minimize the shuffling proceeds between several responses and several observations. Suppose a research instrument contains 120 responses and the observations have been collected from 200 respondents, a simple summary of one response from all 200 observations would require shuffling of 200 pages. The process is quite tedious if several summary tables are to be prepared from the instrument. The transcription process helps in the presentation of all responses and observations on data sheets, which can help the researcher to arrive at preliminary conclusions as to the nature of the sample collected, etc. Transcription is, thus, an intermediary process between data coding and data tabulation.

Tabulation: The transcription of data can be used to summarize and arrange the data in compact form for further analysis. The process is called tabulation. It is a process of summarizing raw data displaying them on compact statistical tables for further analysis. The process involves counting the number of cases falling into each of the categories identified by the researcher. Tabulation can be done manually or through the computer. The choice depends on the size and type of study, cost considerations, time pressures, and the availability of software packages. Manual tabulation is suitable for small and simple studies.

Construction of frequency table: Frequency tables provide a 'shorthand' summary of data. The importance of presenting statistical data in tabular form needs no emphasis. Tables facilitate comprehending masses of data at a glance; they conserve space and reduce explanations and descriptions to a minimum. They gives give a visual picture of relationships between variables and categories. These tables facilitate summation of item and the detection of errors and omissions and provide a basis for computations. It is important to make a distinction between the general purpose tables and specific tables. The general purpose tables are primary or reference tables designed to include large amount of source data in convenient and accessible form. The special purpose tables are analytical or derivate ones that demonstrate significant relationships in the data or the results of statistical analysis. Tables of government reports on population, vital statistics, agriculture, industries, etc. are of general purpose type. They represent extensive repositories and statistical information. Special purpose tables are found in monographs, research reports and articles and reused as instruments of analysis. In research, we are primarily concerned with special purpose tables.

Types of Graphs and General Rules

The most commonly used graphic forms may be grouped into the following categories:

- Line graphs or charts
- Bar charts
- Segmental presentations
- Scatter plots
- Bubble charts
- Stock plots
- Pictographs
- Chesnokov faces

Measures of Central Tendency

Arithmetic mean, geometric mean and harmonic mean are mathematical averages. Median and mode are positional averages. These statistical measures enable one to understand how individual values in a distribution concentrate to a central value such as average. If the values of distribution approximately come near to the average value, we conclude that the distribution has central tendency.

Dispersion

Dispersion is the tendency of the individual values in a distribution to spread away from the average. Many economic variables like income, wage, etc. are widely varied from the mean. Dispersion is a statistical measure that understands the degree of variation of items from the average.

Correlation Analysis

The simplest way to find out qualitatively the correlation is to plot the data. In the case of our example, as seen from Figure 7.1, a strong *positive* correlation between y and x is **evident,** i.e., the plot reveals that, as the weight increases, the fuel consumption increases as well. How can we quantify the degree of correlation? This is usually done by specifying the correlation coefficient R, defined as where μ_x and σ_x denote the sample mean and the sample standard deviation, respectively for the variable x, and μ_y and σ_y denote the sample mean and the sample standard deviation, respectively for the variable y.

Now, let's assume that a perfect linear relationship exists between the variables x and y, i.e., $y_i = ax_i + b$ for $i = 1, 2, \ldots, n$ with $a \neq 0$. Now, verify using the definitions of the mean and the variance that $\mu_y = a\ \mu_x + b$ and $\sigma_y = |a|\ \sigma_x$. This implies that $R = a/|\ a|$. Or, in other words, $R = 1$ if $a > 0$ and $R = -1$ if $a < 0$. The case $R = 1$ corresponds to the maximum possible linear positive association between x and y, meaning that all the data points will lie exactly on a straight line of the positive slope. Similarly, $R = -1$ corresponds to the maximum possible negative association between the statistical variables x and y. In general, $-1 \leq R \leq 1$ with the magnitude and the sign of R representing the *strength* and *direction* respectively of the association between the two variables. So, for, $R = 0.977$, implying a strong positive correlation between the fuel consumption and the weight of the automobile.

Types of correlation analysis

Correlation can be:

- Positive or negative
- Linear or nonlinear
- Simple, multiple or partial

Coefficient of Determination

Besides probable error, another important method of interpreting coefficient of correlation is the coefficient of determination which is the square of correlation or r. For instance, suppose the coefficient of correlation between price and supply is 0.8. We calculate the coefficient of determination as r, which is .8 or .64. It means that 64% of 22, i.e. the variation in supply is on account of changes in price.

REPORT WRITING

The report should be written in a simple, lucid and systematic manner.

1. **Rough draft:** First, a *rough draft* of the report is required to be prepared on the basis of outlines. Necessary changes should be made in the report before it is presented in its final form to the concerned authority.
2. **Method of report writing:** A report can be written in two ways:
   - Report in the letter form
   - Report in the headings and sub-headings form

3. **Accuracy in recording facts and figures:** The report should be written quickly without interrupting the continuity of thought. Proper attention should be given towards need for coherence, unity and logical arrangement of ideas, accuracy in recording facts and figures, correlation of illustrations with the text, and cross-referencing proper documentation.
4. **Concentration on subject matter:** Here, the concentration should be on the subject-matter spelling, punctuation, and other details can be checked in the final draft.
5. **Proper draft and sufficient margin:** The draft should be written properly and sufficient margin should be left on both the sides of the paper so that revisions and corrections can be made.
6. **Numbering of pages:** The pages should be properly numbered as in the case of the draft.
7. **Table of contents:** It is essential to give a table of contents in the beginning of the report. It gives a complete picture of the report.
8. **Preface:** The report should begin with Acknowledgement (if separate) and Preface. The Preface should include the names of the Chairman, secretary and the members of the committee appointed certain details such as type of investigation used, method of research, nature of questionnaire, and interviews taken.
9. **Use of charts, diagrams exhibits:** The diagrams, charts and exhibits should be clear and precise. Suitable captions must be given to them. Also, the labels in the diagrams and charts should be clear and readable.
10. **Appendix:** The supporting and technical data should be separated from the main body and should be included on the report as an appendix. Thus, due prominence can be given to the presentation of facts.

Finally, you should give a suitable title and mention the date of submission of the report.

SUMMARY

Research really begins when the researcher experiences some difficulty, i.e., when a problem demands a solution within the subject on from some other discipline.

The problem selected for research may initially be a vague topic. The process of defining a problem includes:

- Developing the title
- Building a conceptual model
- Defining the objective of the study

Research problem is the situation that causes the researcher to feel apprehensive, confused and ill at ease. It is the demarcation of a problem area within a certain context involving the who or what, the where, the when and the why of the problem situation. These differ in terms of the degree of formality, physical form, scope, style and size.

The contents of a report include the following:

I. Prefatory Items

- Title page
- Declaration
- Certificates
- Preface/Acknowledgements
- Table of contents
- List of tables
- List of graphs/figures/charts
- Abstract or synopsis

II. Body of the Report

- Introduction
- Theoretical background of the topic
- Statement of the problem
- Review of literature
- The scope of the study
- The objectives of the study
- Hypothesis to be tested
- Definition of the concepts
- Models, if any
- Design of the study
- Methodology
- Method of data collection
- Sources of data
- Sampling plan
- Data collection instruments
- Field work
- Data processing and analysis plan
- Overview of the report
- Limitation of the study
- Results: findings and discussions
- Summary, conclusions and recommendations

III. Reference Material

- Appendix
- Copies of data collection instruments
- Technical details on sampling plan
- Complex tables
- Glossary of new terms used
- Bibliography

DISCUSSION QUESTIONS

1. How is a research problem formulated?
2. What are the concepts of measurement techniques used in marketing research?
3. Explain the different scales of measurement.
4. Write Short Notes on:
   (a) Review of literature
   (b) Communicating to a specific audience
   (c) Secondary sources of data

FURTHER READING

Beri, G.C. (1997): *Marketing Research*, New Delhi: Tata McGraw-Hill.

Blankenship, A.B. and Doyle, J.B. (1971): *Marketing Research Management*, Bombay: Tarapore Wala Sons & Co.

Green, Paul E., Tull Donald S., and Albaum Gerald (2010): *Research for Marketing Decisions*, 5th ed., New Delhi: PHI Learning.

8 Overview of Sampling Methods and Sample Size Determination

Chapter Outline

- Why Sampling?
- Types of Sampling
- Probability Sampling Methods
- Non-probability Sampling Methods
- The Sample Size
- Discussion Questions

Learning Objectives

After going through this chapter, you will be able to:

- Appreciate why sampling is so common in managerial situation.
- Identify the potential sampling errors.
- List the various sampling methods with their strengths and weaknesses.
- Distinguish between probability and non-probability sampling.
- Know when to use the proportional or the disproportional stratified sampling.
- Understand the role of multistage and multiphase sampling in large sampling studies.
- Appreciate why and how non-probability sampling is used in spite of its theoretical weaknesses.
- Recognize the factors that affect the decision on sample size.

INTRODUCTION

Let us take a look at the following five situations to find out the common features among them, if any:

1. An inspector from the Weights and Measures Department of the government goes to a unit manufacturing vanaspati. He picks up a few packed containers from the day's production, pours out the contents from each of these selected containers, and weighs them individually to determine if the manufacturing unit is packing enough vanaspati in its containers to conform to what is claimed as the net weight in the label.
2. The Personnel Department of a large bank wants to measure the level of employee motivation and morale so that it can initiate appropriate measures to help improve the same. It hands out a questionnaire to about 250 employees from different branches and offices all over India selected from a total of about 30,000 employees and analyzes the information contained in these 250 filled-in questionnaires to assess the morale and motivation levels of all employees.
3. The Product Development Department of a consumer products company has developed a "new improved" version of its talcum powder. Before launching the new product, the Marketing Department gives a container of the old version first and, after a week, a container of the new version to a group of 400 consumers and gets the feedback of these consumers on various attributes of the products. The responses of these consumers will form the basis for assessing the consumer perception of the new talcum powder as compared to the old talcum powder.
4. The Quality Control Department of a company manufacturing fluorescent tubes checks the life of its products by picking up 15 of its tubes at random and letting them burn till each one of them fuses. The life of all its products is assessed based on the performance of these 15 tubes.
5. An industrial engineer takes 100 rounds of the shop floor over a period of six days and based on the 100 observations, assesses the machine utilization on the shop floor.

What is Sampling?

On the face of it, there is little that is common among the five situations described above. Each one refers to a different functional area, and the nature of the problem also differs widely from one situation to another. However, on closer observation, it appears that in all these situations, one is interested in measuring some attribute of a large or infinite group of elements by studying only a part of that group. This process of inferring something about a large group of elements by studying only a part of it, is referred to as **sampling**.

Most of us use sampling in our daily life, e.g. when we go to buy provisions from a grocery on buying fruits from a fruit shop. We might sample a few grains of rice or wheat to infer the quality of the grain on taste an apple or grapes before buying them. In this unit we shall study why sampling works and the various methods of sampling available so that we can make the process of sampling more efficient.

Some Basic Concepts

We shall refer to the collection of all elements about which some inference is to be made as the **population**. For example, in situation 2 above, the population is the set of 30,000 employees working in the bank and, in situation 3, the population comprises all the consumers of talcum powder in the country.

We are basically interested in measuring some **characteristics** of the population. This could be the average life of a fluorescent tube, the percentage of consumers of talcum powder who prefer the "new improved" talcum powder to the old one or the percentage of time a machine is being used as in situation 5 above. Any characteristic of a population will be referred to as a **parameter** of the population.

In sampling, some population parameter is inferred by studying only a *part* of the population. We shall refer to the part of the population that has been chosen as a *sample*. Sampling, therefore, refers to the process of choosing a sample from the population so that some inference about the population can be made by studying the sample. For example, the sample in situation 2 consists of the 250 employees from different branches and offices of the bank. Any characteristic of a sample is called a **statistic.** For example, the mean life of the sample of 15 tubes in situation 4 above is a sample statistic.

Conventionally, population parameters are denoted by Greek or capital letters and sample statistics by lower case Roman letters. There can be exceptions to this form of notation, e.g. population proportions is usually denoted by p and the sample proportion by p.

Figure 8.1 shows the concept of a population and a sample in the form of the Venn diagram, where the population is shown as the universal set and a sample is shown as a true subset of the population. The characteristics of a population and a sample and some symbols for these are presented in Table 8.1.

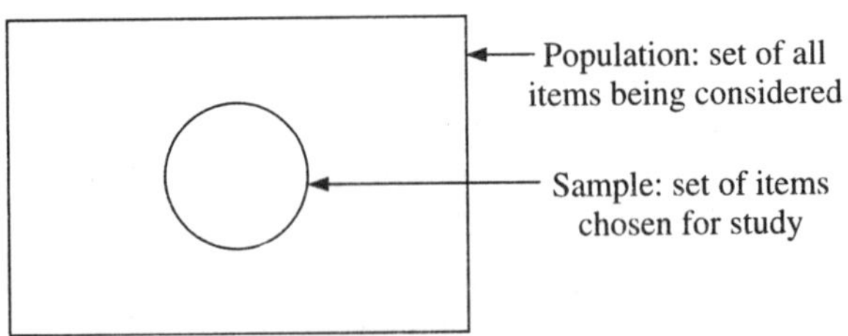

FIGURE 8.1 Illustration of population set and sample: through Venn Diagram.

TABLE 8.1 Symbols of Population and Samples

	Population	Sample
Characteristics	Parameter	Statistic
symbols	Population size = N	Sample size = n
	Population mean = μ	Sample mean = x
	Population s.d. = σ	Sample s.d. = s
	Population proportion = p	Sample proportion = p

Sampling is not the only process available for making inferences about a population. For small populations, it may be feasible and practical, and sometimes desirable to examine every member of the population, e.g. for inspection of some aircraft, components. This process is referred to as census or complete enumeration of the population.

WHY SAMPLING?

In the example situations given in the Introduction, the reasons for resorting to sampling should be very clear. We now give the various reasons which make sampling a desirable and, in many cases, the only course open for making an inference about a population.

1. Inferring from a sample can be *much faster* than from a complete enumeration of the population because fewer elements are being studied. In situation 3 given in the Introduction, a complete enumeration of all consumers, even if feasible, would perhaps take so much time that it is unacceptable for product launch decisions.
2. Sampling also helps in substantial *cost reductions* as compared to censuses and, as we shall see later in this unit, a better sample design could reduce the cost of the study further. In many cases, for example, in situation 3 above, it may be too costly, although feasible, to contact all the employees in the bank and get information from them.
3. In many situations the element being studied gets destroyed while being tested. The fluorescent tubes in situation 4 above, which are chosen for testing their lives, get destroyed while being tested. In such cases, a *complete enumeration is impossible* as there would be no population left after such an enumeration.
4. Quite often, it is not feasible to do a complete enumeration due to many practical difficulties. For example, in situation 3 above, it would not be feasible to collect information from all the consumers of talcum powder in India. Some consumers would have moved from one place to another during the period of study, some others would have stopped consuming talcum powder just before the period of study, whereas some others would have been users of talcum powder during the period of study but would have stopped using it some time later. In such situations, although

it is theoretically possible to do a complete enumeration, it is practically not feasible to do so.

5. In many cases, sampling provides adequate information so that *not much additional reliability can be ensured* with complete enumeration in spite of spending large amount of additional money and time. It is also possible to quantify the magnitude of possible error on using some types of sampling as will be explained later.
6. For large populations, complete enumeration also suffers from the possibility of *spurious* or *unreliable data* collected by the enumerators. On the other hand, there is greater confidence on the purity of the data collected in sampling as there can be better interviewing, better training and supervision of enumerators, better analysis of missing data, and so on.

TYPES OF SAMPLING

There are two basic types of sampling depending on whom or what is allowed to govern the selection of the sample. We shall call them *probability sampling* and *non-probability sampling*.

Probability Sampling

In probability sampling, the decision whether a particular element is included in the sample or not is governed by chance alone. All probability sampling designs ensure that each element in the population has some nonzero probability of getting included in the sample. This would mean defining a procedure for picking up the sample, based on chance, and avoiding changes in the sample except by way of a pre-defined process again. The picking up of the sample is therefore totally insulated against the judgment, convenience or whims of any person involved in the study. That is why probability sampling procedures tend to become rigorous and at times quite time-consuming to ensure that each element has a nonzero probability of getting included in the sample. On the other hand, when probability sampling designs are used, it is possible to quantify the magnitude of the likely error in the inference made, and this is of great help in many situations in building up confidence in the inference.

Non-probability Sampling

Any sampling process which does not ensure some nonzero probability for each element in the population to be included in the sample would belong to the category of non-probability sampling. In this case, samples may be picked up based on the judgment or convenience of the enumerator. Usually, the complete sample is not decided at the beginning of the study, but it evolves as the study progresses.

However, the very same factors which govern the selection of a sample, e.g. judgment or convenience, can also introduce biases in the study. Moreover, there is no way that the magnitude of errors can be quantified when non-probability sampling designs are used.

Often, samples are selected by interviewers or enumerators "at random", meaning that the actual sample selection is left to the discretion of the enumerators. Such a sampling design would also belong to the non-probability sampling category, and not the category of probability or random sampling.

Probability Sampling Methods

In the category of probability sampling, we shall discuss the following four designs:

1. Simple random sampling
2. Systematic sampling
3. Stratified sampling
4. Cluster sampling

We can also use sampling designs which are combinations of the above four types of sampling.

Simple Random Sampling

Conceptually, simple random sampling is one of the simplest sampling designs and can work well for relatively small populations. However, there are many practical problems when we try to use simple random sampling for large populations.

What is simple random sampling? Suppose we have a population having N elements and that we want to pick up a sample of size n ($< N$). Obviously, there are many possible samples of size n. Simple random sampling is a process that ensures that each of the samples of size n has an equal probability of being picked up as the chosen sample. As we shall see later in this section, this also implies that, under simple random sampling, each element of the population has an equal probability of getting included in the sample.

All other forms of probability sampling use this basic concept of simple random sampling but it is only applied to a part of the population at a time and not to the whole population.

Let us consider a small example to illustrate what simple random sampling is. Our population is a family of five members, two adults and three children, viz. A, B, C, D and E respectively. There are 10 different samples possible of size three as listed in Table 8.2. As shown in the table, if each of the 10 samples has an equal probability of 1/10 of being picked up, this implies that the probability that any particular element, say A or B, is included in the sample is the same, i.e. 10.

TABLE 8.2 Simple Random Sampling

P[ABC] = 1/10	P[ADE] = 1/10
P[ABD] = 1/10	P[BCD] = 1/10
P[ABE] = 1/10	P[BCE] = 1/10
P[ACD] = 1/10	P[BDE] = 1/10
P[ACE] = 1/10	P[CDE] = 1/10

In general, there are $\binom{N}{n}$ different samples of size n that can be picked up from a population of size N. Simple random sampling ensures that any of these samples has the same probability of getting picked up, i.e. $\frac{1}{\binom{N}{n}}$.

Population of size 5: (A, B, C, D and E)

Let P [ABC] be the probability that the sample of size 3 containing elements A, B and C is chosen. Therefore,
The probability that element A is in the sample

$$P(\text{A}) = P[\text{ACC}] + P[\text{ABD}] + P[\text{ABE}] + P[\text{ACD}] + P[\text{ACE}] + [\text{ADE}] = \frac{6}{10}$$

$$P(\text{B}) = P[\text{ABC}] + P[\text{ABD}] + P[\text{ABE}] + P[\text{BCD}] + P[\text{BCE}] + P[\text{BDE}] = \frac{6}{10}$$

Similarly,

$$\text{P(C)} = \frac{6}{10} \quad \text{P(D)} = \frac{6}{10} \quad \text{P(E)} = \frac{6}{10}$$

If we want to find the probability that element A (or any other element for that matter) is included in the sample picked up, we have to find the number of different samples in which this element A occurs. There are $(n - 1)$ positions available in the sample (since 1 is occupied by A) which can be picked up from any of the $(N - 1)$ elements of the population (since A is not available to be picked up) and so there are different samples in which element A occurs.

$$\binom{N}{n}$$

Therefore, the probability that element A is included in the sample is

$$\frac{\binom{N-1}{n-1}}{\binom{N}{n}} = \frac{(N-1)!}{(n-1)!\,(N-n)!} \times \frac{n!\,(N-n)!}{N!} = \frac{n}{N}.$$

The fact that every element of the population has an equal probability of getting included in the sample is made use of in actually picking up simple random samples.

Sampling with and without replacement: We have implicitly assumed above that we are sampling without replacement, i.e. if an element is picked up once, it is not available to be picked up again. This is how most practical samples are, but as a concept, it is possible to think in terms of sampling with replacement, in which case, an element, after being picked up and included in the sample, is replaced in the population so that it can be picked up again.

What is important for us to note at this stage is that even in the case of simple random sampling with replacement, each element has an equal probability of getting included in the sample.

How is simple random sampling done? It is imperative to have a list of all the members of the population before a simple random sample can be picked up. Such an exhaustive list of all population members is called a *sampling frame*.

Suppose we write the name of one such member on a chit of paper and thus have N chits in a bowl, one chit for each member of the population. We can then mix the chits well and pick up one chit at random to represent one member of the sample. If we want a sample of size n, we have to repeat this process n times and we shall have a simple random sample of size n consisting of the names of members appearing on the chits picked. It is easy to see that if we replace the chits in the bowl after noting down the name of the element, we will have a simple random sample with replacement and one without replacement if we do not.

As the population size increases, it becomes more and more difficult to work with chits, and one can simulate this process on a computer or by using a table of random numbers. We can associate a serial number with each member of our population and then instruct a computer to pick up a member from 1 through N using its pseudo-random number generator. This ensures that every number from 1 through N has an equal probability of getting picked up and so the sample selected is a simple random sample.

We can also use a table of random numbers to pick up a simple random sample. In a table of random numbers, there is an equal probability for any digit from 0 to 9 to appear in any particular position. Table 8.3 gives five-digit random numbers containing 100 such numbers. The most important point to remember in using a random number table is to specify to the minutest detail the sequence of steps that has been decided before the table is actually referred to. We shall demonstrate this with an example.

Suppose we have a population of size 900 with each number being given a serial number ranging from 000 through 899 and we want to pick up a simple random sample of size 20. We start with the procedure.

1. Starting point and direction of movement.

We may decide to start with the top left-hand number and consider the first three digits (from left) as the three-digit random number picked up, e.g. the first number would then be 121. We also specify that we shall move down a column to pick up further numbers, e.g. the second number would be 073, If there is no further number down the column, we shall go to the top of the next column of five-digit numbers and pick up the first three digits (from left), e.g. after 851 our next number shall be 651.

TABLE 8.3 Random Numbers

7369	49031	45451	10724	95051
70387	53186	97116	32093	95612
93451	53493	56442	67121	70257
74077	66687	45394	33414	15685
73627	54287	42596	5544	76826
51353	56404	74106	66185	23145
46426	12855	48497	5532	36299
57126	99010	29015	65778	93911
37997	89034	79788	94676	32307
41283	42498	73173	21938	22024
76374	68251	71593	93397	26245
51668	47244	13732	48369	60907
17698	32685	24490	56983	81152
12448	902	7263	16764	71261
52515	93269	61210	55526	71912
43501	10248	34219	83416	91239
45279	19382	82151	57365	84915
11437	98102	58168	61534	69495
85183	38161	22848	6673	35293

Checking the number picked up

If the number picked up is in the range 000 to 899, we accept the number, but if it is outside this range, we shall discard it and pick up the next number, e.g. after the third number 703, we discard 934, and the fourth member of the sample would be 740. Similarly, if we are doing sampling without replacement and a number is picked up again, it is discarded and we move to the next three-digit number.

Using this process, if we want a sample of size 10, our sample would contain members with the following numbers: 121, 073, 703, 740, 736, 513, 464, 571, 379 and 412.

Simple random sampling in practice: Simple random sampling, as described here, is not the most efficient sampling design, either statistically or economically, in all practical situations. However, it forms the basis for all other forms of probability sampling which are used on parts of the population or sub-population and not on the population as a whole.

As already mentioned, listing all members of the population, viz. a frame is required before a simple random sample can be chosen. In many situations the frame is not available nor is it practical to prepare the frame in a time and cost-effective manner. Obviously, under such conditions, simple random sampling is not a viable sampling design.

Most large populations are not homogeneous and can be broken down into more homogeneous units. In such conditions, one can design sampling schemes which are statistically more efficient, meaning that they allow the same precision from smaller sample sizes.

Similarly, by picking up members from geographically closer areas, the cost efficiency of the sampling design can be improved. Cluster sampling is based on this concept.

The process of picking up a simple random sample through using a table of random numbers or any other such aids, as discussed earlier, is rather cumbersome and not very purposeful to the uninitiated interviewer. Simpler forms of sampling overcome this handicap of simple random sampling.

Systematic Sampling

Systematic sampling proceeds by picking up one element after a fixed interval depending on the sampling ratio. For example, if we want to have a sample of size 10 from a population of size 100, our sampling ratio would be $n/N = 10/100 = 1/10$. We would, therefore, have to decide where to start from among the first 10 names in our frame. If this number happens to be 7, for example, then the sample would contain members having serial numbers 7, 17, 27, …, 97 in the frame. It is to be noted that the random process establishes only the first member of the sample, the rest are preordained automatically because of the known sampling ratio.

Systematic sampling in the previous example would choose one out of ten possible samples, each starting with either No. 1, or No. 2, or No. 10. This is usually decided by allowing chance to play its role, e.g. by using a table of random numbers.

Systematic sampling is relatively much easier to implement as compared to simple random sampling. However, there is one possibility that should be guarded against while using systematic sampling: the possibility of a strong bias in the results if there is any periodicity in the frame that parallels the sampling ratio. One can give some ridiculously simple example to highlight the point. If you were making studies on the demand for various banking transactions in a bank branch by studying the demand on some days randomly selected by systematic sampling, be sure that your sampling ratio is not, say, 1/7 or 1/14. Otherwise, you would always be studying the demand on the same day of the week and your inferences could be biased depending on whether the day selected is a Monday or a Friday, and so on. Similarly, when the frame contains addresses of flats in buildings all alike and having, say, 12 flats in one building, systematic sampling with a sampling ratio of 1/6, 1/60, or any other such fraction would bias your sample with flats of only one type, e.g. a ground floor corner flat, i.e., all types of flats would not be members of your sample; and this might lead to biases in the inference made.

If the frame is arranged in an order, ascending or descending, of some attribute, then the location of the first sample element may affect the result of the study, for example, if our frame contains a list of students arranged in a descending order of their percentage in the previous examination and we are picking a systematic sample with a sampling ratio of 1/50. If the first number picked is 1 or 2, then the sample chosen will be academically much better off compared to another systematic sample with the first number chosen as 49 or 50. In such situations, one should devise ways of nullifying the effect of bias due to starting number by insisting on multiple starts after a small cycle or other such means.

On the other hand, if the frame is so arranged that similar elements are grouped together, then systematic sampling produces almost a proportional stratified sample and would therefore, be, more statistically efficient than simple random sampling.

Systematic sampling is perhaps the most commonly used method among the probability sampling designs and for many purposes, e.g. for estimating the precision of the results, systematic samples are treated as simple random samples.

Stratified Sampling

Stratified sampling is more complex than simple random sampling, but where applied properly, stratification can significantly increase the statistical efficiency of sampling.

The concept: Suppose we are interested in estimating the demand of non-aerated beverages in a residential colony. We know that the consumption of these beverages has some relationship with the family income and that the families residing in this colony can be classified into three categories, viz., high income, middle income, and low income families. If we are doing a sampling study, we would like to make sure that our sample does have some members from each of the three categories—perhaps in the same proportion as the total number of families belonging to that category—in which case, we would have used proportional stratified sampling. On the other hand, if we know that the variation in the consumption of these beverages from one family to another is relatively large for the low income category then there is not much variation in the high income category, and we would perhaps pick up a smaller than proportional sample from the high income category and a larger than proportional sample from the low income category. This is what is done in disproportional stratified sampling.

The basis for using stratified sampling is the existence of strata such that each stratum is more homogeneous within and markedly different from another stratum. The higher the homogeneity within each stratum, the higher the gain in statistical efficiency due to stratification.

What are strata?: The strata are so defined that they constitute a partition of the population, i.e. they are mutually exclusive and collectively exhaustive. By definition, every element of the population belongs to one stratum, and not more than one stratum.

A stratum can therefore he conceived of as a sub-population which is more homogeneous than the complete population. The members of a stratum are similar to each other and are different from the members of another stratum in the characteristics that we measure as shown in Figure 8.2.

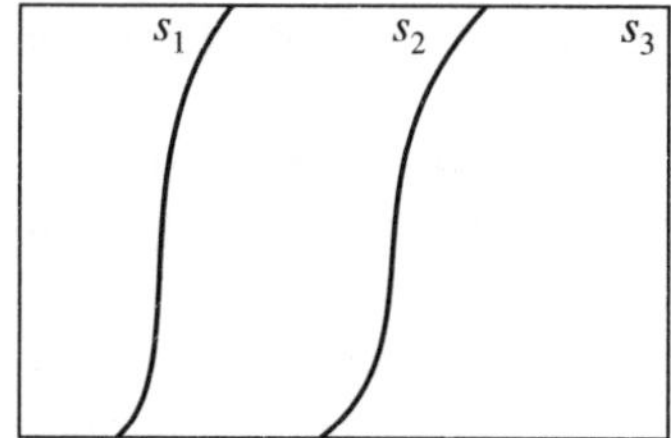

FIGURE 8.2 A population with three strata.

Proportional stratified sampling: After defining the strata, a simple random sample is picked up from each of the strata. If we want to have a total sample of size 100, this number is allocated to the different strata, either in proportion to the size of the stratum in the population or otherwise.

If the different strata have similar variances of the characteristic being measured, then the statistical efficiency will be the highest if the sample sizes for different strata are in the same proportion as the size of the respective stratum in the population. Such a design is called proportional stratified sampling (see Table 8.4).

TABLE 8.4 Proportional Stratified Sampling

Stratum No. (i)	No. of elements in Stratum (N_1)	Sample size n_1	Sampling ratio n_1/N_1
1	200	10	1/20
2	300	15	1/20
3	500	25	1/20
Total	**1000**	**50**	**1/20**

If we want to pick up a proportional stratified sample of size n from a population of size N, which has been stratified to p different strata with sizes $N_1, N_2, \ldots, N_p$, respectively, then the sample sizes for different strata, viz. $n_1, n_2, \ldots, n_p$, are given by

$$\frac{n_1}{N_1} = \frac{n_2}{N_2} = \cdots = \frac{n_p}{N_p} = \frac{n}{N}$$

The strata and the samples from each stratum are shown in the form of a Venn diagram in Figure 8.3, where $S_1, S_2, \ldots$ refer to the stratum 1, stratum 2, and so on.

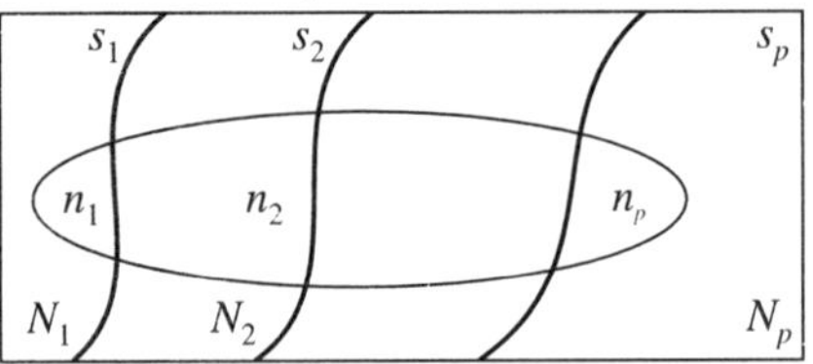

FIGURE 8.3 Stratified sampling

Disproportional stratified sampling: If the different strata in the population have unequal variances of the characteristic being measured, then the sample size allocation decision should consider the variance as well. It would be logical to have a smaller sample from a stratum where the variance is smaller than from another stratum where the variance is higher. In fact, if $\sigma_1^2, \sigma_2^2, \ldots, \sigma_p^2$, are the variance of the p strata, respectively, then the statistical efficiency is the highest when

$$\frac{n_1}{N_1\sigma_1} = \frac{n_2}{N_2\sigma_2} = \cdots = \frac{n_p}{N_p\sigma_p}$$

where the other symbols have the same meaning as in the previous example.

Suppose the variances of the characteristic we are measuring were different for each of the three strata of the earlier example and were actually as shown in Table 8.5. If the total sample size was still restricted to 50, the statistically optimal allocation would be as given in Table 8.5 and we can compare this table with Table 8.4 above to find that the sampling ratio would fall for stratum 3 as the variance is smaller here and would go up for stratum 2, where the variance is large.

TABLE 8.5 Disproportional Stratified Sampling

Stratum No. (i)	No. of elements in stratum (N_i)	Stratum variance (σ_1^2)	Stratum s.d. (σ_i)	Sample size (n_i)	Sampling ratio (n_i/N_i)
1	200	2.25	1.5	13	0.065
2	300	4.00	2.0	26	0.087
3	500	0.25	0.5	11	0.022
Total	**1000**			**50**	

Stratified sampling in practice: Stratification of the population is quite common in managerial applications because it also allows drawing separate conclusions for each stratum. For example, if we are estimating the demand for a non-aerated beverage in a residential colony and have stratified the population based on the family income, then we would have data pertaining to each stratum which might be useful in making many marketing decisions.

Stratification requires us to identify the strata such that the intra-stratum differences are as small as possible and inter-strata differences as large as possible. However, whether a stratum is homogeneous or not-in the characteristic that we are measuring, e.g. the consumption of non-aerated beverage in the family in the given earlier example, can be known only at the end of the study whereas stratification is to be done at the beginning of the study and that is why some other variable like family income is to be used for stratification. This is based on the implicit assumption that family income and consumption of non-aerated beverages are very closely associated with each other. If this assumption is true, stratification would increase the statistical efficiency of sampling. In many studies, it is not easy to find such associated variables which can be used as the basis for stratification and then stratification may not help in increasing the statistical efficiency although the cost of the study goes up due to the additional costs of stratification.

Cluster sampling: Let us take up the situation where we are interested in estimating the demand for a non-aerated beverage in a residential colony again. The colony is divided into 11 blocks, called Block A through Block K as shown in Figure 8.4.

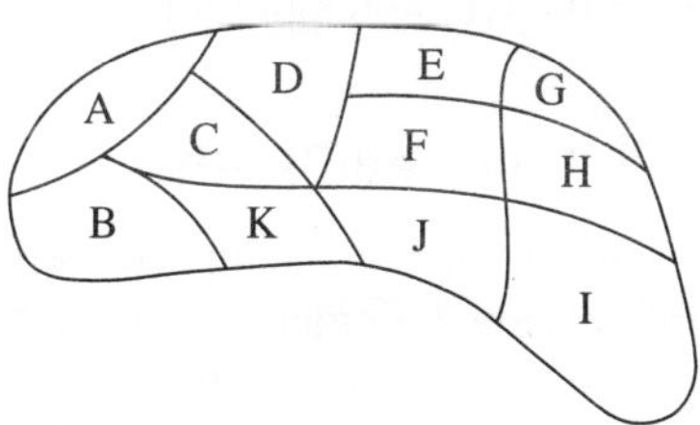

FIGURE 8.4 Blocks in a residential colony.

We might use cluster sampling in this situation by treating each block as a cluster. We will then select two blocks out of the 11 blocks at random and then collect information from all families residing in those two blocks. **Cluster** vs. **stratum:** We can now compare cluster sampling with stratified sampling. Stratification is done to make the strata homogeneous within, and different from other strata. Clusters, on the other hand, should be heterogeneous within, and the different clusters should be similar to each other. A clusture, ideally, is a mini-population and has all the features of the population. The criterion used for stratification is a variable which is closely associated with the characteristic we are measuring, e.g. income level when we are measuring the family consumption of non-aerated beverages in the example quoted earlier. On the other hand, convenience of data collection is usually the basis for cluster definitions. Geographic contiguity is quite often used for clusture definitions, as in Figure 8.4 above; in such cases, cluster sampling is also known as **area sampling**. There are much fewer strata and we need to pick up a random sample from each of the strata for drawing inferences. In cluster sampling, there are many clusters, out of which only a few are picked up by random sampling and then the clusters are completely enumerated.

Cluster sampling in practice: Cluster sampling is used primarily because it allows for great economy in data collection costs since the travel related costs, etc. are smaller. Although it is statistically less efficient than simple random sampling in most cases, this deficiency may be more than offset by the high economic efficiency that it offers. For example, to get a certain precision level, we may need a sample size of 100 under simple random sampling and a sample size of 175 under cluster sampling. However, if the cost of data collection is Rs. 20 under simple random sampling and only Rs. 5 under cluster sampling, it would be cost effective to use cluster sampling.

Cluster sampling is rarely used in single-stage sampling plans. In a national survey, a district might be treated as a cluster, and cluster sampling used in the first stage to pick up 15 districts in the country. Some other form of probability sampling like stratified sampling, cluster sampling, etc. is then used to go to a smaller sampling unit.

If a frame has to be developed, then cluster sampling allows us to save on the cost of developing a frame because frames need to be developed only for the selected clusters and not for the whole population.

Multistage and Multiphase Sampling

In most large surveys, we use multistage sampling, where the sampling unit is something larger than an individual element of the population in all stages but the final. For example, in a national survey on the demand of fertilizers, we might use stratified sampling in the first stage with a district as a sampling unit and the average rainfall in the district as the criterion for stratification. Having obtained 20 districts from this stage, cluster sampling may be used in the second stage to pick up 10 villages in each of the selected districts. Finally, in the third stage, stratified sampling may be used in each village to pick up frames in each of the strata defined with land holding as the criterion.

Multiphase sampling, on the other hand, is designed to make use of the information collected in one phase to develop a sampling design in a subsequent phase. A study with two phases is often called **double sampling.** The first phase of the study might reveal a relationship between the family consumption of non-aerated beverages and the family income, and this information would then be used in the second phase to stratify the population with family income as the criterion.

NON-PROBABILITY SAMPLING METHODS

Probability sampling has some theoretical advantages over non-probability sampling. The bias introduced due to sampling could be completely eliminated and it is possible to set a confidence interval for the population parameter that is being studied. In spite of these advantages of probability sampling, non-probability sampling is used quite frequently in many sampling surveys. This is so because all sampling methods are based on practical considerations.

Probability sampling requires a list of all the sampling units and this frame is not available in many situations. It is also not practically feasible to develop a frame of, say, all the households in a city or zone or ward of a city. Sometimes, the objective of the study may not be to draw a statistical inference about the population but to get familiar with extreme cases or other such objectives. In a dealer survey, our objective may be to get familiar with the problems faced by the dealers so that we can take some corrective actions, wherever possible. Probability sampling is rigorous and this rigour, e.g. in selecting samples, adds to the cost of the study. And, finally, even when we are doing probability sampling, there are chances of deviations from the laid out process, especially where some samples are selected by the interviewers at site, say, after reaching a village. Also, some of the sample members may not agree to be interviewed or may be not available for interview, and our sample may turn out to be a non-probability sample in the strictest sense of the term.

Convenience Sampling

In this type of non-probability sampling, the choice of the sample is left completely to the convenience of the interviewer. The cost involved in picking up the sample is minimum and the cost of data collection is also generally low, e.g. the interviewer can go to some retail shops and interview some shoppers while studying the demand for non-aerated beverages. However, such samples can suffer from excessive bias from known or unknown sources and also there is no way that the possible errors can be quantified.

Purposive Sampling

In convenience sampling, any member of the population can be included in the sample without any restriction. When some restrictions are put on the possible inclusion of a member in the sample, the sampling is called *purposive*.

Judgment Sampling

In judgment sampling, the judgment or opinion of some experts forms the basis for sample selection. The experts are persons who are believed to have information on the population which can help in giving us better samples. Such sampling is very useful when we want to study rare events, or when members have extreme positions, or even when the objective of the study is to collect a wide cross-section of views from one extreme to the other.

Quota Sampling

Even when we are using non-probability sampling, we might want our sample to be representative of the population in some defined ways. This is sought to be achieved in quota sampling so that the bias introduced by sampling could be reduced.

If in our population, 20% of the members belong to the high income group, 30% to the middle income group, and 50% to the low income group, and we are using quota sampling, we will specify that the sample should also contain members in the same proportion as in the population, e.g. 20% of the sample members should belong to the high income group, and so on.

The criteria used to set quotas could be many. For example, family size could be one of the criteria and we can set quotas for families with family size up to 3, between 4 and 5, and above 5. However, if the number of such criteria is large, it becomes difficult to locate sample members satisfying the combination of the criteria. In such cases, the overall relative frequency of each criterion in the sample is matched with the overall relative frequency of the criterion in the population.

The Sample Size

How large a sample should be taken in a study? So far in this unit, we have not addressed ourselves to this question. At this stage, we only mention that some factors affect the sample size decision and in later units some of these ideas will be gone into in more depth.

One of the most important factors that affect the sample size is the extent of variability in the population. Taking an extreme case, if there is no variability, i.e. if all the members of the population are exactly identical, a sample of size 1 is as good as a sample of 100 or any other number. Therefore, the larger the variability, the larger is the sample size required.

A second consideration is the confidence in the inference made—the larger the sample size, the higher is the confidence. In many situations, the confidence level is used as the basis to decide the sample size as we shall see in Chapter 9.

In many real-life situations, the overriding consideration is the cost of the study and the problem then becomes one of designing a sampling scheme to achieve the highest statistical efficiency subject to the budget for the study. It is here that cluster sampling and convenience sampling score over other more statistically efficient methods of sampling since the unit cost of data collection is lower.

SUMMARY

In this chapter we have looked at various sampling methods available when we want to make some inferences about a population without enumerating it completely. We started by looking at some situations where sampling was being done and then found that in many situations sampling may be the only feasible way of knowing something about the population—either because of the time or cost involved, or because of the physical impossibility or practical infeasibility of observing the complete population. Also, sampling can give us adequate results in many applications and can be preferred over complete enumeration as it ensures a higher purity of the data collected, especially when the population is large.

We noted that there are two basic methods of sampling—probability sampling which ensures that every member of the population has a calculable nonzero probability getting included in the sample—and non-probability sampling where there is no such assurance. Probability sampling is theoretically superior to non-probability sampling as it helps us in reducing the bias and also allows us to quantify the possible error involved, but non-probability sampling is less rigorous, easy to use, practically feasible, and gives adequate results in some applications.

Among the probability sampling methods, simple random sampling works the best when the population is homogeneous but may have many practical limitations when the population is large. Simple random sampling ensures that each of the possible samples of a particular size has an equal probability of getting picked up as the sample selected and it also implies that each element of the population has an equal probability of being included in the sample. Systematic sampling starts with a random start and picking up members after a fixed interval down a list of all members called the sampling frame. If the population can be broken down into smaller, more homogeneous sub-populations or strata, then stratified sampling should be used, which allows higher economic efficiency as the cost of data collection per element is reduced if members are physically or otherwise closer to each other as they are in a cluster. Most large studies are based on multistage sampling where different sampling methods are used at each stage. In some studies multiphase sample is also used, especially where the information collected in one phase is used in the sampling design of a later phase.

We have also discussed some of the non-probability sampling methods used in practice. If any member of the population could be included in the sample, we would get a convenience sample. On the other hand, if the entry is subject to the judgment of some expert or experts who have a better knowledge of the population, we would have used judgment sampling and, if the sample is made representative of the population by setting quotas for elements satisfying different criteria, this is called *quota sampling*. Purposive sampling is a genuine name for all non-probability sampling methods where restrictions are used on entry. We have looked at all of these sampling methods to gauge their strengths and weaknesses and also to find their applicability under different conditions.

DISCUSSION QUESTIONS

1. List the various reasons that make sampling so attractive in drawing conclusion about the population.

2. What is the major difference between probability and non-probability sampling?

3. A study aims at quantifying the organizational climate in any organization by administering a questionnaire to a sample of its employees. There are 1000 employees in a company with 100 executives, 200 supervisors and 700 workers. If the employees are **stratified** based on this classification and a sample of 100 employees is required, what should the sample size be from each **stratum** if proportional **stratified** sampling is used?

4. In Q. 3 above, if it is known that the standard deviation of the response for executives is 1.9, for supervisors is 3.2, and for workers is 2.1, what should the respective sample sizes be? Please state for each of the following statements, which of the given responses is the most correct.

5. To determine the salary, the sex, and the working hours structure in a large multistoried office building, a survey was conducted in which all the employees working on the third, the eighth and the thirteenth floors were contacted. Which of the following sampling schemes can be used?

(a) Simple random sampling
(b) Stratified sampling
(c) Cluster sampling
(d) Convenience sampling

6. We do not use extremely large sample sizes because

(a) the unit cost of data collection and data analysis increases as the sample size increases, e.g. it costs more to collect the thousandth sample member as compared to the first;
(b) the sample becomes unrepresentative as the sample size is increased;
(c) it becomes more difficult to store information about large sample size;
(d) As the sample size increases, the gain in having an additional sample element falls, and so after a point, is less than the cost involved in having an additional sample element.

Find out the most appropriate option.

7. If it is known that a population has groups which have a wide amount of variation within them, but only a small variation among the groups themselves, which of the following sampling schemes would you consider appropriate:

- cluster sampling
- stratified sampling
- simple random sampling
- systematic sampling

8. One of the major drawbacks of judgement sampling is that
   (a) the method is cumbersome and difficult to use
   (b) there is no way of quantifying the magnitude of the error involved
   (c) it depends **on** only one individual for sample selection
   (d) it gives us small sample sizes

FURTHER READING

Levin, R.I. (1987): *Statistics for Management*, New Delhi: Prentice-Hall of India.

Mason, R.D. (1986): *Statistical Techniques in Business and Economics*, Homewood: Richard D. Irwin, Inc.

Mendenhall, W., Scheaffer, R.L. and Wackerly, D.D. (1981): *Mathematical Statistics with Applications*, Boston: Danbury Press.

Plane, D.R. and Oppermann, E.B. (1986): *Business and Economic Statistics;* Business Publications, Inc. Plan.

9 Methods and Techniques of Data Collection

After going through this chapter, you will be able to:

- Discuss the necessity and usefulness of data collection;
- Distinguish between primary and secondary data;
- Describe different methods of collecting primary data with their merits and demerits;
- Design questionnaire for collection of primary data;
- Develop skills in conducing interview;
- Identify the sources of secondary data;
- Examine the reliability, suitability and adequacy of secondary data

INTRODUCTION

The increasingly complex nature of business and government has focused attention on the uses of research methodology in solving managerial problems. The credibility of the results derived from the application of such methodology is dependent on the upto date information about the various pertinent characters included in the analysis. To illustrate, the demand for discs has dropped dramatically after cassettes have entered the market commercially. This information must be taken into consideration for formulating marketing strategy by a dealer selling musical products.

Information expressed in appropriate quantitative form is known as *data.* The necessity and usefulness of information gathering or data collection cannot be overemphasized in government policies. For example, the government must be aware of the actual scenario of the acceptance of family planning before it can formulate any policy on this matter. The components of this scenario are provided by appropriate data to be collected from various families. In industrial disputes regarding wages, cost of living index, a data-based indicator of inflation is often accepted as a guideline for arbitration.

In short, neither a business nor a governmental decision can be made in a casual manner in the highly involved environment prevailing today. It is through appropriate data and their analysis that the decision maker becomes equipped with proper tools of decision making.

PRIMARY AND SECONDARY DATA

Primary data are those which are collected afresh and for the first time, and thus happen to be original in character. Such data are published by authorities who themselves are responsible for their collection.

Secondary data, on the other hand, are those which have already been collected by some other agency and which have already been processed Generally speaking, secondary data constitute information which has previously been collected by some organization to satisfy its own need but is being used by the department under reference for an entirely different reason. For example, the census figures are published every tenth year by the Registrar General of India. But these figures are also used by demographers and other social scientists for planning and research. Thus, the officials of the Department of Registrar General will visualize the census figures as primary data. But a demographer using the same figures to prepare a mortality table will consider them as secondary data.

Even when an organization is interested in collecting primary data, it is necessary to take the help of various types of secondary data to design a proper sampling scheme. This aspect of the use of secondary data will be covered in the next unit.

METHODS OF COLLECTING PRIMARY DATA

The collection of primary data for business research is of paramount importance to assist the management in making decisions. Generally, information on a large number of characteristics is necessary to analyze any problem pertaining to management. For instance, a study relating to employment in rural areas requires data on income, wages, types of crops, and land holdings. The collection of primary data thus requires a great deal of deliberation and expertise. Depending on the nature of information necessary, the methods of collecting primary data are the: Observation Method, Questionnaire Method, Mailed Questionnaire Method, and Telephonic Interview, which are now discussed.

Observation Method

The investigator collects the requisite information personally through observation. For example, in order to study the conditions of students residing in a university, the investigator meets the students in their hostels and collects necessary data after personal discussions. The information about the extent of damage caused by natural calamities like flood can be collected by personal observation by a trained investigator. As the investigator is solely responsible for collection of data by this method, his training, skill and knowledge play an important role in the quality of primary data obtained.

A slight variation of this procedure is *indirect oral investigation* where data are collected through indirect sources. Persons who are likely to have information about the problem are interrogated and, on the basis of their answers, primary data become available. Most of the Commissions of Enquiry or Committees appointed by the government collect primary data by this method. The accuracy of the primary data collected by this method depends largely on the type of persons interviewed, and hence these persons have to be selected very carefully.

Questionnaire Method

A popular and common method of collection of primary data is by personally interviewing individuals, and recording their answers in a structured questionnaire. The complete enumeration of Indian decennial census is performed by this method. The enumerators visit the residences of individuals and elicit answers to the queries contained in the questionnaire. Occasionally, a part of the questionnaire is unstructured so that the interviewee can feel free to share information about intimate matters with the interviewer.

As the data are collected by the field staff personally, it is also known as *personal interview method.* Much of the accuracy of the collected data, however, depends on the ability and tactfulness of investigators who should be subjected to special training as to how they should elicit correct information through friendly discussions.

Mailed Questionnaire Method

Here, a set of questions relevant to the subject of enquiry are mailed to a selected list of persons with a request to return them duly filled in. Supplementary instructions on the definitions of terms used and the methods of filling up the forms should also accompany the questionnaire. This method can only be used when the respondents are literate and can answer the questions in writing. The questions should be very clear without any ambiguity, keeping in mind that there is no investigator to help the respondent.

The method of collecting data by mailing the questionnaires to the respondents is most extensively employed in various business and economic surveys. This method saves both time and cost and can cover a large area. The absence of an investigator, however, renders the responses less reliable. The method also suffers from a large degree of non-response.

Telephonic Interview

This method of collecting information consists in contacting respondents on the telephone itself. It is inexpensive but limited in scope as respondents must possess a telephone. The telephone interview method is used in industrial surveys, especially in developed regions.

Merits and Demerits of Different Methods of Collecting Primary Data

Generally speaking, the conditions under which the data are to be obtained will predetermine the method of data collection. If only a few items of information are sought quickly covering a number of industries and funds are limited, telephone interviews should be recommended for collection of data. If depth interviews and probing techniques are to be employed, it is necessary to employ investigators to collect data.

Thus, each method has its uses and none is superior in all situations. The joint use of more than one data collection method is sometimes preferred for a variety of reasons. When a wide geographic area is being covered, the use of mail questionnaires supplemented by personal interviews will yield more reliable results than either method alone.

Designing a Questionnaire

A questionnaire is a proforma containing a sequence of questions to elicit information from the interviewees. The questionnaire is used for personal interview. At the same time, the questionnaire is also mailed to individuals who are requested to write the answers against each question and to return the completed proforma by post.

The questionnaire is the heart of the primary data collection technique. Hence, its drafting requires utmost skill. The questions must be clear, simple, and to the point. They must be well organized from the point of view of the respondent and be formulated in such a manner as to provide the data insofar as possible in the desired form. This is especially true of a mail questionnaire which essentially has to speak for itself. If it is not clear, not only the replies may be vague and of little value but many potential respondents may not bother about returning the questionnaire at all.

A questionnaire may be said to possess the following:

- The general form
- The question sequence
- The question wording

These properties are now briefly discussed.

The General Form

The form of a questionnaire will depend partly on the type of data being sought and partly on the data collection method to be used. The choice lies between two extremes. On the one hand, there is the highly structured questionnaire in which all questions and answers are specified and the respondents' own words are held to a minimum. At the other end is the unstructured questionnaire in which the interviewer is provided with a general brief on the sort of information to be obtained but the exact question is largely his own responsibility.

The **unstructured** questionnaires are useful in carrying out in-depth interviews where the aim is to probe for attitudes and reasons. They may also be effectively employed in pretesting, the result of which can be used as a basis for constructing a structured questionnaire at a later stage. Thus, in order to ascertain the expectation of the television viewers about a programme, interviews may be conducted with unstructured questionnaires. The resulting range of answers may then be used to prepare a structured questionnaire for use in the main part of the study.

The major disadvantage with any unstructured questionnaire is that it requires personal interview. It cannot be used in the mailed questionnaire method of data collection. A structured questionnaire usually has fixed alternative answers to each question. It is simple to administer and relatively inexpensive to analyze. The questionnaires have, however, their limitations. It is not possible to record the responses made by the respondent in their own words. They are considered inappropriate in investigations where the aim probably is to probe for attitudes and feelings.

The Question Sequence

The introduction to the questionnaire should be as short and simple as possible. The introductory letter accompanying the mailed questionnaire should also be made very brief. The introduction lays the foundation for establishing the rapport with the respondent in addition to making the interview possible. Once the rapport is established, the questions will generally seek substantive information of value to the study. As a general rule, questions that put too great a strain on the memory or the intellect should be reserved for a later period. Likewise, questions relating to personal wealth and personal character should be avoided in the beginning.

Following the opening phase should come the questions that are really vital to the interview. Even here, substantive questions should be surrounded by more interesting ones in order that the attention does not wane. Awkward questions, which create the risk that the respondent may discontinue the interview, are usually relegated to the end. By the time the interview is over, some information is already available with the interviewer.

Ideally, the question sequence should conform to the respondents' way of thinking, and this is where unstructured interviews are highly advantageous. The interviewer can rearrange the order of the questions to fit the discussion in each particular case. With structured questionnaire, the best that can be done is to determine with pretesting the question sequence which is likely to produce good rapport with most people

The Question Wording

It has been stated that the wording and formulation of the question are more of an art than a science. Science does enter, however, in testing the stability and the adequacy of replies for business and management decisions. The wording of the questions should be impartial so as not to give a biased picture of the true state of affairs. Colourful adjectives and undue descriptive phrases should be avoided. In general, the questions should be worded such that they are (a) easily understood; (b) simple; (c) concrete and conform to respondents' way of thinking.

Multiple choice questions constitute the basis of a structured questionnaire, particularly in a mailed questionnaire method. But in addition to these questions, various open-ended questions are generally inserted to provide a more complete picture of the respondent's feelings and attitudes.

A questionnaire with an objective to collect information concerning the loanees who have taken loan from a bank during the last five years under the Self-Employment to Educated.

Unemployed Youth Scheme is presented now. Note that the first few questions make the interviewer familiar with the subject. "The substantive information commences from question 9, but the two embarrassing questions, namely questions 11 and 12, are followed by a sympathetic question 13. Although the questionnaire is structured, an unstructured part has been included in the answer of question 14 to record different kind of replies.

Bank of New Delhi
Self-Employment to Educated Unemployed Youth Scheme

1. Questionnaire No ....

2. Name of Loanee..

3. Address..

4. Educational Qualifications: (General)

   Below Matriculation ☐

   Matriculation and above but below Graduate ☐

   Graduate and above ☐

5. Educational Qualifications: (Technical)

   None ☐

   Technical Diploma ☐

   Technical Degree ☐

6. Date of Birth..

7. When did you start your Business?...

   Not yet started ☐ Less than one year back ☐ One year and above but less than two years back ☐ Two years and above but less than three years back ☐ Three years and above but less than four years back ☐ Four years and above but less than five years back ☐

8. Type of Business

Agro based	☐	Supply of Material	☐
Manufacturing	☐	Retail Selling	☐
Chemical	☐	Transport	☐
Service	☐	Other, please specify	☐

9. From which branch of the bank did you borrow money?

   Branch A ☐ Branch B ☐ Branch C ☐ Branch D ☐

10. When did you borrow money?

    Less than one year back ☐

    One year and above but less than two years back ☐

    Two years and above but less than three years back ☐

    Three years and above but less than four years back ☐

    Four years and above but less than five years back ☐

11. What was the amount of loan?

    Upto ₹. 10,000 ☐

    Above ₹ 10,000 but less than or equal to ₹ 25,000 ☐

    Above ₹ 25,000 but less than or equal to ₹ 50,000 ☐

    Above ₹ 50,000 ☐

12. How many instalments have you repaid so far?

    None ☐

    Upto five ☐

    More than five but less than or equal to ten ☐

13. What difficulties are you facing in your project?

    Lack of customer demand ☐

    Lack of raw material ☐

    Lack of power ☐

    Lack of skilled worker ☐

    Difficulty in procuring trade license and other Government papers ☐

    Other, please specify ☐

14. Your suggestions to overcome these difficulties

    ....

    ....

Signature of the Investigator ....

Name of the Investigator...

Date if Interview ....

PRETESTING A QUESTIONNAIRE

The pretest is a valuable indicator of the effectiveness of a questionnaire to collect data. The pretesting of questionnaire consists in selecting, approaching and interviewing a small segment in the same manner to be followed in the full scale operation and then analyzing the results in light of the objectives of the study.

We can understand from the pretest whether the replies provide the type of information needed or whether the respondents are misinterpreting any of the questions. In addition, results obtained in a pretest can at times suggest new ideas or hypotheses worthy of further examination.

If a pretest indicates any change of importance, a further pretest may be warranted to review the questionnaire. Thus, the mere fact that the wording of a question originally misunderstood has been changed does not of itself ensure the clarity of the new form. A few interviews with the new question form are highly desirable.

Pretests are sometimes conducted in an informal manner.

EDITING OF PRIMARY DATA

Editing involves reviewing the data collected by investigators to ensure maximum accuracy and unambiguity. It should be done as soon as possible after the data have been collected. If the size of the data is relatively small, it is desirable that only one person edit all the data for the entire study. The different steps of editing involves checking for the following:

1. **Legibility:** Obviously, the data must be legible to be used. If a response is not presented clearly, the investigator concerned should be asked to rewrite it.
2. **Completeness:** An omitted entry on a fully structured questionnaire may mean that no attempt was made to collect data from the respondent or that the investigator simply did not record the data. If the investigator did not record the data, prompt editing and questioning of the investigator may provide the missing item. If an entry is missing because of the first possible cause, there is not much that can be done, except to make another attempt to get the missing data. Obviously, this requires knowing why the entry is missing.
3. **Consistency:** The editor should examine each questionnaire to check for inconsistency or inaccuracy, if any, in the statement. The income and expenditure figures may be unduly inconsistent. The age and the date of birth may disagree. The area of an agricultural plot may be unduly large. The investigators concerned should be asked to make the necessary corrections. If there is any repetitive response pattern in the reports of individual investigators, they may represent investigator bias or perhaps attempted dishonesty.

Technique of Interview

The general qualities that an interviewer should possess can be identified as extroversion, impartiality to different points of view, friendliness without getting personal, ability to remain calm under many different circumstances, conscientiousness, perseverance, accuracy of reporting, and adaptability. In addition, the interviewer must plan in advance and should fully know the problem under consideration. He must choose a suitable time and place so that the interviewee may feel at ease during the interview. In order to establish proper rapport, especially in the rural areas if a significant part of the respondents are women, a female interviewer must be employed to obtain the responses. If the questionnaire is in English, the translation in the regional languages must be available so that the interviewer has no ambiguity about the questions.

While collecting data on various industrial problems, the interviewer should proceed very cautiously and systematically as the success of his project would depend entirely on the cooperation of others. The interviewer is also expected to be familiar with all the material already published by the organization. In an administrative hierarchy, it is preferable to begin interviews by contacting the officials at the middle and lower levels and to collect all relevant materials available with them.

The selection, training and supervision of interviewers are very important administrative functions for collection of reliable data.

Collection of Secondary Data

Secondary data refer to those data which have been collected and analyzed by some other agency.

The sources of secondary data could be:

1. *Various publications of central, state and local governments*: The important official publications are Statistical Abstract, India-Annual; Monthly Abstract of Statistics (both published by Central Statistical Organization); Indian Agricultural Statistics (Annual), published by Ministry of Food and Agriculture; Index Number of Wholesale Prices in India (Weekly), published by Ministry of Commerce and Industry; Reserve Bank of India Bulletin (Monthly), published by Reserve Bank of India.
2. *Various publications of foreign governments or of international bodies:* The important publications are publications of international bodies like UNO, FAO, WHO, UNESCO, ILO, Statistical Year Book (published by the Statistical Office of the United Nations), Yearbook of Labour Statistics (published by ILO, Geneva).

   The secondary data provided by such publications are authentic, but along with other things, one must be specially careful about the units in respect of currency, weight, etc., which vary widely from one country to another.

3. *Journals of trade, commerce, economics, engineering, etc. published by responsible trade associations, Chambers of Commerce provide secondary data in respect of some important items:* Some examples of such publications are Annual Report of the Chief Inspector of Mines in India (issued annually by the Office of the Chief Inspector of Mines, Dhanbad) and *Indian Textile Bulletin* (issued monthly by the Textile Commissioner, Mumbai).
4. *The other sources of secondary data are books, magazines and newspapers, reports prepared by various universities, historical documents, diaries, letters, unpublished biographies and autobiographies.*

SCRUTINY OF SECONDARY DATA

Primary data are to be scrutinized after the questionnaires are completed by the interviewers. Similarly, the secondary data are to be scrutinized before they are compiled from the source. The scrutiny should be made to assess the suitability, reliability, adequacy and accuracy of the data to be compiled and to be used for the proposed study.

1. Suitability: The compiler should satisfy himself that the data contained in the publication will be suitable for his study. In particular, the conformity of the definitions, units of measurement and timeframe should be checked. For example, one US gallon is different from one British gallon.

2. Reliability: The reliability of the secondary data can be ascertained from the collecting agency, mode of collection, and the time period of collection. For instance, secondary data collected by a voluntary agency with unskilled investigators are unlikely to be reliable.

3. Adequacy: The source of data may be suitable and reliable but the data may not be adequate for the proposed enquiry. The original data may cover a bigger or narrower geographical region or the data may not cover suitable periods. For instance, the per capita income of Pakistan prior to 1971 is inadequate for reference during the subsequent periods as it became separated into two different countries, with considerable variation in standard of living.

4. Accuracy: The user must be satisfied about the accuracy of the secondary data. The process of collecting raw data, the reproduction of processed data in the publication, the degree of accuracy desired and achieved should also be satisfactory and acceptable to the researcher.

SUMMARY

The pattern of business and industry in the present-day environment has become quite complex and involved due to a variety of reasons. Any meaningful decision to be made in this context must be objective and fact based in nature. This is achieved by collecting and analyzing appropriate data. Data may broadly be divided into two categories: primary data and secondary data.

The primary data are those collected for the first time by the organization which is using them. The secondary data, on the other hand, are those that have already been collected by some other agency but also can be used by the organization under consideration. Primary data may be collected by observation, oral investigation, and questionnaire method, or by telephone interviews. Questionnaires may be used for data collection by interviewers. They may also be mailed to prospective respondents. The drafting of a good questionnaire requires great skill.

The process of interviewing also requires a great deal of tact, patience and competence to establish rapport with the respondent. Secondary data are available in various published and unpublished documents. The suitability, reliability, adequacy and accuracy of the secondary data should, however, be ensured before they are used for research problems.

DISCUSSION QUESTIONS

1. The following paragraphs show an unstructured questionnaire

(a) We want to know about major purchases of goods and services (over ` 1000) made by the respondent or his family during the last five years. What were the prices and how were they paid, e.g. cash, installment, borrowing, etc.? Of particular interest are the following: television, refrigerator, vacation, children's education.

(b) We are also interested to know if the respondent or members of his family are planning to spend money on any of the above items during the next two years. If they do, we want to have an indication of its cost and its mode of payment. Prepare a structured questionnaire on the basis of this unstructured questionnaire.

2. A local newspaper wants to ascertain the extent to which the inclusion of a daily stock market page might increase its circulation. Prepare a questionnaire to collect the pertinent information.

3. Explain what is wrong in the following forms of questions in a questionnaire.

(a) Do you have a Savings Account ?

(b) What is the profession of your husband ?

(c) What is the price you paid for a piece of soap 'Brand A'?

(d) Why do you prefer it?

(e) Is the bus service reasonably good?

(f) Isn't this a nice colour?
(g) How many razor blades do you use annually?
(h) Did you decide to buy the scooter after the loan was approved?
(i) Do you believe borrowing from personal finance companies is faster and more pleasant than borrowing from banks?

4. Describe the various methods of collecting primary data and comment on their relative advantages and disadvantages.

5. Define secondary data. State their chief sources and point out the dangers involved in their use and the precautions necessary to use them. Illustrate with examples. Which method is most suitable for conducting enquiry regarding family welfare programme in India? Explain its merits and demerits.

6. Examine the merits and demerits of the observation method in collecting data. Illustrate your answer with suitable examples. What are the major considerations in the construction of questionnaire? Explain. You have been assigned the task of finding the various problems of local train commuters in Mumbai. Design a suitable questionnaire to be used in this study.

7. The Chamber of Commerce has appointed you to ascertain the reaction of the Finance Bill, 1990. Design a suitable questionnaire to be mailed to collect information in this matter.

FURTHER READING

Gopal, M.H. (1964): *An Introduction to Research Procedure in Social Sciences*, Bombay: Asia Publishing House.

Kothari, C.R. (1989): *Research Methodology: Methods and techniques*, New Delhi: Wiley Eastern.

Sadhu, A.N. and A. Singh (1980): *Research Methodology in Social Sciences*, New Delhi: Sterling Publishers.

Wilkinson, T.S. and Bliandarkar, P.L. (1979): *Methodology and Techniques of Social Research*, Bombay: Himalaya Publishing House.

10 Data Processing and Analysis

- Types of Data
- Coding of Data
- Preparing a Master Chart
- Analysis of Quantitative Data
- Use of Computer in Data Processing and Tabulation
- Discussion Questions

After going through this chapter, you will be able to:

- Define quantitative and qualitative data.
- Prepare code book and master chart.
- Prepare analytic model for data analysis.
- Make various types of tables for presenting data.

INTRODUCTION

In Chapter 9, we dealt with the nature of various tools used in the collection of data. These data are mostly expressed in quantified terms. However, quantitative data may not be available in certain cases. In such a situation, the researcher has to consider the phenomenon as a whole without breaking it down into measurable or quantifiable components. As such, he should be familiar not only with the two types of data—quantitative and qualitative—but also with the processing of data and the various methods of data analysis.

The aim of this chapter is to make you understand the nature of quantitative and qualitative data, the procedures for classifying and tabulating quantitative data, presenting them in tabular form, and the various methods used in data analysis.

TYPES OF DATA

The data collected through the administration of various types of tools on the selected samples are of two types: **quantitative** and **qualitative**. In quantitative data, numerical values are assigned to the characteristics or properties of objects or events, according to logically accepted rules. It is a process wherein a number system like figures, ratings or scores is imposed on empirical data. However, when the researcher takes into consideration the phenomenon as a whole and does not attempt to analyze it in measurable or quantifiable terms, the characteristics or properties of objects or events are known as *qualitative data*. We look at the characteristics of both quantitative and qualitative date in the following sections.

Quantitative Data

Quantitative data describe an empirical event or phenomenon in a numerical system with the help of different scales of measurement: nominal, ordinal, and interval or ratio measurements.

Nominal scales of measurement are used when a set of objects among two or more categories is to be differentiated on the basis of certain clearly known characteristics. For example, we may assign individual categories such as sex (male or female), nationality (French or Indian), type of education (formal and non-formal), etc. The ordinal scales of measurement correspond to quantitative classification of a set of objects done with the help of ranking on a continuum. For example, we may rank students according to their height from the lowest to the highest. The interval scale of measurement is based on equal units of measurement.

The scale of measurement talks in how much or how little of a given characteristic or attribute is present. For example, the difference in the amount of an attribute possessed by individuals with test scores of 60 and 61 is assumed to be equivalent to that between individuals with scores of 50 and 51. Ratio scale is the highest level of measurement. Since this scale assumes the existence of absolute zero, this type of measurement is almost non-existent in educational and psychological measurements. Thus, quantitative data are expressed in nominal, ordinal, interval and ratio scales of measurement.

Types of quantitative data: Quantitative data may be classified into two categories: (i) Parametric, and (ii) Non-parametric. Parametric data are obtained by applying interval or ratio scales of measurement. Scores of the tests of ability, achievement, attitude, interest, values, personality, etc. are examples of interval scales of measurement. In the study of reaction time, we use ratio scale. In this type of experiment, the zero point in the absolute sense is known and it makes sense to look at the ratio of the time taken to respond in different treatment situations.

Non-parametric data are either counted or ranked. In counted data, we make use of the nominal scale. Each individual can be a member of only one category and all the members of that category have the same defined characteristics. For example, we may categorize a group as a sample of 'female students' of a particular 'Study Centre' of an open university. The categorization of teacher at different educational levels—school, college and university—is another example of nominal data.

In ranked data, we apply the ordinal scale of measurement. The sets or classes of objects are ordered on a continuum in a series ranging from the lowest to the highest according to the characteristics we wish to measure. The ranking of students in a class for height, weight or academic achievement are examples of ordinal data.

Processing and analysis of quantitative data: Once data are collected, the researcher turns his focus on processing the data. In this section, we discuss about one of the most important stages of the research process, i.e. data processing and analysis.

A researcher has to make his plan for each and every stage of the research process. Hence, a good researcher makes a perfect plan of processing and analysis of data. To some researchers, data processing and analysis is not a very serious activity. Many a time they feel that data processing is a job of a computer assistant. Consequently, they have to be contended with the results given by the computer assistant, which may not help them to achieve their objectives. To avoid such situations, it is essential that data processing be planned in advance and instruction be given to assistants accordingly. Here we discuss about data processing and data analysis.

Data processing refers to certain operations such as editing, coding, computing of the scores, preparation of master charts, etc. After collection of filled-in questionnaires, editing of entries therein are not only necessary but also useful in making subsequent steps simpler. Many a time, a researcher or the assistant either enters the entries wrongly in the questionnaires or enters responses which are not legible. This sort of discrepancies can be resolved by editing the schedule meticulously.

Another problem comes up at the time of tabulation of data when the researcher asks for tabulation of responses from consecutive questions. In cases where data are not cleaned, there should be inconsistency in the tabulations, the researcher has to be very particular about, consecutive questions where category 'not applicable' exists. In the process of editing, the researcher has to be very careful about consecutive questions having 'not applicable' as a response.

Coding of Data

Coding of data involves assigning of symbols (numerical) to each response of the question. The purpose of giving numerical symbols is to translate raw data into numerical data which may be counted and tabulated. The task of the researcher is to give numbers to response carefully. As we have already discussed various types of questions (e.g. an open-end question) in the previous block, the coding scheme will vary accordingly. For example, a close-end question may be already coded, and hence it has to be just included in the code book, whereas coding of open-end questions involves operations such as classification of major responses and developing a response category of 'others' for responses which were not given frequently.

The classification of responses is primarily based on similarities or differences among the responses. Usually, in the case of open-end questions, to classify responses, the researcher looks for major characteristics of the responses and puts them accordingly.

In the case of attitude scales, the researcher has to keep in mind the direction or weightage of responses. For example, a response "strongly agrees" is coded as 'five'. The subsequent codes would be in order. Therefore, if there are responses like "agree", "undecided", "disagree" and "strongly disagree", they have to be coded as 4, 3, 2, and 1. Alternatively, if "strongly agree" is coded as –2, the subsequent responses would be coded as –1, 0, +1, and +4. The matrix questions have to be coded by taking into consideration each cell as one variable. For example, if the column of matrix represents employment status, namely, 'permanent' and 'temporary', and row represents employers or type of employer, namely, 'government' and 'private', the first cell would represent a variable government-permanent. The second cell would represent 'government-temporary', and so on. In order to demonstrate the points discussed above, a section of a code book used in a study is reproduced in Table 10.1.

TABLE 10.1 A Section of a Code Book

Q. No.	Var. No.	Information sought	Responses	Code	Col. No.	Remarks
		Respondents No.			1–3	
2	1	Age	Actual	–	4–5	
3	2	Designation	Worker Supervisor Manager	1 2 3	6	
4	3	Establishment	Public Private	1 2	7	
5	4	Level of education	Graduate Intermediate High School Middle School Primary Illiterate Other	1 2 3 4 5 6 7	8	
6	5	Marital status	Married Unmarried Widow Divorce	1 2 3 4	9	
36	35	Nature of work	Yes No	1 2	10	
	36	Duration of work	Yes No	1 2	11	
	37	Wages	Yes No	1 2	12	
	38	Promotion	Yes No	1 2	13	
43	42	Attitude of employer Preference for male employees	Agree Undecided Disagree	1 2 3	14	

Preparing a Master Chart

After a code book is prepared, the data can be transferred either to a master chart or directly to computer through a statistical package. Going through a master chart to computer is much more advantageous than entering data directly to computers because one can check the wrong entries in the computer by comparing 'data listing' as a computer output and master chart. Entering data directly to computer is disadvantageous as there is no way to check wrong entries, which will show inconsistencies in tabulated data at the later stages of tabulation. A sample of master chart prepared in accordance with the code book is presented in Table 10.2.

TABLE 10.2 A Sample Master Chart

Corresponding No.				Variable Lables									
				Age	Designation	Establishment	Education	Marital Status	Nature of work	Duration of work	Wages	Promotions	Attitude of employer
				Question/Variable/Col. No.									
1	2	3	4	5	6	7	8	9	10	11	12	13	14
0	0	1	1	4	1	2	1	2	3	2	3	4	3
0	0	2	2	1	1	3	4	5	6	7	8	9	5
0	0	3	3	3	3	3	4	2	6	7	2	6	3
0	0	4	4	5	7	8	9	1	3	5	6	1	1
0	0	5	5	4	5	1	4	2	1	1	4	3	5
0	0	6	6	3	1	2	3	4	5	6	3	1	5
0	0	7	7	5	4	5	6	9	7	8	5	2	4
0	0	8	8	1	4	2	5	3	6	3	7	8	9
0	0	9	9	2	2	4	2	6	7	8	2	1	5
0	0	0	0	9	5	6	8	7	9	2	4	4	3
0	0	1	1	2	2	8	4	9	3	4	7	3	8
0	0	2	2	2	5	7	9	5	1	4	2	4	3
0	0	3	3	2	9	4	5	6	7	2	6	9	6
0	0	4	4	2	8	7	9	5	2	4	6	2	3
0	0	5	5	3	5	4	8	7	9	2	4	2	3
0	0	6	6	2	4	8	7	9	5	8	4	5	6
0	0	7	7	8	7	4	9	4	3	4	6	3	4

ANALYSIS OF QUANTITATIVE DATA

The purpose of data analysis is to prepare data as a model where relationships between the variables can be studied. Analysis of data is made with reference to the objectives of the study and research questions, if any. It is also designed to test the hypothesis. Analysis of data involves re-categorization of variables, tabulation, explanation and casual inferences.

The first step in data analysis is a critical examination of the processed data in the form of frequency distribution. This analysis is made with a view to draw meaningful inferences and generalization.

The process of categorization, in accordance with the objectives and hypothesis, is completed with the help of frequency distributions. Re-categorization is a process to arrange categories with the help of statistical techniques. This helps the researcher to justify the tabulation. We have seen earlier that the responses to a statement may be assigned scores or weightage. These scores or weightage are summated and re-categorized on the bases of high, medium and low. The basic principle in the process of categorization or re-categorization is that the categories thus obtained must be exhaustive and mutually exclusive. In other words, the categories have to be independent and not overlapping.

Univariate Analysis

Univariate analysis refers to tables which give data relating to one variable. Univariate tables which are more commonly known as **frequency distribution tables** show how frequently item repeats Tables 10.3–10.5 are examples of frequency tables. The distribution may be symmetrical or asymmetrical. The characteristics of the sample while examining the percentages are further properties of a distribution can be found out by various measures of central tendencies. However, the researcher is required to decide which characteristic is most suited for this analysis. To know how much is the variation, the researcher has to calculate measures of dispersion. Usually, frequency distribution tables are prepared to examine each of the independent and dependent variables. While Tables 10.3 and 10.4 represent two independent variables, Table 10.5 represents one dependent variable.

A frequency distribution of a single variable is the frequency of observation in each category of a variable. For example, an examination of the pattern of response to variable "awareness of the respondents" in Table 10.3 would provide a description of the number of respondents who have high, medium, and low levels of awareness.

TABLE 10.3 Table Showing Awareness of Respondents (Independent Variable)

Level of awareness	Distribution of respondents	
	Frequency percentage	Percentages
High	110	39.3
Medium	106	37.9
Low	64	21.8
Total	**280**	**100.00**

TABLE 10.4 Table Showing Respondents by Regional Development (Independent Variable)

Regional development	Distribution of respondents	
	Frequency percentage	Percentages
High	142	55.7
Medium	86	29.7
Low	52	14.6
Total	**280**	**100.00**

TABLE 10.5 Table Showing Wage Differentials of Respondents (Dependent Variable)

Wage differentials	Distribution of respondents	
	Frequency percentage	Percentages
High	78	27.9
Medium	134	47.9
Low	68	24.2
Total	**280**	**100.00**

In the case of nominal variables, categories can be listed in any arbitrary order. Thus, the variable "Religion" may be described with the category 'Hindu' or the category 'Christian' listed first. However, the categories of 'ordinal', 'interval' and 'ratio' variables are arranged in order. Let us consider the frequency distribution (Tables 10.3, 10.4 and 10.5) which describes the awareness, wage differentials and regional development of respondents. The tables have four rows, the first three being the categories of variables, which appear in the left-hand columns; the right-hand columns show the number of observation in each category. The last rows are the totals of all frequencies appearing in tables. To analyze the data, it is necessary to convert the frequencies into figures that can be interpreted meaningfully. Note, for instance, while distribution of respondents by regional development displayed in Table 10.4 clearly shows the predominance of respondents from 'high' development region, distribution of respondents by wage differential in Table 10.5 indicates that the proportions of respondents with 'high' and 'low' wage differentials are almost equal.

Bivariate Analysis

A researcher might be interested in knowing the relationships between the variables. To know the relationship between the variables, the data pertaining to the variables are cross-tabulated. Hence, a bivariate table is also known as *cross table*. A bivariate table presents data of two variables in column percentages and row percentages simultaneously. An example of a bivariate table is given in Table 10.6:

TABLE 10.6 Table Showing Levels of Awareness Towards the Act and Wage Differentials of the Respondents

Awareness about the Act	Wage differentials			Total
	High	*Medium*	*Low*	
High	94 (66.2)	9 (10.5)	7 (13.5)	110 (39.3)
Medium	37 (26.1)	58 (67.4)	11 (21.2)	106 (37.9)
Low	11 (7.7)	19 (22.1	34 (65.3)	64 (22.8)
Total	**142** (57.70)	**86** (30.7)	**52** (14.6)	**280** (100.0)

The table presents data with regard to two variables namely, awareness about the Equal Remuneration Act and the level of wage differential. The first row presents data on the respondents who were aware of the Act. The second row presents data on those who were not aware. Similarly, the first column gives data pertaining to workers who have low wage differentials. The second column presents data of workers whose differentials were medium, and the last column represents the respondents who felt high wage differentials. For example, the first cell (in the left-hand corner) represents 94 respondents who were fully aware of the Act and perceived high wage differentials.

The association between two variables can be explained either by comparing the percentages of respondents column wise or row wise. The relationship between the variables can also be examined by various statistical techniques (the details about all these measures are given in Chapter 3 of this block) depending on the level of measurement of the data. Apparently, the two variables are associated therefore with more people who were aware of the Act and have perceived low wage differentials than those who were not aware of the Act. Alternatively, comparatively smaller percentage of people who were aware of the Act has perceived high wage differentials than people who were not aware of the Act.

Trivariate Analysis

Sometimes, the researcher might be interested in knowing whether there is a third variable which is affecting the relationships between two variables. In such cases, the researcher has to examine the bivariate relationship by controlling the effects of the third/variable. This is performed in two ways. One way of controlling the effects of a third/variable is to prepare partial tables and examine the bivariate relationship, and the second method of assessing the effects of a third/variable is to compare the coefficient of partial correlations. Let us take an example. In the above table, if the researcher wants to examine whether there is effect of regional development on the bivariate relationship, he may prepare three partial tables giving data relating to awareness of the Act and wage differential for high, medium and low regional development (Tables 10.7–10.9).

TABLE 10.7 Regional Development = High (N = 142)

Awareness about the Act	**Wage differentials**			**Total**
	High	*Medium*	*Low*	
High	7 (21.9)	10 (21.8)	3 (9.3)	20
Medium	13 (40.6)	26 (33.3)	9 (28.1)	48
Low	12 (37.5)	42 (53.8)	20 (62.5)	74
Total	**32**	**78**	**32**	**142**

TABLE 10.8 Regional Development = Medium ($N = 86$)

Awareness about the Act	Wage differentials			Total
	High	*Medium*	*Low*	
High	8 (6.4)	11 (25.6)	4 (19.0)	23
Medium	9 (40.9)	17 (39.5)	8 (38.1)	34
Low	5 (34.9)	15 (34.9)	9 (42.9)	29
Total	**22**	**43**	**21**	**86**

TABLE 10.9 Regional Development = Low ($N = 52$)

Awareness about the Act	Wage differentials			Total
	High	*Medium*	*Low*	
High	14 (58.3)	7 (53.8)	7 (46.7)	28
Medium	8 (33.3)	4 (30.8)	6 (40.0)	18
Low	2 (8.3)	2 (15.4)	2 (13.3)	6
Total	**24**	**13**	**15**	**52**

On examination of these three partial tables, if the researcher finds out that bivariate relationships do not hold good, she may infer that it is the third variable, "regional development" which is affecting the bivariate relationship. In the partial tables for higher regional development, the proportion of people perceiving high wage differential represents those who are having high level of awareness about the Act.

A similar trend can be noticed in the remaining two partial tables, which means regional development does not affect the bivariate relationships between wage differential and awareness about the Act.

In the other method, the researcher tries to find out the effect of the third variable on the bivariate relationship with the help of partial correlation. To find out whether the third variable affects the bivariate relationship between awareness (X) and wage differentials (Y), the researcher considers the work experience of respondents.

To examine this, the researcher calculates the correlation coefficients between 'awareness' and 'wage differential' keeping 'experience' as a constant. The results are given as follows.

X_1 = Awareness (independent variable)

X_2 = Wage differential (independent variable)

X_3 = Experience (control variable)

$\gamma 1$ and 2 (Correlation coefficient between X_1 and X_2) = .70
$\gamma 1$ and 3 (Correlation coefficient between X_1 and X_3) = .40
$\gamma 2$ and 3 (Correlation coefficient between X_2 and X_3) = .50

The researcher on examination of the results of the partial correlation finds that even after controlling the third variable, the relation between the first two variables, "awareness" and "wage differentials" is statistically significant. Thus, the researcher concludes that the relationship between awareness and wage differentials is not spurious.

Multivariate Analysis

When a researcher is interested in assessing the joint effect of three or more variables she uses the techniques of *multivariate analysis.* The most common statistical technique used for multivariate analysis is *regression analysis.* In the first step of multivariable analysis, the researcher has to obtain the correlation between the variables which are having statistically significant correlation. These variables are put in the regression analysis. One important point in applying correlation and regression analysis is that the data must be measured on ratio or interval level. Another point a researcher has to keep in mind is that these two statistical techniques are based on certain assumptions. Thus, before applying these techniques, the researcher has to see whether the sample selected by her fulfills those conditions.

USE OF COMPUTER IN DATA PROCESSING AND TABULATION

Research involves large amounts of data, which can be handled manually or by computers. Computers provide the best alternative for more than one reason. Besides, its capacity to process large amounts of data, the computer also analyzes data with the help of a number of statistical procedures. Computers carry out processing and analysis of data flawlessly and with a very high speed. The statistical analysis that took months earlier takes now a few seconds or a few minutes. Today, all over the world availability of statistical software and access to computers has considerably increased over the last few years.

While there are many specialized software application packages for different types of data analysis, Statistical Package for Social Sciences (SPSS) is one such package that is often used by researchers for data processing and analysis. It is a preferred choice for social work research analysis due to its easy-to-use interface and comprehensive range of data manipulation and analytical tools.

Basic Steps in Data Processing and Analysis by Computer

There are four basic steps involved in data processing and analysis using SPSS.

1. Entering of data into SPSS
2. Selection of a procedure from the menus
3. Selection of variables for analysis
4. Examination of the outputs.

SUMMARY

In this chapter, we have discussed the nature of quantitative and qualitative data, the various methods of representing the quantified data graphically, and the methods used in the analysis of quantitative and qualitative data. The main points are as follows:

1. The data collected through the administration of various tools on the selected samples are of (i) quantitative and (ii) qualitative nature.
2. Quantitative data are expressed in nominal, ordinal, interval or ratio scales of measurement. These data are classified into two categories: (i) parametric and (ii) non-parametric. The parametric data are obtained by applying interval or ratio scales of measurement, whereas non-parametric data are either enumerated or ranked. In the enumerated data we make use of nominal scale, and in the ranked data, we apply ordinal scale.
3. 'Data processing' refers to certain operations such as editing, coding, computing of the scores, preparation of master charts, etc.
4. Many a time, a researcher or the assistants either miss entries in the questionnaires or enter responses, which are not legible. This sort of discrepancies can be resolved by editing the questionnaires.
5. Coding of data involves assigning of symbols (numerical) to each response of **Data** the question. The purpose of giving numerical symbols is to translate raw data into numerical data, which may be counted and tabulated.
6. With the help of a codebook the data can be transferred to a master chart.
7. Tabulation is a process of presenting data in rows and columns in such a way as to facilitate comparisons and show the relations involved.
8. Keeping in view the objectives of research study, we set up analytic models which diagrammatically represent variables and their interrelationships.
9. Univariate analysis refers to tables which give data relating to one variable.
10. A bivariate table presents data of two variables in column percentages and row percentages simultaneously.
11. Trivariate analysis is undertaken to know whether there is a third variable which is affecting the relationships between the two variables.
12. When a researcher is interested in assessing the joint effect of three or more variables, he uses the techniques of multivariate analysis.

DISCUSSION QUESTIONS

1. What is trivariate analysis? Discuss the process of examining the effect of the third variable on the bivariate relationship.
2. Define quantitative data. Describe the various types of quantitative data along with examples.
3. Briefly discuss the processing and analysis of quantitative data.

FURTHER READING

Bailey, Kenneth, D. (1978): *Methods of Social Research,* London: The Free Press.

Baker, L. Therese (1988): *Doing Social Research,* New York: McGraw-Hill.

Blalock, Hubert, M. (1972): *Social Statistics,* New York: McGraw-Hill.

J.T., Doby et al. (1953): *An Introduction to Social Research,* London: Stackpole Co.

Kerlinger, Fred R. (1964): *Foundations of Behavioural Research,* Delhi: Surjeet Publications.

Lal Das, D.K. (2000): *Practice of Social Research: A social work perspective,* Jaipur: Rawat Publications.

Monete, Duane R., et al. (1986): *Applied Social Research,* Tool for the Human Services, Chicago: Holt.

Nachmias, D and Nachmias, C. (1981): *Research Methods in the Social Sciences,* New York: St. Martins Press.

Sellitz, G. et. al. (1973): *Research Methods in Social Relations,* 3rd ed., New York: Rinehart and Winston.

Sjoberg, G. and Nett., B. (1968): *A Methodology of Social Research,* New York: Harper & Row.

Wilkinson, T.S. and Bhandarkar, P.L. (1977): *Methodology and Techniques of Social Research:* Bombay: Himalaya.

11 Statistical Techniques

After going through this chapter, you will be able to:

- Know what are various measures of central tendency such as arithmetic mean, median and mode.
- Understand the meaning of various measures of dispersion such as range, variance, standard deviation, and coefficient of variation.
- Comprehend the intricacies correlation and regression techniques; and analyze time series data.

INTRODUCTION

In chapter 10, we explained the methods of presenting data in the form of tables and graphs. However, many a time we need a single summary value that would describe a series. For example, we have data on the number of visitors to a library on a daily basis. Such data can be presented in the form of a table or in the form of a line graph. But if we want a single summary figure, the arithmetic mean would give us the average number of visitors to the library. Statistical techniques are more suitable for quantitative data although certain techniques do exist for qualitative data also. Recall that quantitative data can be of two types: **discrete** and **continuous**. We will explain various techniques for both types of variables. We begin with measures of central tendency.

MEASURES OF CENTRAL TENDENCY

Measures of central tendency provide us with a summary that describes some central or middle point of the data. There are five important measures of central tendency: (i) arithmetic mean; (ii) median; (iii) mode; (iv) geometric mean; and (v) harmonic mean. Of these, geometric mean and harmonic mean have specific uses and thus are less frequently used. Therefore, we will discuss the measures (i)–(iii) in this chapter.

Before dealing with these measures, let us be familiar with certain notations that we will use. The standard notation is: X is a variable that takes values N X_1, X_2, X_3, ..., X_n. Let us consider the data given in Table 11.1 on the number of books issued to borrowers. You know that it is a discrete variable and the number of books that can be issued to each borrower varies between 0 and 5, viz., 0, 1, 2, 3, 4, and 5. The corresponding frequency for each observation is: 10, 23, 25, 17, 15 and 10.

TABLE 11.1 Books Issued to Borrowers

No. of books issued	No. of borrowers
0	10
1	23
2	25
3	17
4	15
5	10
Total	**100**

In the above example, we denote the variable "number of books issued" as X and the values assumed by it as X_1, X_2, X_3, X_4, X_5, X_6. The corresponding frequencies are $f_1, f_2, ..., f_6$. We call a typical observation as the ith observation and denote it as X_i with frequency f_i. In the example on the number of books issued i ranges between 0 and 5.

In the case of continuous variable, we take the mid-values of class intervals as n $X_1, X_2, X_3, \ldots, X_n$, and the corresponding frequencies as $f_1, f_2, \ldots, f_n$.

Arithmetic Mean

Arithmetic mean is also called *mean* or *average*. It is denoted by a bar above the variable being averaged. It is defined as the sum of all observations divided by the number of observations.

Let us calculate arithmetic mean for observations arranged in a frequency distribution.

If $X_1, X_2, X_3, \ldots, X_n$ are the observations and the corresponding frequencies are $f_1, f_2, \ldots, f_N$, then the arithmetic mean is given by $\overline{X}$ (read it as "X-bar") and is defined as

$$\overline{X} = \frac{f_1X_1 + f_2X_2 + \cdots f_nX_n}{f_1 + f_2 + \cdots f_n}$$

It can be reduced to

$$\overline{X} = \frac{\Sigma fx}{\Sigma f}$$

$$\overline{X} = \frac{\Sigma fx}{N} \qquad (11.1)$$

where N is the total number of observations and is equal to f_i. The symbol Σ ('sigma') denotes the sum of a variable.

When observations are classified into class intervals, in the case of continuous data, individual observations within a class interval are not separately identifiable. To overcome this difficulty, it is assumed that every observation falling into a class interval has a value equal to the mid-value of the class interval.

Example 11.1. Calculate the average number of books issued to borrowers on the basis of Table 11.2.

TABLE 11.2 Data on Number of Books Issued to Borrowers

No. of books issued	No. of borrowers
0	10
1	23
2	25
3	17
4	15
5	10
Total	**100**

We prepare a table (Table 11.3) for calculating arithmetic mean.

TABLE 11.3 Data on Calculating Arithmetic Mean

No. of books issued (X_i)	No. of borrowers (f_i)	$f_i X_i$
0	10	0
1	23	23
2	25	50
3	17	51
4	15	60
5	10	50
Total	**100**	$f_i X_i$ = **234**

Secondly, we fill in the values from the table in the formula given in Eq. (11.1) where, $N = 100$, and $f_i X_i = 234$. Therefore,

$$\bar{X} = \frac{1}{100} \times 234 = 2.34$$

Thus, the average number of books issued to borrowers is 2.34.

Example 11.2. Table 11.4 gives the monthly expenditure (₹) on purchase of books by 100 persons. What is the monthly average expenditure?

TABLE 11.4 Monthly Expenditure (₹) on Purchase of Books

Class Interval	Frequency
100–200	12
200–300	18
300–400	28
400–500	19
500–600	13
600–700	7
700–800	3
Total	**100**

In the case of continuous data, we have to find out the mid-value of the class intervals and then apply formula (11.1), as illustrated in Table 11.5.

TABLE 11.5 Method of Finding out Mid-value of Class Intervals

Class-interval	Mid-value	Frequency	$f_i X_i$
100–200	150	12	1800
200–300	250	18	4500
300–400	350	28	9800
400–500	450	19	8550
500–600	550	13	7150
600–700	650	7	4550
700–800	750	3	2250
Total		f_i = **100**	$f_i X_i$ = **38,600**

By applying the relevant values from Table 11.5 in (11.1), that is, arithmetic mean = $\bar{X}$, we get

$$\bar{X} = \frac{\Sigma fx}{N}$$

Here, $N = 100, f_1X_1 = 38,600.$

Therefore, $\bar{X} = \frac{1}{100} \times 38600 = 386$

Thus, the average monthly expenditure on purchase of books by the groups of individuals is ₹ 386.

Median

Median gives us the observation in the middle in a series so that half of the observations remain on each side of the median. For example, if you have five observations, viz., 2, 5, 9, 14 and 20, then 9 is the middle observation and two observations remain on both sides of it. Thus, the median of the above series is 9.

Let us consider another series where there are six observations: 3, 8, 15, 25, 35, and 43. In this case, the median could be any number between 15 and 25 because two observations will remain on both sides. Conventionally, we take the average of the two numbers in the middle. Here it will be

$$\frac{15+25}{2} = \frac{40}{2} = 20$$

Thus, in this case the median is 20.

However, when the number of observations is too large or data is arranged in a frequency distribution, it is not that easy to locate the median. If there are N observations, the median observation should correspond to the nth observation. We first find out the cumulative frequency of the distribution and then find out the class interval in which the $N/2$th observation lies. This class interval is our *median class*.

Thirdly, we apply the following formula to get the median value.

$$M_d = l_m + \frac{h(N/2 - cf)}{f_m} \qquad (11.2)$$

where

l_m = The lower limit of the median class, i.e., the class in which the median lies

N = The total frequency

c.f = The cumulative frequency of classes preceding the median class

f_m = The frequency of the median class

h = The width of the median class.

Example 11.3. For the data given in Example 11.2 above, find out the median, and monthly expenditure on purchase of books. To solve the above problem, we go by the following steps:

1. Calculate the cumulative frequency distribution.
2. Find out the median class.
3. Apply formula (11.2).

TABLE 11.6 Cumulative Frequency Distribution

Expenditure (₹)	No. of persons (Frequency)	Cumulative frequency
100–200	12	12
200–300	18	30
300–400	28	58
400–500	19	77
500–600	13	90
600–700	7	97
700–800	3	100
Total	**100**	

There are 100 observations. So the median value corresponds to 50th observation, which lies in the class interval 300–400. Therefore, the median will remain somewhere between 300 and 400. Thus the median class is 300–400. In this case

$$l_m = 300, \quad C = 30, \quad N = 100, \quad f_m = 28, \quad h = 100,$$

By applying (11.2), we obtain the median value as

$$M_d = 300 + \frac{100(100/2 - 30)}{28} = 300 + 71.43 = 317.43$$

Mode

Mode is the observation with the highest frequency. For discrete data, it is easier to find out the mode. But in the case of continuous data, we have to identify the 'modal class', that is the class interval having the highest frequency. We have to see that the width of the classes is the same. Otherwise, large class intervals are likely to include large number of observations and smaller class intervals are likely to have only a few observations. Mode is computed by the following formula:

$$M_o = \frac{l_m + h(f_m - f_1)}{2f_m - f_1 - f_2} \tag{11.3}$$

l_m= lower limit of the modal class, i.e. the class in which the mode lies
f_m= frequency of modal class
f_1= frequency of pre modal class
f_2 = frequency of post class
h = the width of modal class

MEASURES OF DISPERSION

Measures of central tendency provide us with a summary figure for the data set. However, in many situations these measures do not represent the distribution of data. For example, note the following three sets of data:

1. Set A: 2, 5, 17, 17, and 44.
2. Set B: 17, 17, 17, 17, and 17.
3. Set C: 13, 14, 17, 17, and 24.

Calculate the mean, median and mode for all three sets and you will find that they are the same, that is, 17 in all the three sets. Still these sets are so different! While in Set B all the observations are equal, in Set A they are so dispersed. Definitely we need another measure, which will account for such dispersion of data.

The word 'dispersion' gives the degree of heterogeneity in the data. It is an important characteristic indicating the extent to which observations vary amongst themselves.

The dispersion of a given set of observations will be zero, only when all of them are equal as in Set B given above. The wider the discrepancy from one observation to another, the larger would be the dispersion. Thus dispersion in Set A should be larger than that in Set C. A measure of dispersion should capture such variability in data.

There are quite a few measures of dispersion. We will discuss range, mean deviation, variance and standard deviation in this Section.

Range

Range is defined as *the difference between the largest and the smallest observations*. Thus for the data given at Set A, the range is 44 – 2 = 42. Similarly, for Set B the range is 17 – 17 = 0, and for Set C it is 11. In the case of grouped data, individual observations are not identifiable. In such cases we take the difference between two extreme boundaries of the classes.

Variance

Variance is the most widely used measure of dispersion. It is denoted by the symbol σ^2 and is defined as

$$\text{Variance} = \sigma^2 = \Sigma \frac{(X_i - \bar{X})^2}{n} \tag{11.4}$$

where $i = 1, 2, \ldots, n$

In the case of frequency distribution, variance is given by

$$\sigma^2 = \Sigma \frac{f_i(X_i - \bar{X})^2}{N} \tag{11.5}$$

where N = total frequency

Standard Deviation

Standard deviation is another widely used measure of dispersion. It is defined as the positive square root of variance and denoted by S. Remember that standard deviation cannot be negative.

Example 11.4. The following tabulated data give the range of marks obtained by students in a class. Find out the standard deviation.

Marks	No. of students
15–25	8
25–35	12
35–45	20
45–55	10
55–65	6
65–75	4
Total	**60**

In order to calculate the standard deviation, we have to take the following steps:

1. Calculate the mid-values of the classes.
2. Calculate arithmetic mean.
3. Apply formula (11.5) to find out variance.
4. Prepare a table with the required columns. We have prepared one table (Table 11.7) for applying formula (11.5).
5. Find out the variance.
6. Find out the positive square root of variance.

TABLE 11.7 Calculation of Standard Deviation

Marks	No. of students f_i	Mid-value X_i	X_i	$(X_i - \bar{X})$	$(X_i - \bar{X})^2$	$f_i(X_i - \bar{X})^2$
1	*2*	*3*	*4*	*5*	*6*	*7*
15–25	8	20	160	−21	441	3528
25–35	12	30	360	−11	121	1452
35–45	20	40	800	−1	1	20
45–55	10	50	500	9	81	810
55–65	6	60	360	19	361	2166
65–75	4	70	280	29	841	3364
Total	**60**		**2460**			**11340**

In the above table, we first find out the arithmetic mean, which is 41. Next we find out the variance as

$$\sigma = \sqrt{\frac{\Sigma f_i (X_i - \bar{X})^2}{N}}$$

So the σ, i.e. the variance, is 189. Thus the Standard Deviation is $\sqrt{189} = 13.75$ marks.

Coefficient of Variation

Quite often, we have to compare the variability among different series of data. If the units are measured in different units, we obtain different values for standard deviation. For example, let us compare the economic status of households in two villages. The summary figures of monthly calorie intake of households for the two villages are obtained as follows:

	Village A	*Village B*
No. of households	817	561
Mean calorie intake	2417	2235
SD of calorie intake	418	232

The problem is to identify the village that has more inequality as far as calorie intake is concerned. We find that village A has higher mean calorie intake but has larger standard deviation and larger number of households as compared to village B. Thus, village A may actually have more number of poorer households than in village B. In order to compare such situations we use the coefficient of variation (CV). It is defined as percentage standard deviation per unit of mean, i.e.,

$$\text{CV} = \frac{\sigma}{X} \times 100 \tag{11.7}$$

Since and have same unit of measurement, CV is a pure number and it is not affected by the choice of unit of measurement.

For village A,

$$\text{CV} = 418/2417 \times 100 = 17.29$$

For village B,

$$\text{CV} = 232/2235 \times 100 = 10.38.$$

Since the coefficient of variation in village A is greater than the coefficient of variation in village B, the inequalities are greater in village A as compared to village B

CORRELATION

So far we have dealt with a single characteristic of data. But, there may be cases when we would be interested in analyzing more than one characteristic at a time. For example, you may like to study the relationship between the age and the number of books a person reads. Such data, having two characteristics under study are called **bivariate data**. One of the measures to find out the extent or degree of relationship between two variables is correlation coefficient.

An analysis of the covariation of two or more variables is usually called **correlation**. If two characteristics vary in such a way that movement in one is accompanied by movement in the other, these characteristics are correlated. For example, there is relationship between price and supply, income and expenditure, etc. With the help of correlation analysis, we can measure in one figure the degree of relationship existing between two variables.

Scatter Diagram

If we are interested in finding out the relationship between two variables, the simplest way to visualize it is to prepare a dot chart called **scatter diagram**. Using this method, the given data are plotted on a graph paper in the form of dots. For example, for each pair of *X* and *Y* values, we put a dot and thus obtain as many points as the number of observations. Now, by looking into the scatter of various dots, we can ascertain whether the variables are related or not. The greater the scatter of the plotted points on the chart, the lesser is the relationship between the two variables. The more closely the points come to a straight line, the higher the degree of relationship. We now give some illustrations of correlations between two variables (see Figures 11.1–11.3).

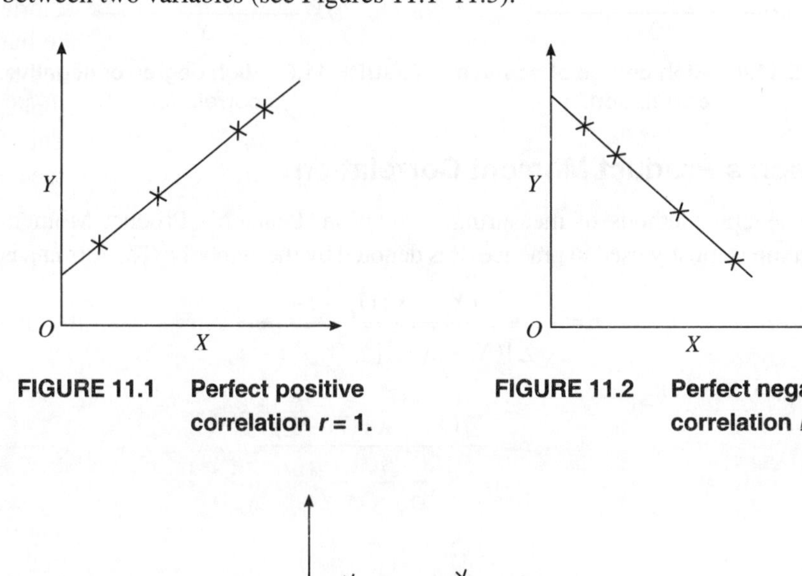

FIGURE 11.1 Perfect positive correlation $r = 1$.

FIGURE 11.2 Perfect negative correlation $r = -1$.

FIGURE 11.3 No Correlation $r = 0$.

Note that the scatter diagram gives a rough idea of the degree of relationship between two variables.

As we are considering a relationship between the two variables here, there might be a relationship between more than two variables. In the case of 10 variables, we can plot the points on a two-dimensional graph paper, i.e., on a space with *x* and *y* axes. But the scatter diagram has the limitation that it cannot be plotted where more than two variables are involved. Secondly, it does not give an exact figure on the degree of relationship between variables.

To reach an exact figure on the extent of relationship between variables and also to overcome the limitation of considering more than two variables at a time, we calculate the correlation coefficient, which is shown in Figures 11.4 and 11.5 respectively.

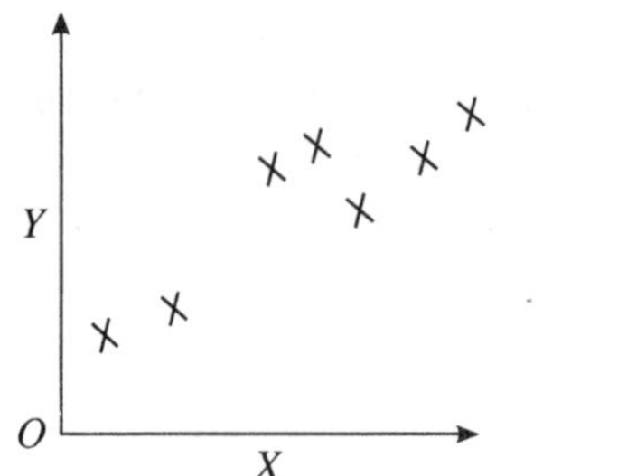

FIGURE 11.4 High degree of positive correlation.

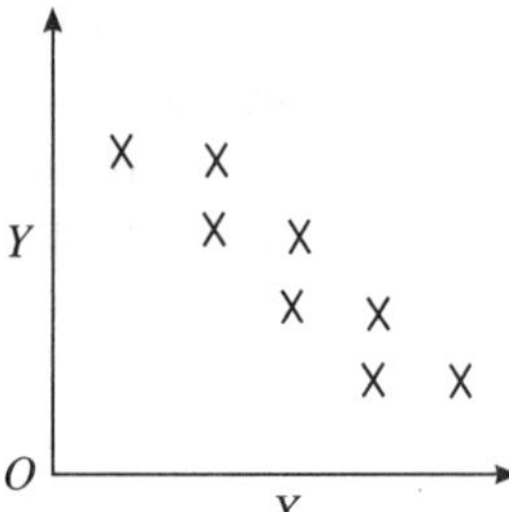

FIGURE 11.5 High degree of negative correlation.

Pearson's Product Moment Correlation

Of the several methods of measuring correlation, Pearson's Product Moment Correlation is mostly used in practice. It is denoted by the symbol r. The formula is

$$r = \frac{\Sigma (X_i - \bar{X})(Y_i - \bar{Y})}{\sqrt{\Sigma [(X_i - X)^2][\Sigma (Y_i - Y)^2]}}$$

where $i = 1, 2, \ldots, n$.

$$r = \frac{\dfrac{\Sigma (X_i - \bar{X})(Y_i - \bar{Y})}{n}}{\sigma_x \times \sigma_y}$$

$$r = \frac{(\bar{X}_i - X)(\bar{Y}_i - Y)}{n\sigma_x \times \sigma_y}$$

where $i = 1, 2, \ldots, n$.

When we get the value of $r = +1$, it means there is perfect positive correlation between variables. When $r = -1$, there is perfect negative correlation and, when $r = 0$, it means that there is no correlation between the two variables. The correlation coefficient can take any value between +1 and –1, i.e., it cannot exceed +1 and cannot be less than –1.

Usually, in real-life analysis, we get values which lie between +1 and –1 such as +0.6, –0.5, ...

Remember that correlation indicates the degree of association between variables X and Y. It merely shows whether the variation in one variable is accompanied by the variation in the other or not. Correlation coefficient does not indicate a cause and effect relationship between the variables. We cannot say X causes Y or vice versa. The second point one should remember is that a $r = +0.6$ does not imply greater relationship than $r = 0.6$. The positive or negative sign indicates the direction of relationship. If $r = +0.6$, then it is very likely than an increase in X is accompanied by an increase in Y. On the other hand,

$r = -0.6$ indicates the inverse relationship between X and Y. Thirdly, correlation coefficient is neutral to change in scale and origin. This means that in illustration –8, for example, if we divide the X variable by any figure, say, 5 and variable Y by 2 (or any other figure), we get the same value for r-value. This is called a change in scale. For instance, when you convert the height in cm. To that in inches, the correlation coefficient does not change. Similarly, if you change the origin, i.e., deduct or add certain figure to all the observations, the correlation coefficient does not change. You may find this out yourself by deducting 10 from X and 5 from Y and then by calculating the correlation coefficient.

Fourthly, the correlation coefficient indicates the linear relationship between the variables.

For higher order relationships, the correlation coefficient does not reflect the proper degree of relationship. For example, for two variables, X and Y, if $X = Y_2$ for every value of Y then r may turn out to be zero. But this does not mean that X and Y are not related, so what we can say is that when two variables are independent $r = 0$, but from the mere knowledge of $r = 0$, we cannot infer that the two variables are independent.

The following example will enable you to find out the value of r.

Example 11.5. Table 11.8 shows the data on height and weight of 10 children. Find out the product moment correlation coefficient.

TABLE 11.8 Data on Height and Weight of 10 Children

Children	Height (cm)	Weight (kg)	Children	Height (cm)	Weight (kg)
1	110	26	6	140	38
2	110	21	7	135	30
3	125	22	8	130	30
4	130	24	9	140	40
5	145	36	10	135	43

Let the height (cm) be termed X and weight be Y.

Solution

TABLE 11.9 Calculation of Co-relation Coefficient

X_i	Y_i	$x_i = (X_i - \bar{X})$	$y_i = (Y_i - \bar{Y})$	$x_i y_i$	x_i^2	y_i^2
110	26	–20	–5	100	400	25
110	21	–20	–10	210	400	100
125	22	–5	–9	45	25	81
130	24	0	–7	0	0	49
145	36	15	5	75	225	25
140	38	1	7	70	100	49
135	30	5	–1	–5	25	1
130	30	0	–1	0	0	1
140	40	10	9	90	100	81
135	43	5	12	60	25	144
1300	310			645	1300	

Spearman's Rank Correlation

In Chapter 10, while mentioning the types of data, we had distinguished between ratio scale and ordinal scale of measurement. Pearson's product moment correlation coefficient can be applied only when the data are measured in the ratio scale. But when, instead of actual magnitude of the observations, we have only the ranks, Pearson's '*r*' becomes inapplicable. In such cases, Spearman's rank correlation (r_s) is used.

The method of calculating *r* is quite simple. The first step is to identify the rank or the *i*th observation in *X* and *Y* in their respective series of *n* items. The second step is to find out the difference between the rank in *X* and the rank in *Y*. Let this difference be termed D_i. The third step is to apply the following formula.

$$r_x = \frac{1 - 6\sum D_i^2}{n(n^2 - 1)}$$

The Spearman's rank correlation also ranges from +1 to –1. Thus, positive values indicate direct relationship between the variables, while negative values indicate inverse relationship. The value $r = 0$ indicates absence of association between the variables.

One note of caution is that Spearman's rank correlation should not be used just because it is easier to compute than Pearson's product moment correlation coefficient *r* is less interpretive than *r*. We cannot strictly say that the change in *X* is associated with proportionate change in *Y* because equal differences in ranks do not imply equal differences in the characteristics.

Example 11.6. The following data give rank of 12 journals by two different methods used to compute rank correlation coefficient. This is illustrated in Table 11.10. Therefore,

$$r_s = 1 - 1.454 = 0.454$$

TABLE 11.10 Rank Correlation Coefficient r_s

S. No.	Rank according to the No. of publication *X*	Rank according to the No. of citation *Y*	D_1	D_1^2
1	1	12	–11	121
2	2	9	–7	49
3	3	6	–3	9
4	4	10	–6	36
5	5	3	+2	4
6	6	5	+1	1
7	7	4	+3	9
8	8	7	+1	1
9	9	8	+1	1
10	10	2	+8	64
11	11	11	0	0
12	12	1	+11	121
				D^2 416

REGRESSION ANALYSIS

Regression analysis assumes that one variable is the cause and other(s) the effect. In general terms, we can say that, variables are of two types: **independent variables** and **dependent variables**. The independent variable is the *cause* and dependent variable is the **effect**.

Regression analysis is a statistical tool, that helps understand the relationship between variables and predicts the unknown values of the dependent variable from known values of the independent variable.

Let us assume that the number of books in circulation in a library is related to the number of users. For example, it can be postulated that, as the number of users increases, the number of books in circulation also increases. Here, the number of users is the independent variable and the number of books in circulation is the dependent variable.

Let us denote the dependent variable as Y and the independent variable as X. In regression analysis, we gather data over a period of time or across units at a point of time. Let us assume that n pairs of observations in X and Y are collected. The next step is to find out the relationship X and Y.

The relationship between X and Y can take many forms. Generally we express the relationship in terms of some mathematical equations. The simplest of these equations is the *linear equation*. This means that the relationship between X and Y is in the form of a straight line. When the equation represents curves (not a straight line), the regression is called **nonlinear** or **curvilinear**.

Now the question arises, "How do we identify the equational form?" There is no hard and fast rule as such. The form of equation depends on the reasoning and assumptions made by the researcher. However, the researcher may plot the X and Y variables on a graph paper to prepare a scatter diagram. From the scatter diagram, the location of the points on the graph paper helps in identifying the equational form. If the points are more or less in a straight line, then the linear equation is assumed. If the points are not in a straight line and are in the form of a curve, a suitable nonlinear equation, which resembles the scatter, is assumed.

The researcher has to make another assumption: namely, identification of independent and dependent variables. The again depends on the logic of the researcher and purpose of analysis: whether Y depends on X or X depends on Y. Thus, there may be two regression lines from the same data (a) when Y is assumed to be dependent on X, this is termed 'Y on X' line and, (b) when X is assumed to be dependent on Y, it is termed 'X on Y' line.

Let us take an example of a linear equation with Y as the dependent variable and X as the independent variable:

$$Y = 3 + 2X$$

By taking in different values of X, we can determine the values of Y, e.g., when $X = 1$, $Y = 5$; when $X = 2$, $Y = 7$, and so on. If we plot these pairs of points (1, 5), (2, 7), ... on a graph paper, we get a straight line.

Generalizing the above relationship, it can be said that a linear equation of Y on X takes the form $Y = a + bX$, where a and b are constants. Similarly, non-linear equations can be specified in many forms. A simple example is $Y = a + bX + cX_2$.

Linear Regression

Let us consider the following data. The number of visitors and the number of books issued during weekdays in a week are given:

No. of visitors to a library (X)	6	2	10	4	8
No. of books issued (Y)	8	4	10	7	8

If we plot the data on a graph paper, the scatter diagram will be similar to Figure 11.6.

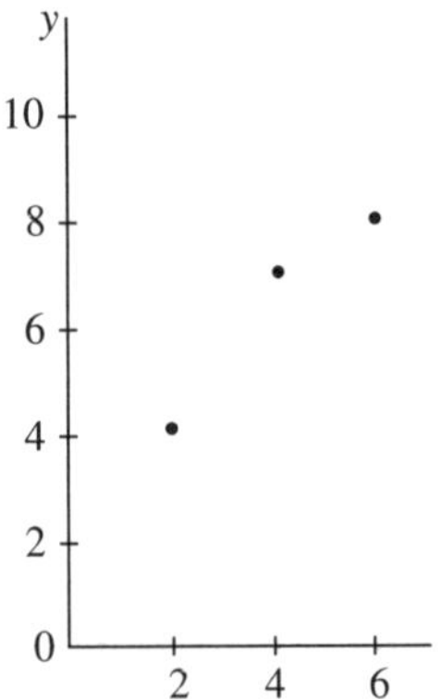

FIGURE 11.6 Scatter Diagram for number of visitors to a library and Books issued.

As is obvious from Figure 11.6, the points do not strictly lie in a straight line. But they show an upward rising tendency where a straight line can be fitted. If we plot the straight line along with the scattered points, the diagram looks like Figure 11.6. The difference between the regression line and the observations is the 'error'. For example, against an X value of 2, the Y value is 4. This is called the **observed value**.

But the regression line shows Y value of 4.8 against X value of 2. This value, which is calculated from the regression line, is the **expected value**. The difference between the observed value and the expected value is termed as the **error value**. So we see that observed value is the sum of expected value and error value.

Our objective in fitting a regression line is to minimize the error values. This is usually done by the method of 'least squares'. The method of least squares minimizes the value of E which is the difference between the observed and expected values.

We will not go into the details of the method here. Instead, the two equations derived on the basis of least squares method and known as normal equations are

$$Y = na + bx$$

As a rule of thumb, we can say that these normal equations are derived by multiplying the coefficients of a and b to the linear equation and summing over all observations.

Here the linear equation is $Y = a + bx$. The first normal equation is simply the linear equation $Y = a + bx$ summed over all observations, where x and y are the variables, and

$$SY = a + SbX \quad \text{or} \quad SY = na + bSX$$

The second normal equation is the linear equation multiplied by X and summed over all observations. Thus,

$$SXY = SaX + SbX^2$$

or

$$SXY = aSX + bSX$$

It is evident that all the terms in these equations are given numbers, calculated from the data, except a and b.

The values of a and b need to be calculated for getting the estimated value of the dependent variable. This is done in the following manner.

Table 11.11 shows that data on X and Y variables are given in the first two columns. The succeeding two columns in the table give the calculations necessary to solve two normal equations given above. The expected value of Y and error value are given in the last two columns.

TABLE 11.11 Computations of Data for Regression Analysis

1	2	3	4	5	6
X	*Y*	X^2	*XY*	*Expected value of Y*	*Error*
6	8	36	48	7.4	0.6
2	4	4	8	4.8	−0.8
10	10	100	100	10.0	0.0
4	7	16	28	6.1	0.9
8	8	64	64	8.7	−0.7
Total 30	**37**	**220**	**248**	**37**	**0.0**

As the normal equations are

$$Y = na + b\,X \tag{11.9}$$

we substitute the respective values from Table 11.11. Thus,

$$37 = 5a + 30b \tag{11.10}$$

$$248 = 30a + 220b \tag{11.11}$$

If we multiply Equation (11.10) by 6 and subtract the product from Equation (11.11), we get

$$\begin{array}{r} 248 = 30a + 220b \\ 222 = 30a + 180b \\ - \quad - \\ \hline 40b = 26 \end{array}$$

or $$b = 0.65$$

Substituting the value of b in equation (11.10), we obtain

$$37 = 5a + 30 \times 0.65$$

or $$5a = 17.5 \quad \text{or} \quad a = 3.5$$

So the regression line is

$$Y = 3.5 + 0.65X \tag{11.12}$$

If we substitute the values of X in the regression line that is Equation (11.12), we get the expected values of Y. For example, when $X = 2$,

$$Y = 3.5 + 0.65 \times 2 = 4.8$$

But our observed value of Y against $X = 2$ is 4. This difference between the observed value and the expected value $(4 - 4.8 = -0.8)$ is the error e.

The expected values of Y and e are given in the Table 11.11 in columns 5 and 6.

Notice that the sum of errors for the sample is zero, i.e., $Se = 0$.

For computational purposes, we may use the following formulae to find out the value of a and b.

Let us take

$$X = (X - \overline{X}), \qquad Y = (Y - \overline{Y})$$

$$XY = (X - \overline{X})(Y - \overline{Y})$$

where X and Y are the arithmetic means of X and Y variables, respectively. This formula gives

$$b = \frac{xy}{x^2} \tag{11.13}$$

$$a = \overline{y} - b\overline{x} \tag{11.14}$$

Since these formulae are derived from the normal equations, we get the same values for a and b in this method also.

The steps involved in computation are:

1. Find out the values of X and Y.
2. Find out $x = (X - \overline{X})$ and $y = (Y - \overline{Y})$.
3. Find out the values of xy.
4. Find out the values of x_2.
5. Apply the formulae in Equations (11.13) and (11.14) above.

On applying the above formulae in the example given in Table 11.11, we get the data given in Table 11.12.

TABLE 11.12 Computation of Regression Equation: The short-cut method

X	Y	$X = (\bar{X} - X)$	$Y = (\bar{Y} - Y)$	xy	X^2
6	8	0	0.6	0	0
2	4	−4	−3.4	13.6	16
10	10	4	2.6	10.4	16
4	7	−2	−0.4	0.8	4
8	8	2	0.6	1.2	4
Total = 30	**37**			**26.0**	**40**

$$X = \frac{\Sigma X}{n}$$

$$\bar{X} = \frac{30}{5} = 6, \qquad b = \frac{xy}{x^2} = \frac{26}{40} = 0.65$$

$$\bar{Y} = \frac{\Sigma y}{n},$$

$$\bar{Y} = \frac{37}{5} = 7.4, \qquad a = \bar{y} - b\bar{x} = 3.5$$

Needless to mention that the values for a and b are the same as those derived earlier.

Properties of Regression Coefficient

The coefficient b is called the *regression coefficient*. Note that we can draw two regression lines from the data on X and Y.

(i) Y on X line, $y = a + bx$
(ii) X on Y line, $x = A + By$

The coefficient B represents the change in the value of dependent variable x for a unit change in the value of independent variable y and is called the coefficient of regression of x an y.

The two coefficients, b and β, demonstrate some interesting properties. First, the product of both regression coefficients is equal to the square of r (correlation coefficient), i.e., $b\beta = r^2$.

So once we know both regression coefficients, we can find out the value of r^2. By taking the square root of r^2, we get r. Second, if the regression coefficients are negative in sign, then the correlation coefficients also are negative. If the regression coefficients are positive, then the correlation is positive. Third, you know that, r lies between −1 and +1.

Therefore, r^2 lies between zero and +1. The regression coefficient can take finite value. But is one regression coefficient > 1 the other regression coefficient < 1. Both regression coefficients cannot exceed unity. Also, it follows that the product of both, which is r^2, cannot exceed unity. The square of correlation coefficient is called the *coefficient of determination* and implies important characteristics. If r^2, the coefficient of determination, is closer to 1, we can infer that the independent variable explains the movements in the dependent variable. If the coefficient of determination is closer to zero, the independent variable does not explain the variation in the dependent variable.

Prediction

A major interest in studying regression lies in its ability to forecast. In the illustration at the beginning, we assumed that the number of books issued depends on the number of visitors. We fitted a linear equation to the observed data and obtained the relationship

$$Y = 3.5 + 0.65\, X$$

From this equation, we can forecast the number of books issued given the number of visitors. For example, if the number of visitors goes up to 30, then the number of books issued will be

$$Y = 3.5 + 0.65 \times 30 = 23$$

The procedure is to substitute the X value in the regression equation and get the expected Y value. The question that arises here is: Will the predicted value come true? It depends on the coefficient of determination. If the coefficient of determination is closer to 1, there is greater likelihood that the prediction will be realized. However, the predicted value is constrained by elements of randomness involved with human behaviour and other unforeseen factors.

Time Series Analysis

In regression analysis, we discussed the cause and effect relationship between the dependent and the independent variables. The independent variable can be any characteristic based on our reasoning. When the independent variable is 'time', we call it *time series.* We assume that the dependent variable depends on time or varies according to time.

In our day-to-day life, we encounter several instances where certain characteristics vary according to time. The stock in a library, the expenditure on user facilities, etc. are a few examples.

One of the important tasks before librarians and information managers is to make estimates for the future. For example, a publisher may want to know his probable sales for the next year, so that he can properly plan and take steps to avoid the possibility of unsold stocks or lack of supply of some books published by him. A librarian may wish to study the trend of books issued in order to take appropriate measures while making his future plans. For all these purposes, they require data, which have been collected and recorded at successive intervals of time Such statistical data are referred to as *time series data.*

An example of time series data is the number of books on Library and Information Science issued during 1995–2004. These data may be recorded as follows:

TABLE 11.13 Hypothetical Data Recorded on Books Issued over Time

Year	No. of books issued
1995	356
1996	350
1997	391
1998	289
1999	408
2000	412
2001	405
2002	482
2003	497
2004	469

A close look at the data would show that the demand for the books has increased with some fluctuations. There may be several reasons for increase or decrease during a certain period.

Components of Time Series

The fluctuations in time series may be classified into the following types:

1. Secular trend
2. Seasonal variation
3. Cyclical variation
4. Irregular variation

A time series may have the above components in combination as well.

Secular trend: Changes which take place as a result of general tendency of the data to increase or decrease are known as *secular movement.* The general movement persisting over a long period of time is called *secular trend.* The above time series example for data on books issued is an example of secular trend.

Seasonal variation: Changes or variations, which seasonally occur within a period of one year as a result of changes in climate, weather, important happenings, etc. are called *seasonal variations*. It may be possible that in the data on books issued in the above example (If made available on a month to month basis), the year starts with a low figure in the beginning, reaches its peak in the middle and decreases at the end of the year. This type of fluctuation within a span of a year is called *seasonal variation*.

Cyclical variation: Changes that take place due to cyclic fluctuations like prosperity and depression may be termed as cyclical variations. In every business cycle there are four periods: (i) prosperity, (ii) decline, (iii) depression, and (iv) improvement. Cyclical variations are of a longer duration—they last more than a year.

Irregular variation: Changes which take place due to the factors that could not be predicted, such as violent riots, and natural calamities come under irregular variation.

The components of time series data, namely, seasonal, trend, cyclical and irregular, can be separated. In a traditional time series analysis, it is assumed that there is a multiplicative relationship among these four components. This may be represented symbolically as follows:

$$Y = T \times S \times C \times I$$

where T = secular trend

S = seasonal variation

C = cyclical variation

I = irregular variation

This is called the **multiplicative model.**

In another approach, it is assumed that

$$Y = T + S + C + I$$

A model formulation of this category is called *additive model.*

Measurement of Secular Trends

There are various methods for determining secular trends. The most frequently used methods are:

- Moving average method
- Method of least squares.

(i) Method of moving average: It is a method of smoothing out fluctuations by calculating a series of averages by allowing overlapping periods of the time series. Before the moving average is calculated, it is necessary to select a proper period of moving average, for example, three yearly, five- yearly ...

If the period chosen is m years, the moving averages are obtained by calculating a series of mean values of m consecutive values covering overlapping periods of the series. The mean of the first m values, given by $(Y + Y + \cdots + Y_m)$. It is placed at the mid-point of the period covering the first m years. It would be the first moving average value. The second moving average value will be obtained by calculating mean of values covering the second period to $(m + 1)$th years. For example:

$$\frac{1}{m}(Y_1 + Y_2 + \cdots + Y_{m1})$$

will be the next moving average, and so on. This process is repeated till the last observation is done.

The formula of the three-yearly moving average is

$$\frac{1}{3}(Y_1 + Y_2 + Y_3), \frac{1}{3}(Y_2 + Y_3 + Y_4), \frac{1}{3}(Y_3 + Y_4 + Y_5), \cdots$$

and that of five-yearly moving average will be

$$\frac{1}{5}(Y_1 + Y_2 + Y_3 + Y_4 + Y_5), \frac{1}{5}(Y_2 + Y_3 + Y_4 + Y_5 + Y_6), \cdots$$

The above procedure will be easy to understand from the following illustration

Illustration. Calculate a three-yearly moving average from the sales figures of a publisher given Table 11.14.

TABLE 11.14 Hypothetical Data for Computation of Moving Average

Year	Sales (hundred units)
1990	5
1991	7
1992	9
1993	12
1994	11
1995	10
1996	8
1997	12
1998	13
1999	17
2000	19
2001	14
2002	13
2003	12
2004	15

Data on sales of books for 15 years are given in Table 11.4. To calculate the three-yearly moving average, to begin with, we take the first three years total. This is 5 + 7 + 9 = 21, and place this value against the middle observation, i.e., against 1971. In column 4 of Table 11.15, the moving average, i.e., the three-yearly total divided by the period (which is 3 in this case), is given. Thus, 21/3=7 for the first entry.

TABLE.11.15 Computation of Three-Yearly Moving Average

Year	Sales (hundred units)	Yearly totals	Yearly moving average
1990	5		
1991	7	21	7
1992	9	28	9.33
1993	12	32	10.67
1994	11	33	11.00
1995	10	29	9.67
1996	8	30	10.00
1997	12	33	11
1998	13	42	14
1999	17	49	16.33
2000	19	50	16.67
2001	14	46	15.33
2002	13	39	13.00
2003	12	40	13.33
2004	15		

Following a similar procedure, other calculations are made and the results are presented as in the above table.

From Table 11.15, it may be noted that we do not get moving average value for the beginning and end years. In the case of a five-yearly moving average, we lose moving averages for the beginning two years and the two years at the end. This loss of information increases as the 'period' of moving average increases. Secondly, from the moving averages, we cannot predict the figures for the future. It is just an analysis of past behaviour.

(ii) Method of least squares: We used this method earlier to obtain the regression lines. The procedure here is very similar to the fitting of regression lines. Here the independent variable is time t. The first step is to form the equation of 'secular trend'. As you know, both straight lines and curves can be fitted by the least squares method. If Y is the dependent variable, the straight line to be fitted is $Y = a + bt$. Again, we have to minimize the error between the observed and the expected values. The method of least squares suggests that the sum of squares of the error terms should be the minimum. From this method, the relationship between dependent and independent variables is estimated from the normal equations.

For a linear equation $Y = a + bt$, the normal equations are:

$$Y = na + bt \qquad tY = at + bt^2$$

The constants a and b are determined from these two equations, and n indicates the number of observations in the sample. We measure the variable t by taking the mid-point of time as the origin. Suppose

$n = 5$ years. Then taking the origin at the third year of the time, we get $t = -2, -1, 0, 1, 2$. It may be seen that $t = 0$ for the third year. In case the number of years covered is even, say 6 years, the origin at the mid-point of the two middle years, i.e., at six months past the third year, is considered. In such cases, t takes the values

$$t = -5, -3, -1, +1, +3, +5$$

To fit a linear trend line by making use of the data given in Table 11.15 above, the necessary computations are summarized in Table 11.16.

TABLE 11.16 Data Computation of Time Trend

Year	t	Sales	tY	t^2
1990	−7	5	−35	49
1991	−6	7	−42	36
1992	−5	9	−45	25
1993	−4	12	−48	16
1994	−3	11	−33	9
1995	−2	10	−20	4
1996	−1	8	−8	1
1997	0	12	0	0
1998	1	13	13	1
1999	2	17	34	4
2000	3	19	57	9
2001	4	14	56	16
2002	5	13	65	25
2003	6	12	72	36
2004	7	15	105	49
Total	**0**	**177**	**171**	**280**

Now, recall that the normal equations are:

$$Y = na + bt$$
$$tY = at + t^2$$

Substituting the respective values from the values given in the table, we get

$$177 = 15a + b0$$
$$171 = a0 + b280$$

or

$$15a = 177 \quad \text{or} \quad a = 11.8$$
$$280b = 171 \quad \text{or} \quad b = 0.61$$

So the trend line is $Y = 1.8 + 0.61t$. Remember that t is the codified time value with 197 as the origin.

The method of least squares enables us to forecast future values for Y. This is done by substituting the t value in the equation $(Y = na + bt)$.

In the illustration given earlier, the sales books (in hundred units) for 2006 will be 17.29, i.e.

$$Y = 11.8 + 0.619 = 17.29$$

In place of t, 9 is substituted since, starting with 1997, the year of origin, 2006 will be nine years. The predicted sales of books (in 100 units) for 2006 will be 17.29.

As you know, nonlinear trends can also be fitted to the observed data. Hence, predictions can also be made on them. In the analysis of trend line, we make the implicit assumption that the past behaviour continues to persist in a future period also. So, a change in the past behaviour would make prediction unreliable.

Measurement of Other Components

Seasonal variation and cyclical fluctuations are periodic and recurring movements in the data. It has been stated above that the seasonal variation is short term by nature and usually the periodicity is less than a year. In contrast to this, the cyclical fluctuation lasts longer than a year.

Just as there are several methods of measuring the seasonal variations, viz., ratio to trend method, ratio to moving averages method and link relative method, the cyclical fluctuations can be measured by harmonic analysis, spectrum analysis, etc. These methods involve tedious calculations and hence are not discussed here. If you are interested in these methods, you may refer to the books given under "Further Reading". However, attempts to separate the time series of its four components–seasonal, trend, cyclical and erratic, may follow some simple procedure. This is briefly spelt out in the following:

1. The seasonal component described above can be estimated with the help of moving average. This component can be eliminated from the original observations through subtraction if we assume an additive model.
2. The trend of the seasonally adjusted data is then estimated by means of least square straight line or some other function fitted by least squares described above. The trend component can be eliminated from the seasonally adjusted data.
3. The residuals, which remain after the elimination of seasonal and trend components from the original time series can be recorded and plotted graphically. This residual variation may be compared visually or through some other method. The remaining variations of the data series are attributed to cyclical and erratic components.

SUMMARY

In this Chapter, we have discussed various statistical techniques for analyzing data. Often, it is necessary to provide a summary figure for a set or series of data.

Such figure could be a measure of central tendency such as mean, median and mode, or it could be a measure of dispersion such as variance, standard deviation and coefficient of variation.

There are cases where more than one characteristic of a sampling unit is measured. In such type of data, we can find out the correlation coefficient or we can fit a regression equation. Remember that correlation does not show a cause and effect relationship between variables. It only shows the strength of relationship. In regression analysis variables are divided into two categories: independent and dependent. Regression equation can be a straight line or a curve depending upon the type of equation fitted.

Often, we have data at certain intervals for a sufficiently long period of time. Such data are called time series and contains certain components, viz., secular trend, cyclical variation, seasonal variation and irregular movements.

DISCUSSION QUESTIONS

1. Calculate the mode for the data set given in Example 11.2. The steps involved are:

(a) Identify the modal class. This is the class interval with highest frequency. In this case, the modal class is 300–400.

(b) Calculate l_m, f_m and h.

(c) Apply formula (11.3) and find the modes.

$$M_o = \frac{l_m + h(f_m - f_1)}{2f_m - f_1 - f_2}$$

$$= 352.63$$

Note that mean, median and mode assume different values for the same data. In the case of data relating to monthly expenditure on purchase of books given in Example 11.2, we find that mean, median and mode are ₹386, ₹371.43 and ₹352.63, respectively.

2. Find out the standard deviation of the following data.

Marks in statistics	*No. of students*
0–20	5
20–40	10
40–60	15
60–80	8
80–100	2

3. Table 11.17 shows the marks obtained by 10 students in Statistics and Mathematics. Find out the correlation coefficient.

TABLE 11.17 Marks Obtained by Students in Statistics and Mathematics

Students	Marks Obtained in	
	Statistics	Mathematics
1	52	48
2	60	40
3	45	38
4	38	28
5	35	42
6	62	65
7	68	53
8	28	25
9	50	28
10	62	33

4. Write the formulae for the following concepts:

(a) Standard Deviation

(b) Variance

(c) Product moment correlation coefficient

(d) Rank correlation

(e) Given below is the data on *X* and *Y*:

X:	15	17	20	22	25	33
Y:	25	22	30	31	37	35

Find out:

(i) the regression line *Y* on *X*.

(ii) the regression line *X* on *Y*.

(iii) the coefficient of determination.

(iv) Pearson's product moment correlation.

FURTHER READING

Rao, I. K. R. (1983). *Quantitative Methods for Library and Information Science*. New Delhi: Wiley Eastern.

Sanders, D. H. (1980). *Statistics*: A fresh approach, New Delhi: Tata McGraw-Hill.

12 Statistical Packages

CHAPTER OUTLINE

- Statistical Problem Areas
- Features of Some Statistical Packages
- Other Software's for Statistical Analysis
- Discussion Questions

LEARNING OBJECTIVES

After going through this chapter, you will be able to:

- Define what is statistics.
- Describe the different data types and data formats.
- Illustrate the role of statistical methods.
- Describe the features of statistical packages like SPSS and MS-Excel.
- Portray some of the popular statistical packages.

INTRODUCTION

One of the features of the modern world is the development of human capacity to convert observations into numerical data. The science, which deals with collecting and analyzing of numerical data in large quantities, especially for the purpose of inferring properties in a whole from those in a representative sample, is called **Statistics**. (The Concise Oxford Dictionary). It assembles data and organizes them in a meaningful way so that information is generated. This information builds up knowledge and thus development goes on. Advances in computing have come handy in this as they help in doing this part of the job accurately, timely, effectively and convincingly.

Computer can help immensely in statistical analysis. There exist numerous statistical tools, and the need is to identify their actual usage. Even with the use of a statistical package, many statistical procedures require a lot of prior knowledge and insight.

In this chapter, we strive to buildup a case for the usage of statistics by first defining statistics and what it can do to your data. We have also given the definition of the data types besides providing an explanation of the common tasks performed in a preliminary analysis. In this chapter we describe two popular packages—MS Excel and SPSS—and give a glimpse of some other statistical packages.

STATISTICAL PROBLEM AREAS

Before giving the definition of statistical packages, we shall revisit the definition of statistics and its functions. In this section, we highlight the problem areas that statistics as a discipline addresses, and the kind of data we get for statistical applications.

Statistical Techniques and Packages

We have already defind statistics in the introduction. There are also statistical techniques for analyzing numerical data. Statistical techniques have many purposes, which include methods and procedures for summarizing, simplifying, reducing, and presenting raw data. Statistics enables one to makes predictions, test hypotheses and infer characteristics of a population from the characteristics of a sample. In other words, Statistics is generally thought of as serving two functions. One function is to describe sets of data, and the other function is to help in drawing inferences. When you are studying only a sample, there is a possibility that your assumption may not be accurate and you can never be certain that you have drawn the correct inference. For this reason, the inferential use of statistics may be thought of as helping you to make decisions under conditions of uncertainty. It is different from guessing because Statistics also provides you with a method of estimating how reliable your conclusions are. With each statistical statement that you make, you indicate the probability that findings like the ones you have made could have been the result of chance factors.

A statistical package is the software for the collection, organization, interpretation, and presentation of numerical information. The need for a statistical package has arisen because of the complexity of calculations involved in making inferences from the data.

The advances in computing technologies have made statistics a very powerful field. According to Ripley (2004),

> The most widely used piece of statistical packages/software for statistics is Excel. SPSS and SAS dominate certain communities, and Minitab is widely used in teaching. Many niche products, e.g. GenStat, Generalised Linear Interactive Modelling (GLIM) package Stata and S-PLUS dominate the high-end, hence is widely seen in methodology papers.

Data Measurement

Statistical data are generally obtained in many formats such as spreadsheets (e.g., MS Excel) or databases (e.g., MS Access). Data may also be received in various open formats such as typically tab-delimited text (*.dat, *.tab, *.txt), comma-separated text or fixed-width text data (*.dat, *.txt).

The data may be of two types—**qualitative** and **quantitative**. Most of the statistical methods are based on quantitative data. Quantitative variable is a variable whose values are numbers with real numeric meaning. It consists of mainly two types of data, viz. **discrete** and **continuous**. A set of data is said to be **discrete** if the values/observations belonging to it are distinct and separate, i.e., they can be counted, e.g., the number of books in a library. On the other hand, a set of data is said to be *continuous* if the values/observations belonging to it may take on any value within a finite or infinite interval.

There are four well-known levels of measurement scales, viz., nominal, ordinal, interval, and ratio. There is a relationship between the level of measurement and the appropriateness of various statistical procedures. For example, it would be impractical to compute the mean of nominal measurements. Data must be measured on an interval or a ratio scale for the computation of means and other statistics to be valid. Therefore, if data are measured on an ordinal scale, the median but not the mean can serve as a measure of central tendency. Let us have a brief discussion of what these scales are.

1. Nominal scale: Nominal measurement consists of assigning items to groups or categories. No quantitative information is conveyed and no ordering of the items is implied. Nominal scales are therefore qualitative rather than quantitative. Religious preference, race, and sex are all examples of nominal scales. Frequency distributions are usually used to analyze data measured on a nominal scale. The main statistic computed is the *mode*. Variables measured on a nominal scale are often referred to as *categorical* or *qualitative variables*.

Nominal variables allow for only qualitative classification. That is, they can be measured only in terms of whether the individual items belong to some distinctively different categories, but we cannot quantify or even rank order those categories

2. Ordinal scale: Measurements with ordinal scales are ordered in the sense that higher numbers represent higher values. However, the intervals between the numbers are not necessarily equal.

Ordinal variables allow us to rank order the items we measure enables one to know which item has less and which item has more of the quality represented by the variable, but still they do not allow us to say "how much more."

3. Interval scale (Cardinal scale): On interval measurement scales, one unit on the scale represents the same magnitude on the trait or characteristic being measured across the whole range of the scale. However, interval scales do not have a true zero point and, therefore, it is not possible to make statements about how many times higher one score is than another. True interval measurement is somewhere between rare and nonexistent in the behavioural sciences. A good example of an interval scale is the Fahrenheit scale for temperature. Interval variables allow us not only to rank order the items that are measured, but also to quantify and compare the sizes of differences between them.

4. Ratio scale: Ratio scales are like interval scales except that they have true zero points. Ratio variables are very similar to interval variables. In addition to all the properties of interval variables, they feature an identifiable absolute zero point. Thus they allow for statements such as x is twice that of y. A typical example of ratio scales is measure of time or space.

Interval scales do not have the ratio property. Most statistical data analysis procedures do not distinguish between the interval and ratio properties of the measurement scales.

Functions of Statistics

Many people intend to use statistical techniques in their research. It is definitely a good practice to substantiate your claims with the help of data. Statistics has various functions, which can be broadly categorized as follows:

1. *Summarize and describe data:* We summarize and describe data in order to view the data at a glance. If it is nominal or ordinal data, we make cross-tabulations and graphs; if it is interval or ratio data, then we calculate z-scores.
2. *Variance and distribution of the data:* In order to measure the spread of the data and know its distributions, we make tables and charts and graphs for nominal/ordinal data and histograms with normal curve or box plots with inter-quartile range for interval/ratio data.

3. *Compare groups:* When we have to compare two or more populations, then we make cross-tabulations for nominal/ordinal data and employ testing of hypothesis for continuous/numeric data divided into groups.
4. *Identify relationships:* In order to identify relationships in the data, we use cross-tabulations for nominal/ordinal data; calculate correlation coefficient and scatter plot for interval/ratio data or go for linear regression/ANOVA for data with one dependent and two or more predictor variables.
5. *Identify groups of similar cases:* Carrying out hierarchical cluster analysis solves the problem of identifying groups of similar cases or k-means cluster analysis. We use discriminant analysis for identifying characteristics of known groups.
6. *Identify groups of similar variables:* Factor analysis is carried out to identify groups of similar variables.

Features of Some Statistical Packages

Advances in computing, especially the advent of the personal computer (PC) has made computing a game of the commoners. Today, you have the computing power to easily load software of your choice or need into your PC. A plethora of read-made computer packages are available today. Now you can find different statistical packages for applications to different disciplines. We now describe two such packages that are ready available and are popular and user friendly. We also give a glimpse of some other packages in the subsequent section.

Microsoft Excel

Microsoft Excel is a big worksheet (it can take data rows in thousands across 256 columns). This worksheet can be used for data entry and for performing calculations by pressing the keyboards. It has a paste function where you can paste any formula from a big list of in-built functions. MS Excel can be used to create tables and graphs and perform statistical calculations. The work done in MS Excel can be easily copied and pasted to many window-based programs for further analysis.

According to Pottel, "Spreadsheets are a useful and popular tool for processing and presenting data. In fact, Microsoft Excel spreadsheets have become somewhat of a standard for data storage, at least for smaller data sets. The fact that the program is often being packaged with new computers, which increases its easy availability, naturally encourages its use for statistical analysis. However, many statisticians find this unfortunate since Excel is clearly not a statistical package. There is no doubt about that, and Excel has never claimed to be one. But one should face the fact that due to its easy availability, many people, including professional statisticians, use Excel, even on a daily basis, for quick and easy statistical calculations. Therefore, it is important to know the flaws in Excel, which, unfortunately, still exist today! ..." "Excel is clearly not an adequate statistics package because many statistical methods are simply not available. This lack of functionality makes it difficult to use it for more than computing summary statistics and simple linear regression and hypothesis testing". However, in MS Excel 2003, aspects of some statistical functions, including rounding off results and precision have been enhanced.

The MS Excel worksheet is a collection of cells. As already stated, there are 65,000 (rows) × 256 (columns) cells in an MS Excel worksheet. Each row or column can be used to enter data belonging to one category. Data entry in MS Excel is as simple as writing on a piece of paper. MS Excel assigns each column a field depending on the type of data. It supports various data formats; you can choose a data format by formatting the cells as shown in Figure 12.1.

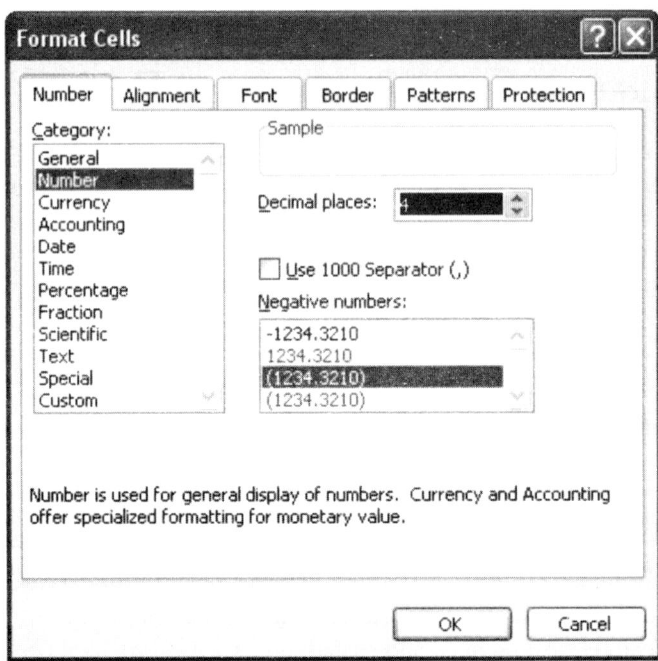

FIGURE 12.1 Screen snapshot of MS Excel for choosing data format.

Once the type of cells is defined, it is easy to enter the data without taking care of the format. MS Excel can perform usual calculations on the data so entered. It has an insert.

The function (f_x) icon contains many in-built functions like sum, count, max/min, standard deviation, etc. In fact, it has a plethora of built-in functions that perform special calculations without even typing the formula. To do a calculation, you have to select a function and specify the range of values on which it has to be applied. These functions are known as **paste functions**.

Insert Function

Search for a function:

Type a brief description of what you want to do and then click Go

Go

Or select a category: Statistical

Select a function:

TINV
TREND
TRIMMEAN
TTEST
VAR
VARA
VARP

TTEST(array1,array2,tails,type)

Returns the probability associated with a Student's t-Test.

Help on this function

OK Cancel

FIGURE 12.2 Screen snapshot of function menu options in MS Excel.

In this chapter, we will concentrate on the statistical functions and see some of the major statistical functions of MS Excel. As can be seen from Figure 12.2, once you go to the function menu and choose "statistical" category, you will be asked to select a function. Suppose you have chosen "T-test". You will be told on the same screen that t-test returns the probability associated with a student's T-test. Now if you are still not comfortable with the description, you may take help on this function, which is at the bottom left of the screen. More help is offered in the following form.

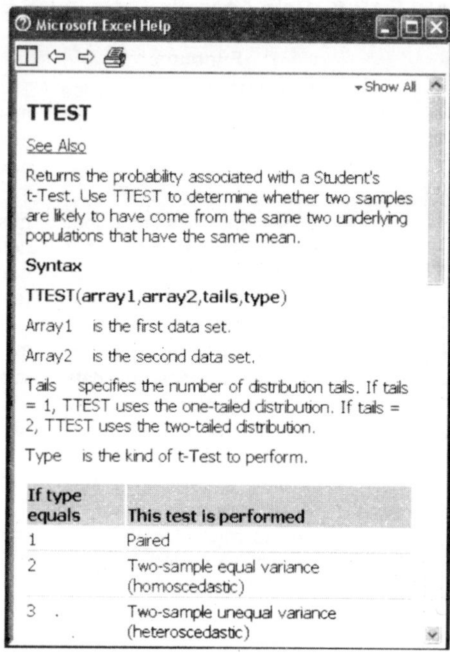

Microsoft Excel Help

Show All

TTEST

See Also

Returns the probability associated with a Student's t-Test. Use TTEST to determine whether two samples are likely to have come from the same two underlying populations that have the same mean.

Syntax

TTEST(**array1**,**array2**,**tails**,**type**)

Array1 is the first data set.

Array2 is the second data set.

Tails specifies the number of distribution tails. If tails = 1, TTEST uses the one-tailed distribution. If tails = 2, TTEST uses the two-tailed distribution.

Type is the kind of t-Test to perform.

If type equals	This test is performed
1	Paired
2	Two-sample equal variance (homoscedastic)
3	Two-sample unequal variance (heteroscedastic)

FIGURE 12.3 Screen snapshot of help for T-test in MS Excel.

MS Excel has a built-in statistical package to enable you to get further details on data analysis. It provides a set of data analysis tools called the **Analysis Tool Pak**, which you can use to save steps when you develop complex statistical analyses. You provide the data and parameters for each analysis; the tool uses the appropriate statistical macro functions and then displays the results in an output table. Some tools generate charts in addition to output tables.

To access these tools, click Data Analysis on the Tools menu.

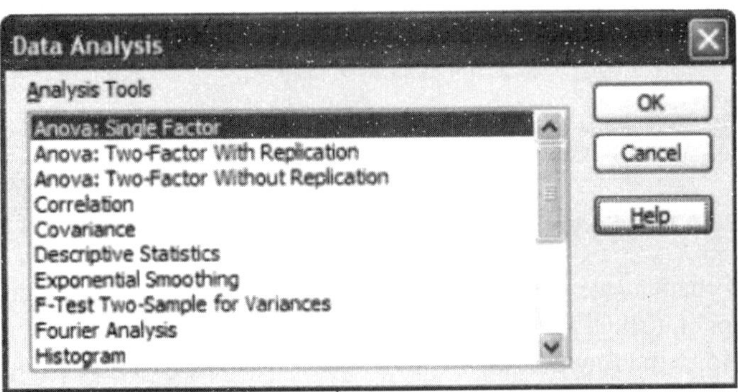

FIGURE 12.4 Screen snapshot of Data Analysis Function in MS Excel.

We now give a brief description of these tools. Table 12.1 highlights their functions and uses.

TABLE 12.1 Data Analysis Tools in MS Excel*

S.No	Tool	Function	Use
1	ANOVA	The ANOVA tools provide different types of variance analysis.	To test of the hypothesis that each sample is drawn from the same underlying probability distribution.
2	Correlation covariance	Calculate the correlation coefficient/Covariance between two variables when measurements on each variable are observed for each of *N* subjects.	To examine each pair of measurement variables to determine whether the two measurement variables tend to move together.
3	Descriptive statistics	Generates a report of univariate statistics for data, providing information about the central tendency and variability of your data.	To describe the data in an interpretable format and show summary statistics like mean, mode, median, SD, skewness, kurtosis, range, etc.
4	Exponential smoothing	Predicts a value based on the forecast for the prior period, adjusted for the error in that prior forecast.	To forecast on the basis of a smoothing constant.
5	F-test	Performs a two-sample F-test to compare two population variances.	To test that these two samples come from distributions with equal variances.

(*Contd.*)

TABLE 12.1 Data Analysis Tools in MS Excel* (*Contd.*)

S.No	Tool	Function	Use
6	Moving average	Projects values in the forecast period, based on the value of the average variable over a specific number of preceding periods.	To forecast trends on the basis of past figures.
7	Regression analysis	Performs linear regression analysis by using the "least squares" method to fit a line through a set of observations.	To analyze how a single dependent variable is affected by the values of one or more independent variables.
8	Sampling analysis	Creates a sample from a population by treating the input range as a population.	To infer about a population on the basis of a sample.
9	t-test, z-test	Determines whether the two z-test samples are likely to have come from distributions with equal population means.	To compare two population means when the population variances are known and unknown.

*Based on the Microsoft Office Excel 2003 help function.

You have seen that MS Excel can do virtually most of the common statistical calculations.

There are two more features that are worth mentioning when we talk about the statistical functions of MS Excel. These two are cross tabulations, pivot tables and graphical features.

MS Excel can be used to create cross tabulations or two-way frequency tables across categorical variables. In MS Excel there is a pivot table wizard which helps in creating tables in multidimensions. Let us explain these concepts with the help of an example. The data given in Table 12.2 is the percentage contribution of a country to world research in a particular subject area.

TABLE 12.2 Percentage Contribution of a Country to World Research in a Particular Area

Country	Chemistry	Engineering	Clinical medicine	Physics	Materials science	Biological sciences
Argentina	0.57	0.26	0.31	0.56	0.36	0.92
Australia	1.56	2.18	2.51	1.36	1.69	4.56
France	6.17	4.9	5.7	7.08	5.81	5.16
Germany	9.38	6.56	8.12	9.89	9.07	6.6
Hungry	0.83	0.44	0.25	0.54	0.41	0.61
India	4.02	2.68	0.85	2.51	4.02	3.49
Ireland	0.22	0.27	0.36	0.21	0.27	0.37
Israel	0.79	1.06	1.26	1.37	0.71	1.11
Italy	3.62	4.02	4.4	4.42	2.48	2.33
Japan	11.33	9.75	8.21	11.14	13.77	6.98

Now suppose you want to make a pivot table that would enable you to visualize a country whose contributions differ in the disciplines of Physics and Chemistry. You can simply show the subjects into rows and columns. This would enable you to see that, say, the shaded countries, Hungary and India, have significantly different contributions as shown in Table 12.3.

TABLE 12.3 Pivot Table

Count of countries	**Chemistry**										**Grand total**
Physics	0.22	0.57	0.79	0.83	1.56	3.62	4.02	6.17	9.38	11.33	1
0.21	1										1
0.54				[illegible]							1
0.56		1									1
1.36					1						1
1.37			1								1
2.51							[illegible]				1
4.42						1					1
7.08								1			1
9.89									1		1
11.14										1	1
Grand total	**1**	**1**	**1**	**1**	**1**	**1**	**1**	**1**	**1**	**1**	**10**

There could be many more such cross-tabulations depending on the need of the researcher. The most pleasant part of working with MS Excel is the ease with which you can drag these fields and have a customized layout as per your wish. It is said that in MS Excel, the most demanding work is to *input the data*, the analysis being the easiest. You can use pivot table effectively to present data where two-dimensional tables are important.

One of the major advantages of this feature is that once the table is prepared, you can change the summary from one characteristic to another.

Similarly, if you want to make a graphical presentation of the data, then you can go to the chart wizard and choose the chart that you want to make. MS Excel has a built-in facility to create graphs and charts. There are several types of charts and graphs supported by MS Excel such as bar charts, line charts, pie charts, and scatter diagrams. The chart wizard menu can be summoned by clicking on the graph icon from the menu bar. The chart wizard looks like the following as shown in Figure 12.5.

So you have seen that it is pretty simple to create a graph and visualize your data once you have some data in your worksheet. These graphs are very useful for common user requirements. You can cut, copy and paste these graphs to any document of MS Word or PowerPoint as shown in Figure 12.6.

FIGURE 12.5 Screen snapshot of chart wizard in MS Excel.

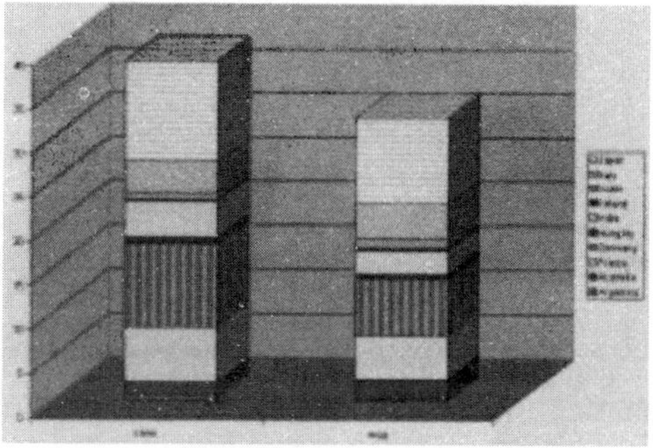

FIGURE 12.6 Screen snapshot of chart companies of the contribution of countries to Chemistry and Engineering.

SPSS

SPSS is the short form for Statistical Package for Social Sciences (SPSS). It is a very popular package due to its features and compatibility with other window-based programs. In the late 1960s, three Stanford University graduate students developed the SPSS statistical software system. SPSS can take data input from many packages like dBase (*.dbf), Excel (*.xls), Lotus 123 (*.w*), and others like *.dat and *.txt. It can filter the data and perform analysis only in selected cases.

Once you open a data file, you can go to the analyze menu and start working on the statistical aspects of the data. Figure 12.7 shows you the menu for the descriptive statistics. You can find the frequencies, cross-tabulations, ratios, etc. You can see that there is a long list of statistical analyses in the analyze menu. We will give you a glimpse of what these functions do.

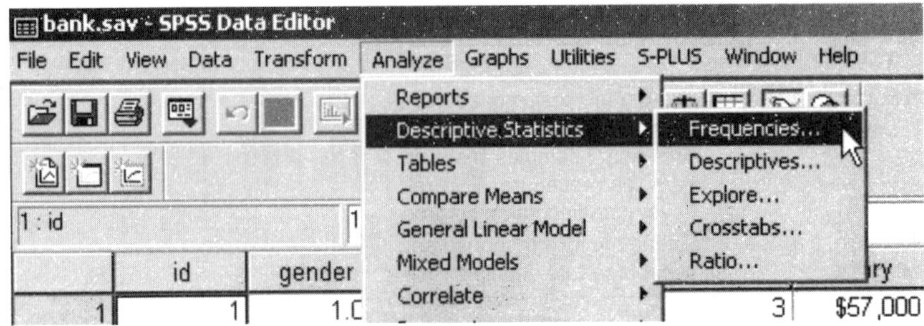

FIGURE 12.7 Screen snapshot of SPSS data editor.

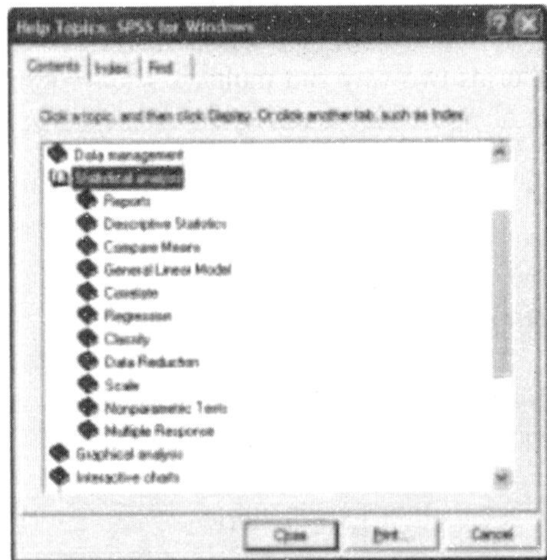

FIGURE 12.8 Screen snapshot of help topics in SPSS.

TABLE 12.4 Functions of Statistical Analysis in SPSS

Tool/ Module	Statistical procedure
Report	OLAP (Online Analytical Processing) cubes, Summarizes procedure, reports summaries in rows, reports summaries in columns.
Descriptive Statistics	Frequencies procedure, Descriptive procedure, Explore procedure, Cross-tabs procedure, Ratio statistics procedure.
Compare means	Means procedure, One-Sample T-Test procedure, Independent-Samples T-Test procedure, Paired-Samples T-Test procedure, One-Way ANOVA procedure.
General Linear Model	GLM univariate procedure
Correlate	Bivariate correlations procedure, Partial correlations procedure, Calculates statistics measuring either similarities or dissimilarities (distances).
Regression	Linear regression procedure, Curve estimation procedure.
Classify	K-Means cluster analysis procedure, Hierarchical cluster analysis procedure, Discriminant analysis procedure.
Data reduction	Factor analysis procedure
Scale	Reliability analysis procedure, Multidimensional scaling procedure.

(*Contd.*)

TABLE 12.4 Functions of Statistical Analysis in SPSS (*Contd.*)

Tool/ Module	Statistical procedure
Non parametric tests	Chi-Square test procedure, Binomial test procedure, Runs test procedure, One-Sample Kolmogorov-Smirnov test procedure, Two-independent-samples tests procedure, Tests for several independent samples procedure, Two related samples tests procedure, Tests for several related samples procedure.
Multiple Response	Define multiple response sets procedure, Multiple response frequencies procedure, Multiple response cross-tabs procedure.

Source: SPSS for Windows Release 11.0 Help

We can see that many of these tools are available in MS Excel also, but the difference is that the output given by SPSS contains many more details on the statistical aspects of the findings as mentioned in Table 12.4. For example, the cross-tabs procedure forms two-way and multi-way tables, in both MS Excel and SPSS, but in SPSS, it also provides a variety of tests and measures of association for two-way tables. The supporting statistics provided in SPSS is Pearson chi-square, likelihood-ratio chi-square, linear-by-linear association test, Fisher's exact test, Yates' corrected chi-square, Pearson's r, Spearman's rho, contingency coefficient, phi, Cramér's V, symmetric and asymmetric lambdas, Goodman and Kruskal's tau, uncertainty coefficient, gamma, Somers' d, Kendall's tau-b, Kendall's tau-c, eta coefficient, Cohen's kappa, relative risk estimate, odds ratio, McNemar test, and Cochran's and Mantel-Haenszel statistics. SPSS is thus more comprehensive.

SPSS also supports several statistical graphs. It displays many statistics on the graph itself. It has a feature that helps you to find a chart that is most suitable for your data, which is called "Chart Galleries by Data Structure" as shown in Figure 12.9.

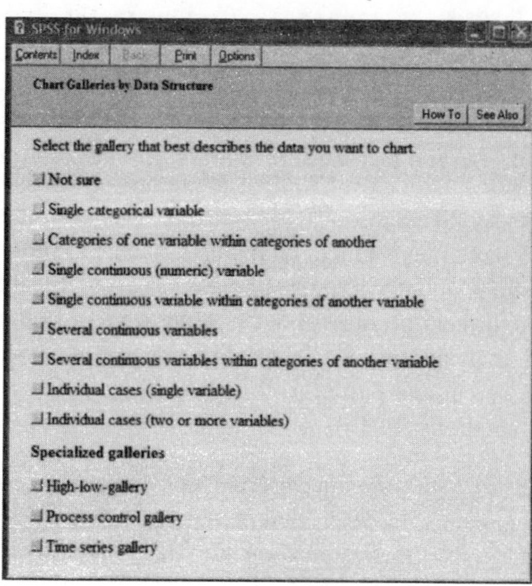

FIGURE 12.9 Screen snapshot of chart galleries by data structure in SPSS.

Now suppose you have chosen a single categorical variable as the gallery that best describes your data. Then the next screen that will appear would be like the one in Figure 12.10. Suppose, here you choose Simple Pareto Counts or Sums for Groups of Cases. Then SPSS will describe what this graph does like, "Creates a bar chart summarizing categories of a single variable, sorted in descending order. A line shows the cumulative sum".

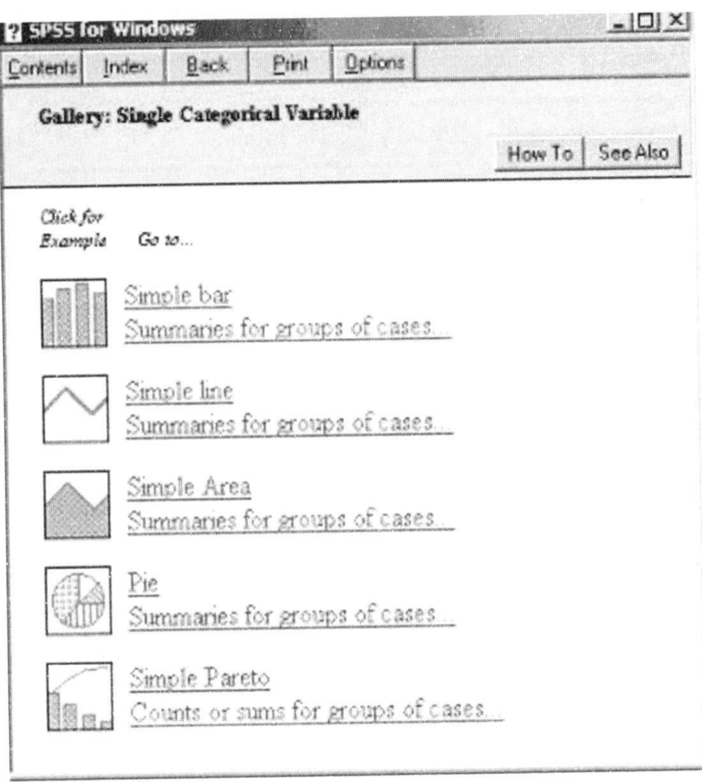

FIGURE 12.10 Screen snapshot of Gallery: Single categorical variable.

Thus, in this way, SPSS also acts as a mentor. Probably, this is the reason for its success. SPSS has a menu called "Statistics Coach", as shown in Figure 12.11 which asks questions about your data like "What do you want to do with your data?" It asks you further questions about your data in four steps and then suggests the right kind of analysis for your dataset. The output of SPSS appears as pivot table, which can be cut and pasted to Word documents, Excel worksheets, and PowerPoint Presentations (PPTs).

According to Wegman and Solka (2005), SPSS supports numerous add-on modules including one for regression, advanced models, classification trees, table creation, exact tests, categorical analysis, trend analysis, conjoint analysis, missing value analysis, map-based analysis, and complex samples analysis.

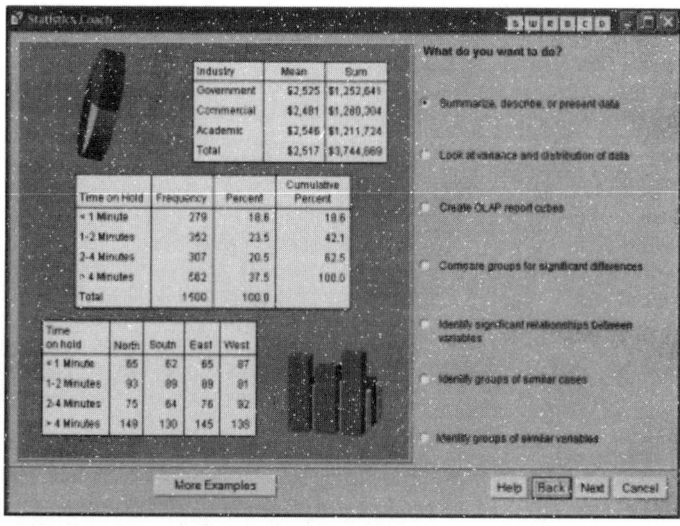

FIGURE 12.11 Screen snapshot of Gallery: Single categorical variable.

OTHER SOFTWARES FOR STATISTICAL ANALYSIS

Modern statistics can perform very large and complex calculations with the help of computers. There are a lot of softwares available in the market. Many of them are shareware, freeware, and online pages that perform statistical calculations. Many of the universities offer statistics online computational resources, e.g. http://www.socr .ucla.edu/ (University of California at LA), Statlib: Data, Software and News from the Statistics Community http://lib.stat.cmu.edu/ (Carnegie Mellon University), and free statistical tools on the web http://www. cbs.nl/isi/ (International Statistical Institute). The list is endless.

We therefore restrict ourselves by giving a brief introduction to some of the popular statistical softwares (Table 12.5).

TABLE 12.5 Brief Description of Some Statistical Softwares

S. No	Its URL	Software and brief description
1	The SAS System http://www.sas.com/	SAS evolved in the late 1960s at North Carolina State University. It has now become a system for complete data management and analysis. As far as statistical software companies are concerned, SAS is similar to Microsoft. The SAS website claims that its software resides at 40,000 sites worldwide including 90 per cent of those companies on the Fortune 500 list. SAS has given due importance to recent "statistical-like" advances like data mining. It has integrated mathematical/statistical methodologies, database technology, and business applications in an effective manner to remain at the top of the commercial statistical software arena.

(Contd.)

TABLE 12.5 Brief Description of Some Statistical Softwares (*Contd.*)

S. No	Its URL	Software and brief description
2	BMDP http://www.statsol.ie/ bmdp/ bmdp.htm	BMDP originated during the 1960s as a biomedical analysis package. It still remains a clear favourite of biomedical field. BMDP has aligned itself with a number of other currently popular statistical products including StatXact 5.0, LogXact 5.0, SOLAS, EquivTest, SigmaPlot, Meta Analysis, and SYSTAT.
3	S-PLUS http://www. insightful.com/	S-Plus is based on statistical analysis language. It provides the user with a fully extensible environment by supporting the user to develop their own functions using the S-PLUS language. S-PLUS contains over 4,200 data analysis functions, which implement modern and robust statistical procedures. It has superb graphical capabilities. It receives strong support from the academic and commercial sectors.
4	MINITAB http://www.minitab.com/	MINITAB combines an array of statistical methods, graphics tools, and project organization features in a user-friendly package. It combines the user-friendliness of MS Excel with the ability to perform complex statistical analysis. Thousands of successful companies worldwide, including GE, 3M, Ford Motor Company, and the leading Six Sigma consultants use MINITAB to make data-driven decisions and achieve world-class quality.
5	GLIM (Generalized Linear Interactive Modelling package) http://www.nag.co.uk/stats/ GDGE_soft.asp	GLIM is a flexible, interactive statistical analysis program developed by the Royal Statistical Society. GLIM is not just a modelling package; it also contains many of the standard statistical procedures and has high-resolution graphics. Professionals, scientists and statisticians worldwide respect GLIM.

Source: Wegman and Solka (2005) and websites of the softwares.

Thus, we have seen that there are many statistical packages that provide the state of the art facilities for performing statistical calculations. All these softwares are extremely handy and it is for the user to work on the one on which he feels most comfortable. There is competition among these softwares for providing enhanced statistical functions, enhanced user-friendliness, better graphics, and sound technical support. Also, there is a trend to move towards "statistics-like" disciplines, e.g. data mining.

SUMMARY

One of the features of the modern world is the development of human capacity to convert observations into numerical data. The science, which deals with collecting and analyzing of numerical data in large quantities, especially for the purpose of inferring properties in a whole from those in a representative sample, is called **Statistics**. (The Concise Oxford Dictionary). Computer can help immensely in statistical analysis. There exist numerous statistical tools and the need is to identify their actual usage. Most of the statistical methods are based on quantitative data. You can find different statistical packages for applications in different disciplines.

In this chapter, we have described two such packages—MS Excel and SPSS. We have also, discussed some of their applications in detail. Besides we have given a brief introduction to some of the popular statistical softwares. This chapter was intended to make you familiar with the basic statistical functions that can be performed with the help of computer and to arouse your interest in the beautiful and huge world of statistical computing.

DISCUSSION QUESTIONS

1. Define a statistical package; describe its need and purpose.
2. Enumerate the data analysis tools in MS-Excel.
3. Enumerate the statistical analysis provisions in SPSS.

FURTHER READING

Box, George E.P., William G. Hunter, and J. Stuart Hunter (1978): *Statistics for Experimenters*: An introduction to design, data analysis, and model building, New York: Wiley.

Johnson R.A., Wichern D.W. (2003): *Business Statistics*: *Decision making with data*, Singapore: Wiley (Asia).

Levin, David M., Stephan, David, Krebhiel, Timothy, C., and Berenson, Mark, L. (2011): *Statistics for Management*: Using Microsoft Excel, 5th ed., New Delhi: PHI Learning.

Microsoft Office Excel 2003. Help Documentation.

Pottel, Hans (2005): *Statistical Flaws in Excel*. Innogenetics NV, Technologiepark 6, 9052 Zwijnaarde, Belgium, http://www.mis.coventry.ac.uk/~nhunt/pottel.pdf. Downloaded 08/11/05.

Ripley, Brian D. (2004): *Statistical Methods Need Software*, Netherlands Statistical Society, 27 April 2004. http://www.stats.ox.ac.uk/pub/bdr/NethStatSoc.pdf Downloaded 08/11/05.

Sarma K.V.S. (2001): Statistics Made Simple—Do it yourself on PC: New Delhi: Prentice-Hall of India.

SPSS for Windows Release 11.0. Help Documentation.

Wegman, Edward J. and Solka Jeffrey L. (2005): Statistical Software for Today and Tomorrow. Fairfax, Virginia: Center for Computational Statistics, George Mason University, 22030. Downloaded 16/11/05 http://www.galaxy.gmu.edu/papers/guide.pdf.

13 Report Writing

Chapter Outline

- Purpose of a Report
- Meaning
- Types of Reports
- Stages in the Preparation of a Report
- Characteristics of a Good Report
- Structure of Research Report
- Check List for the Report
- Discussion Questions

Learning Objectives

After going through this chapter, you will be able to:

- Define a report,
- Explain the need for presenting or writing a report.
- Discuss the subject matter of various types of reports.
- Identify the stages in preparation of a report.
- Explain the characteristics of a good report.
- Describe the different parts of a report.
- Distinguish between a good and a bad report.

INTRODUCTION

The last and final phase of the journey in research is **writing of the report**. After the collected data has been analyzed and interpreted and generalizations have been drawn, the report has to be prepared. The task of the researcher is incomplete till the report is presented. Writing of a report is the last step in a research study and requires a set of skills somewhat different from those called for in respect of the earlier stages of research. This task should be accomplished by the researcher with utmost care.

PURPOSE OF A REPORT

The report may be meant for the people in general, when the investigation has not been carried out at the instance of any third party. Research is essentially a cooperative venture and it is essential that every investigator should know what others have found about the phenomena under study. The purpose of a report is thus the dissemination of knowledge, the spread of generalizations so as to ensure their widest use.

A research report has only one function: **it must inform**. It has to propagate knowledge. Thus, the purpose of a report is to convey to the interested persons the results and findings of the study in sufficient detail, which is so arranged as to enable each reader to comprehend the data, and to determine for himself the validity of conclusions. Research results must invariably enter the general store of knowledge. A research report is always an addition to knowledge. All this explains the significance of writing a report.

In a broader sense, report writing is common to both academics and organizations. However, the purpose may be different. In academics, reports are used for comprehensive and application-oriented learning, whereas in organizations, reports form the basis for decision making.

MEANING

Presenting/Writing reports simply means communicating or informing through reports. The researcher has collected some facts and figures, analyzed the same and arrived at certain conclusions. He has to inform or report the same to the parties interested. Therefore, "reporting is communicating the facts, data and information through reports to the persons for whom such facts and data are collected and compiled".

A report is not a complete description of what has been done during the period of survey/research. It is only a statement of the most significant facts that are necessary for understanding the conclusions drawn by the investigator. Thus, "a report by definition is simply an account"—an account describing the procedure adopted, the findings arrived at, and the conclusions drawn by the investigator of a problem.

Types of Reports

Broadly speaking reports can be classified as follows:

(i) **Oral** or **verbal report:** Verbal report are given in person, for example, presenting the findings in a conference or seminar or reporting orally to the superiors.

(ii) **Written report:** Written reports are more formal, authentic and popular. Written reports can be presented in different ways as follows:

- Textual form reports : Communicating through written text
- Tabular reports : Communicating through tables or exhibits
- Graphic reports : Communicating through graphs and diagrams
- Combined reports : Communicating using all the three of the above. Generally, this is the most popular.

Research reports vary greatly in length and type. In each individual case, both the length and the form are largely dictated by the purpose of the study and problems at hand. For example, business organizations generally prefer reports in letter form, preferably brief letters. Banks, insurance and other financial institutions generally prefer tables and diagrams to illustrate the report. The reports prepared by government bureaux, enquiry commissions, etc., give comprehensive reports on the issues involved. Similarly, research theses/ dissertations usually prepared by students for PG courses and Ph.D. degrees are also elaborate and methodical.

It is, thus, clear that the results of a research enquiry can be presented in a number of ways. They may be termed as a technical report, a popular report, an article, or a monograph.

1. Technical report: A technical report is used whenever a full written report (e.g. Ph.D. thesis) of the study is required, either for evaluation or for record keeping or for public dissemination. The main emphasis in a technical report is on:

- The methodology employed
- The objectives of the study
- Assumptions made/hypotheses formulated in the course of the study
- How and from what sources the data are collected and how the data have been analyzed
- Detailed presentation of the findings with evidence, and their limitations.

2. Popular report: A popular report is one that gives emphasis on simplicity and attractiveness. Its aim is to make the general public understand the findings and implications. Generally, it is simple. Simplicity is sought to be achieved through clear language and minimization of technical details. Attention of the readers is sought to be achieved through attractive layout, liberal use of graphs, charts, diagrams and pictures. In a popular report, emphasis is given on practical aspects and policy implications.

3. Research article: Sometimes, the findings of a research study can be published in the form of a short paper called an *article*. This is one form of dissemination of knowledge. The research papers are generally prepared either to present in seminars and conferences or to publish in research journals. Since one of the objectives of doing research is to make a positive contribution to knowledge in the field, publication (publicity) of the work serves the purpose.

4. Monograph: A monograph is a treatise or a long essay on a single subject. For the sake of convenience, reports may also be classified either on the basis of approach or on the basis of the nature of presentation such as:

- Journalistic report
- Business report
- Project report
- Dissertation
- Enquiry report (Commission report)
- Thesis

Reports prepared by journalists for publication in the media may be **journalistic reports**. These reports have news and information value.

A **business report** may be defined as report for business communication from one departmental head to another, one functional area to another, or even from top to bottom in the organizational structure on any specific aspect of business activity. These are observational reports which facilitate business decisions.

A **project report** is the report on a project undertaken by an individual or a group of individuals relating to any functional area or any segment of a functional area or any aspect of business, industry or society.

A **dissertation**, on the other hand, is a detailed discourse or report on the subject of study. Dissertations are generally used as documents to be submitted for acquisition of higher research degrees from a university or an academic institution. The thesis is an example in point.

An **enquiry report** or a commission of enquiry report is a detailed report prepared by a commission appointed by the government for the specific purpose of conducting a detailed study of any matter of dispute on a major incitant/accident or of a subject requiring greater insight. These reports facilitate action since they contain expert opinions and recommendations.

Stages in the Preparation of a Report

Research reports are the product of slow and painstaking and accurate work. Therefore, the preparation of the report may be viewed in the following major stages:

1. Logical understanding and analysis of the subject matter.
2. Planning/Designing the final outline of the report
3. Write up/Preparation of rough draft
4. Polishing/Finalization of the report.

Logical understanding of the subject matter: It is the first stage which is primarily concerned with the development of a subject. There are two ways to develop a subject: (i) logically, and (ii) chronologically. The logical development is done on the basis of mental connections and associations between one aspect and another by means of logical analysis. Logical treatment often consists of developing material from the simple to the most complex. Chronological development is based on a connection or sequence in time or happening of events. The directions for doing something usually follow the chronological order.

Designing the final outline of the report: It is the second stage in writing the report. Having understood the subject matter, the next stage is structuring the report and ordering the parts and sketching them. This stage can also be called as **planning and organization stage**. Ideas may pass through the author's mind. Unless he first makes his plan/sketch/design, he cannot achieve a harmonious sequence and will not even know where to begin and how to end. Better communication of research results is not only a matter of language but in tact it is much more of planning and organizing the report.

Preparation of the rough draft: The third stage is the writing/drafting of the report. This is the most crucial stage to the researcher, as he/she now sits to write down what he/she has done in his/her research study and what and how he/she wants to communicate the same. Here the clarity in communicating/reporting is influenced by some factors such as who the readers are, how technical the problem is, the researcher's hold over the facts and techniques, the researcher's command over language (his communication skills), the data and completeness of his notes and documentation, and the availability of analyzed results. Depending on the above factors, some authors may be able to write the report with one or two drafts. Some people who have less command over language, no clarity about the problem and subject matter may take more time for drafting the report and have to prepare more drafts (first draft, second draft, third draft, and fourth draft).

Finalization of the report: This is the last stage, perhaps the most difficult stage of all formal writing. It is easy to build the structure, but it takes more time for polishing and giving the finishing touch. Take, for example, the construction of a house. Up to roofing (structure) stage, the work is very quick but the final stages—fixing the doors and windows, roofing, sanitary and electricity work, painting, etc. take up considerable amount of time. The rough draft (whether it is second draft or the *n*th draft) has to be rewritten, and polished in terms of your specific requirements. The careful revision of the rough draft makes the difference between a mediocre and a good piece of writing.

While polishing and finalizing, you should check the report for its weaknesses in logical development of the subject and cohesion in presentation. You should also check the mechanics of writing — language, usage, grammar, spelling and punctuation.

Characteristics of a Good Report

Research report is a channel of communicating the research findings to the readers of the report. A good report is one that does this task efficiently and effectively. It should therefore have the following characteristics/qualities.

1. The report must be clear in informing the what, why, who, whom, when, where and how of the research study.
2. It should be neither too short nor too long. You should keep in mind the fact that it should be long enough to cover the subject matter but short enough to sustain the reader's interest.
3. The report should be written in an objective style and simple language; correctness, precision and clarity should be the watchwords of the scholar. Wordiness, 'beating about the bush', and pompous language are barriers to communication.
4. A good report must combine *clear thinking*, *logical organization* and *sound interpretation*.
5. It should not be dull. The report should be such as to sustain the reader's interest.
6. It must be **accurate**. Accuracy is one of the key requirements of a report. It should be **factual** with objective presentation. Exaggerations and superlatives should be avoided.
7. **Clarity** is another requirement of a report. It is achieved by using familiar words and unambiguous statements, explicitly defining new concepts and unusual terms.
8. **Coherence** is an essential part of clarity. There should be logical flow of ideas (i.e. continuity of thought), and sequence of sentences. Each sentence must be so linked with other sentences in such a way that one thought leads to another automatically.
9. **Readability** is an important requirement of good communication. Even a technical report should be easily understandable. Technicalities should be translated into language understandable by the readers.
10. A research report should be prepared according to the best composition practices. Ensure readability through proper paragraphing, short sentences, illustrations, examples, and section headings, use of charts, graphs and diagrams.
11. Draw sound inferences/conclusions from the statistical tables. But don't repeat the tables in text (verbal) form.
12. Footnote references should be in proper form. The Bibliography should be comprehensive and all the details should be given.
13. The report must be attractive in appearance, neat and clean—whether typed or printed.
14. The report should be free from of all types of errors, viz. language errors, factual errors, spelling errors, calculation errors, etc. The researcher should try to achieve these qualities in his report as far as possible.

Structure of Research Report

The structure of a report includes the format/outline/sketch of that report. A technical report has a number of clearly defined sections. The headings of the sections and their order may differ from one situation to another. The contents of a report can broadly be divided into three parts as:

1. The front matter or prefatory items.
2. The body or text of the report.
3. The end or back matter.

Figure 13.1 summarizes the broad sequence of the contents of a research report.

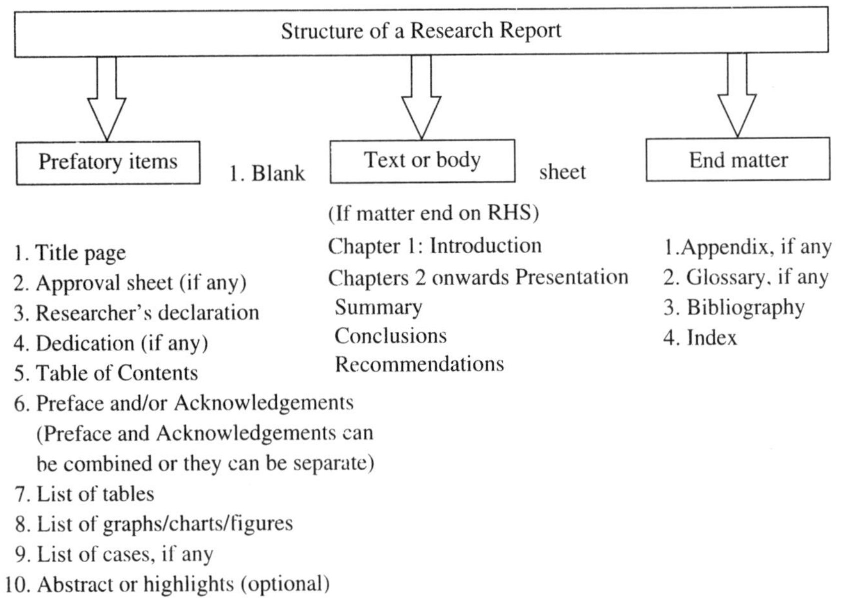

FIGURE 13.1 Structure of research report.

Let us discuss these items one by one in detail.

Prefatory Items

The front page matter or preliminary pages contain the following items:

1. **Title page:** The first page of the report is the title page. The title page should carry a concise and adequately descriptive title of the research study, the name of the author, the name of the institution to whom it is submitted, and the date of presentation.
2. **Approval sheet:** If a certificate of approval is required, either from the research supervisor or from the institution which provided the research facilities, it must be given.

3. **Researcher's declaration:** Generally, the researcher has to declare/certify that it is his/her bonafide and original work.
4. **Dedication:** If the author wants to dedicate the work to whomsoever he/she likes, he/she may do so.
5. **Table of Contents:** The Table of Contents (TOC) gives an outline of the contents of the report. It contains a list of the chapters and their titles with page numbers. It facilitates easy location of topics in the report. The chapter headings may be typed with capital letters.
6. **Preface or Acknowledgements or Both:** A Preface includes the background and reasons for the study. This is an appropriate place for the author to make acknowledgements also. The Acknowledgements can be made separately also especially if there are many people to be acknowledged. In the Acknowledgements, the researcher acknowledges the assistance and support received from individuals and organizations in conducting the research. These are intended to express his/her gratitude to them.
7. **List of tables:** The researcher must have collected lot of data and analyzed these and presented in the form of tables. These tables may be listed chapterwise and the list should be presented with page numbers for easy location and reference.
8. **List of Graphs/Charts/Figures:** If there are many graphs and charts, they should also be listed separately, with page numbers, after the list of tables.
9. **List of Cases/Exhibits:** If there are many cases/exhibits, they should also be listed.
10. **Abstract:** An abstract is a synopsis. It should be as brief as possible and should not be more than one or two pages. It is placed at the prefatory part of the report so that a reader can get a quick overview of the report. It contains a brief and precise statement of the purpose and a bare summary of the findings or the results of the study.

The Text/Body of the Report

After the preliminary items, the body of the report is presented. It is the major or main part of the report. It consists of the text divided into of the study. Normally, the body may be divided into three parts.

1. Introduction
2. Description and discussion of evidence and findings
3. Summary, conclusions and recommendations

Introduction: These are now briefly discussed. Generally, this is the first chapter in the body of the report. It is devoted to introducing the theoretical background of the problem and the methodology adopted for attacking the problem.

It may consist of the following aspects:

- Significance and justification of the topic
- Theoretical background of the topic
- Statement of the problem
- Review of literature
- Objectives of the study
- Hypotheses to be tested
- Definition of special terms, concepts and units of study
- Scope of the study (e.g. geographical scope, i.e. area/places to be covered, content, scope, i.e., aspects to be included/excluded)
- Period of study on the reference period.
- Sources of data, i.e., primary or secondary or both.
- Methods of data collection, i.e., the sample or the census.
- Sampling design.
- Data collection instruments.
- Field work.
- Data processing and analysis plan.
- Limitations of the study, if any.
- An overview of the report or the chapter plan.

Description and discussion of evidence: This is the major on the main part of the report. It is divided into several chapters depending on the number of objectives of the study, each being devoted to presenting the results pertaining to some aspect. The chapters should be well balanced, mutually related and arranged in logical sequence. The results should be reported as accurately and completely as possible explaining as to their bearing on the research questions and hypotheses. Each chapter should be given an appropriate heading. Depending on the need, a chapter may also be divided into sections. The text should be written in a clear and concise manner, the language being single but standard. Each chapter should end with a summary and lead to the next chapter with a smooth transition sentence.

In writing the text matter, the following aspects should be taken care of.

1. Headings
2. Quotations
3. Footnotes
4. Exhibits/Diagrams
5. Tables
6. Illustrations

1. Headings: The following types of headings are commonly used.

Main section heading (For convenience, we may call this 'A' level heading): This may be given at the centre or side. This should preferably be all capitals (though all capitals are somewhat out of style today) and bold.

Main subsection (B level): These heading may be capital and lower case (in printer's language upper/lower). First letter of every word to be capital except prepositions, conjunctions and articles. This should be preferably be on the side.

Sub-subsection (C level): Bold upper/lower (capital and small letter). Only the initial letter to be capital; all others small. This should be side heading.

D level: Upper Lower: Side heading, ordinary italics; only first letter to be cap. Text can continue with heading.

Note:

(a) There should not be more than four levels of heading (maximum) in a research paper.

(b) The reader may refer to this book or any book brought out by reputed publishers (national/international) to see how headings should be shown.

2. Quotations

Quotation marks: Whenever you want to quote something, especially a small quotation, put the quoted matter in double quotes (" ").

Nowadays, longer quotations are displayed, indented on both sides, and put in smaller point to distinguish the quoted matter from the usual text. In such a case, no quotation marks are used and the references to the source also is given, either with a superscript number or author's name (with year in brackets), which refer to the source of quotation.

The quotation within a quotaton is put in single quotes (' ').

Example: He said "To the selfish, 'freedom' is synonymous with licence". Single quotes are also used when you say something and you don't mean it. *Example:* Electrons 'jump'. Single quotes can also be used when you want to give a special meaning to a word.

Note: It is also an accepted style to use single quotes when you want to quote something.

When to use quotation marks: Quotation marks are used for the following:

1. A directly quoted passage or word
2. A word or phrase to be emphasized
3. Titles of articles, chapters, sectio 's of a book, reports, and unpublished works.

Please to note that all quotations should correspond exactly to the original in *wording, spelling, and punctuation.*

There are five ways of introducing a quotation:

(i) ***Introduction:*** He/she said, "The primary test of success in a negotiation is the presence of goodwill on both sides".

(ii) ***Interpolation:*** "The primary test of success in a negotiation", he/she said, "is the presence of goodwill on both sides".

(iii) ***End reference:*** "The primary test of success in a negotiation is the presence of goodwill on both sides", he/she said.

(iv) ***Indented paragraph:*** He/she said:

For the workers no real advance in their standard of living is possible without steady increase in productivity because any increase in wages generally, beyond certain narrow units, would otherwise be nullified by a rise in prices.

(v) ***Run on sentence:*** He/she recommended that "joint management councils be set up in all establishments in the public as well as private sector in which conditions favourable to the success of the scheme exist".

3. Footnotes

Types of footnotes: A footnote either indicates the source of the reference or provides an explanation which is not important enough to include in the text. In the traditional system, both kinds of footnotes are treated in the same form and are included either at the bottom of the page or at the end of the chapter or the book.

In the modern system, explanatory footnotes are put at the bottom of the page and are linked with the text with a footnote number. But source references are incorporated within the text and are supplemented by a bibliographical note at the end of the chapter or the book.

Rationale of footnotes: Footnotes help the readers to check the accuracy of the interpretation of the source by going to the source if they want to. They are also an acknowledgement of the author's indebtedness to the sources. They lend authority to the work and help the readers to distinguish between the author's own contribution and that of others.

Where to put the footnote: Footnotes appear at the bottom of the page or at the end of the chapter.

Numbering of footnotes:

1. For any editorial comment on the chapter or title, an asterisk is used.
2. In the text Arabic numerals are used for footnotes. Each new chapter may begin with number 1, or if the work is not too big, continuous numbering can be used for the whole work.
3. The number is typed half a space above the line or within parentheses. No space is given between the number and the word. No punctuation mark is used after the number.
4. The number is placed at the end of a sentence or, if necessary to clarify the meaning, at the end of the relevant word or phrase. Commonly, the number appears after the last quotation mark. In an indented paragraph, the number appears at the end of the last sentence in the quotation.

4. Exhibits: Exhibits are more common to management literature. Normally they are a mixture of data and diagrammatic representations.

5. Tables: Tables are the most common method of providing data in a convenient form to illustrate the text. Tables are normally set at the **centre** of the page. Each table is given a number, caption and if needed a subtitle.

Column headings: Every table will normally have several column headings which are put in bold or italic type.

Reference and interpretation: Before a table is introduced, it is referred to in the text (e.g., see Table 1.1; refer to Table 1.1; as in Table 1.1; Table 1.1 shows). A table is meant only to expand, clarify, or give visual explanation rather than stand by itself. The text should explain in detail what is contained in the table.

Number of tables: Arabic numerals, instead of Roman numerals or capital letters, are recommended for numbering the tables. Usually, technical monographs and books contain many tables. As the number increases, Roman numerals become more difficult to decipher for the reader. Roman numerals also occupy more space than Arabic numerals. If there are more than 26 tables, capital letters will not be sufficient to identify them.

Tables can be numbered chapterwise, sequentially e.g., 1.1, 1.2, 1.3,... (Chapter 1), 2.1, 2.2, 2.3, ... (Chapter 2), 5.1, 5.2, 5.3, ... (Chapter 5) 20.1, 20.2, 20.3, ... (Chapter 20), and so on. Here, the first number refers to the chapter and the second number to the table.

For the title and subtitle, capital and lower case bold letters may be used.

Abbreviations and symbols are not used in the title or subtitle unless essential.

Checklist: Relevance, accuracy, and clarity are of utmost importance in tables. When entering the table, check the following:

1. Have the explanation and reference to the table been given in the text?
2. Is it essential to have the table for clarity and extra information?
3. Is the representation of the data comprehensive and understandable?
4. Is the table number correct?
5. Are the title and subtitle clear and concise?
6. Are the column headings clearly classified?
7. Are the row captions clearly classified?
8. Are the data accurately entered and represented?
9. Are the totals and other computations correct?
10. Has the source been given?
11. Have all the uncommon abbreviations been spelt out?
12. Have all footnote entries been made?
13. If column rules are used (if necessary), have all rules been properly drawn?

6. Illustrations: Illustrations cover charts, graphs, diagrams, and maps. Most of the instructions given for tables hold good for illustrations.

Illustrations are of different types: figures, charts, maps, screen shots, etc. These should be numbered chapterwise and referred to in the text. The figure number, caption and sub-caption, if any, should be given at the bottom of the figure, screen shot, etc., as is the international style. In diagrams, the lines, curves, etc. should be clear and smooth. Similarly, boxes should be thick. If there are screen shots, they should be very clear.

However, for charts of big company structure, etc. the number and caption can be given at the top in capital and lower case bold as in the case of table. If there are components to a figure, they may be numbered A, B, C, etc. and given subcaptions. The subcaptions can be given either below each component or as continuation to the main captions to the figure.

End Matter

This section follows the text. First comes the Appendices section, then the References and Glossary. Each section is separated by a new page on which only the words APPENDICES, REFERENCES, or GLOSSARY all in capital letters appear. (The reverse of this page will be blank).

All reference section pages are numbered in Arabic numerals in continuation with the page numbers of the text.

Appendices

What goes into an Appendix: (a) Supplementary or secondary references are put in the Appendices section. But all primary reference material of immediate importance to the reader is incorporated in the text. The Appendices help the author to authenticate the thesis and help the reader to check the data.

(b) The material that is usually put in the Appendices is indicated below:

1. Original data
2. Long tables
3. Supportive legal decisions, laws and documents
4. Extensive computations
5. Questionnaires and letters
6. Schedules or forms used in collecting data
9. Transcripts of interviews

Numbering of Appendices: The Appendices can be serialized with capital letters (Appendix A, Appendix B) to differentiate from the chapter or table numbers.

References to Appendices: (a) In the text, the reader's attention is drawn to the Appendices as in the case of tables.

(b) All Appendices are listed in the table of contents.

Glossary: A glossary is a kind of short dictionary or a list of words giving definitions and explanations of the terms and phrases used in the work which are specific to the subject. The meanings of these terms may not be clear to the reader or foreign to the language in which the work is authored.

Glossery is listed in the Table of Contents

Positioning of Glossary: The glossery appears before the References

Order of listing: Items are listed in alphabetical order.

References: References essentially refer only to works cited in the text and which the author would have consulted. **Bibliography**, on the other hand, is a long list of books, articles and journals, reports or PhD theses which the author wants the reader to refer for greater understanding of the subject. The shorter Bibliography is normally called **Further Reading** or **Suggested Further Reading** or **Recommended Reading**. These are all normally given in text and reference books.

References given after the appendix section.

They are separated from the appendices by a new page (written "References"). References are also listed in the table of contents.

Positioning of References: The References come after the Appendices section. They are separated from the Appendices by a new page written REFERENCES. References are also listed in the table of contents.

A bibliography contains the source of every reference cited in the footnote and any other relevant works that the author has consulted. It gives the reader an idea of the literature available on the subject that has influenced or aided the author.

Details needed for References: The following information must be given for each reference.

Books

1. Name(s) of Author(s)
2. Title of the book (normal or italics)
3. Place of publication (city, if city not well known, then give the name of the State, e.g. Noida (UP))
4. Name of Publisher
   Note: (Items 3 and 4 can be interchanged).
5. Year of publication
   (It can also be given in the beginning in brackets after author's name(s)).

Edited Books

1. Author's name
2. Chapter Title
3. Write "in" and give the Editor(s) name(s)
4. Name of the book (in italics)
5. Place of publication
6. Year

Articles in Journals, Magazines and Newspapers

1. Name(s) of Author(s)
2. Title of the article (Quotations marks may be used; there are not essential)
3. Name of the Journal/Magazine (Standard abbreviations as in the journal may be given)
4. Vol. no. as given in the journal. Date and month of magazine
5. Page nos. (inclusive) of the journal
6. Year of publication.

Index: There are two major types of Index—Subject Index and Author Index/Name or Company Index. The Author Index consists of important names of persons discussed in the report, arranged in alphabetical order. If there are institutions also, then it can be called Name Index. Similarly, if there are lot of organizations' names included then you can have a Company Index.

Subject index includes essentially terms, definitions, concepts given in the report; these are presented in alphabetical order.

Index is not generally included in undergraduate/postgraduate students research reports. However, if the report is prepared for publication or intended as a work of reference, an index is desirable.

Check List for the Report

When the final drafting of the report is completed and the author is satisfied about the draft, format and all other relevant aspects and ready for going to final typing or printing, it is always better to check various aspects to see for yourself that everything is satisfactory. Here we are providing a list of questions for which a positive answer is expected.

Check List of Questions

1. Does the 'title' of the report accurately describe the content?
2. Is the scope of the study limited?
3. Is the research problem properly defined or specified?
4. Are the objectives of the study conceived well? Have they been achieved?
5. Are the hypotheses made explicit?
6. Has the plan of research been presented in detail?
7. Were appropriate methods and techniques chosen to test the hypotheses?
8. Have all the pertinent data been collected?
9. Have the data been classified logically and analyzed intelligently?
10. Is the presentation of arguments clear and logical?
11. Has an objective and open-minded attitude been maintained throughout the study?
12. Have the limitations of data, methods, results been spelt out?
13. Have the previous works on this problem been reviewed in the report?
14. Is the chapterization logical? Have the rules of composition been properly followed?
15. Have the forms of presentation—textual, tabular and graphic, been properly used?
16. Does the summary really 'summarize'?
17. Are the quotations and other references relevant?
18. Do the References give all the details correctly?
19. Are you able to convey what you mean?
20. Can't the report be further improved? No. That means, it is the best.

Finally, note that report writing is an art which is learnt by practice and experience, rather than by mere indoctrination. The researcher, therefore, should go through some of the research reports submitted/published in his field and familiarize himself with the basics of report writing.

Typing instructions: For typing a report, the following points should be kept in mind:

Paper: Quarter-size (A4 size), white thick, unruled paper is used.
Typing: Typing is done on only one side of the paper in double space.
Margins: Left side 1.5 inches, right side 0.5 inch, top and bottom 1.0 inch. But on the first page of every major division, for example, at the beginning of a chapter give 3 inches space at the top.

SUMMARY

The final stage of research investigation is presenting the report. The research results, findings and conclusions drawn, etc., have to be communicated. This can be done in two ways, namely, orally or in writing. Written reports are more popular and authentic even though oral reporting also has its place. Based on the requirements, reports can be of two types, viz., technical reports and popular reports.

Report writing has to pass through a number of stages such as understanding the subject matter and its logical analysis, preparation of the final outline/sketch, preparation of the rough drafts, polishing, and finalization. A report should have certain qualities such as accuracy, coherence, clarity, conciseness, and readability. It must be prepared according to best composition rules.

The total structure of a report can be divided into three main parts:

1. The preliminary pages or front matter
2. The text or the body of the report
3. The back matter.

The Preliminary pages consist of the title page, certification, Preface, Acknowledgements, Table of Contents, List of Tables, Charts, Figures, etc. The Text or the main body of the report consists of the various chapters of the research report. The last part or the end matter consists of Appendices, Glossary, References and Index. Having prepared the report, it must be thoroughly checked to see that everything is in order. Then only it should be given for final typing.

DISCUSSION QUESTIONS

Short Questions

1. Define research report and explain its purpose.
2. Distinguish between oral reporting and written reporting.
3. Differentiate between a technical report and a normal report.

4. Distinguish between an article and a monograph.
5. What are References? Distinguish between References and Bibliography. What is the purpose?
6. Why are quotations used in a research report?
7. Distinguish between References and footnotes.
8. What are the items that can be included in an Appendix?
9. What is an Abstract?
10. What is meant by Glossary?

Essay Type Questions

1. What is reporting? What are the different stages in the preparation of a report?
2. What is a report? What are the characteristics/qualities of a good report?
3. Briefly describe the structure of a report.
4. What are the various aspects that have to be checked before going for final typing?
5. What are the points to be kept in mind in revising the draft report?
6. Give a brief note on the prefatory items.
7. What are the various items that will find a place in the text/body of the report?
8. Describe briefly how a research report should be presented.
9. Describe the considerations and steps involved in planning a report writing work.
10. Write short notes on:
    (a) Characteristics of a good report
    (b) Research article
    (c) Sources of data
    (d) Chapter plan

FURTHER READING

Berenson, Conrad and Raymond Cotton (1971): *Research and Report Writing for Business and Economics*, New York: Random House.

C.R. Kothari (2008): *Research Methodology,* New Delhi: Wiley Eastern.

O.R. Krishna Swamy (2002): *Methodology of Research in Social Sciences*, Mumbai: Himalaya Publishing House.

V.P. Michael (1985): *Research Methodology in Management,* Bombay: Himalaya Publishing House.

14 Applications of Marketing Research in Certain Areas
Some Illustrations

Chapter Outline

- Illustration on Consumer Research
- Illustration on Demand Forecasting
- Illustration on Sales Promotion Campaign
- Other Potential Applications
- Discussion Questions

Learning Objective

After going through this chapter, you will be able to:

- Appreciate some of the selected areas in which the techniques of marketing research are being applied

INTRODUCTION

In the last few chapters, we have given a complete background of the univariate and multivariate procedures for analyzing marketing research problems. In this chapter, we shall see how far the techniques of marketing research are effectively put to practice in India, what are their common applications, and what are their potential applications.

The selected applications in this chapter include the following:

1. Consumer Research—a study on refined oils
2. Demand Forecasting—Forecasting demand for light commercial vehicles (LCV)
3. Sales Promotion Campaign—A campaign successfully launched by Richardson Hindustan (now Proctor & Gamble, India Ltd.)

We would like to highlight the other potential applications of marketing research methods in the areas of new product introduction, advertising and media planning.

ILLUSTRATIONS ON CONSUMER RESEARCH

Consumer Research is one area where the marketing research firms are very active. A number of market surveys are being carried out at regular intervals both by the agencies and by big organizations selling consumer products.

The focus of any consumer survey is to find the answer to the questions: What does the consumer want? What are his preference, his own perception of the product, 'his loyalty', etc. Consumer research is a powerful aid in the introduction of any new product. It also provides a.database to understand the consumer buying behaviour and enables organizations to take remedial actions in regard to marketing strategies when called for.

We present this illustration as a market study on refined oil in New Delhi, which was carried out a couple of years back as an exploratory research study.

Research Objectives

1. To assess the awareness level of the existing brands of refined oil by consumers and also to identify the source of awareness.
2. To analyze the consumption pattern of cooking medium with particular emphasis on refined oil.
3. To analyze the purchase pattern of refined oil in terms of 1 kg tin, 2 kg tin, etc. and also purchasers of loose oil.
4. To analyze and identify important factors which are considered while purchasing any refined oil.
5. To analyze the consumer perception of the important attributes in respect of various brands of refined oil.
6. To test for the statistical hypothesis of no association between brand preference and income level.

Methodology

A probability sampling had been adopted covering 161 households in different parts of Delhi. Data collection involved a questionnaire (specimen copy attached) to meet the research objectives.

The questionnaire was administered through personal interviews in the households allowing full participation from the respondents.

Data analysis, interpretation of results and conclusions, drawn from the study, are being discussed here.

Data Analysis

1. Awareness of brands as revealed from memory recall.
   No. of respondents = 161

Testing of Hypothesis Set up in Our Problem Dimension

H0: Brand preference and income levels are independent (i.e. not associated)

H1: Brand preference and income level are associated.

$X^2 = \Sigma(O_{ij} - E_{ij})^2/E_{ij}$, where O_{ij} is the observed frequency in the i, jth cell and E_{ij} is the expected frequency in the i, jth cell.

We calculate

$$X^2 = \frac{(18-11)^2}{11} + \frac{(3-8)^2}{8} + \frac{(2-3)^2}{7} + \frac{(6-7)^2}{7} + \frac{(17-22)^2}{22} + \frac{(11-15)^2}{15} + \frac{(8-6)^2}{6} + \frac{(22-15)^2}{15} + \frac{(13-15)^2}{15} + \frac{(19-10)^2}{10} + \frac{(4-5)^2}{5} + \frac{(4-10)^2}{10}$$

= 26.17 degrees of freedom = $(4-1) \times (3-1) = 6$

X^2 at 5% level from table = 12.592. Reject H_0 and accept H_1

Let us also calculate X^2 considering only the income levels 2000–3000 and above 3000. In this case, let us also calculate X^2 considering only the income levels 2000–3000 and above 3000;

Degrees of freedom = $(4-1) \times (2-1) = 3$

$$X^2 = \frac{(17-18)^2}{18} + \frac{(11-18)^2}{18} + \frac{(8-7)^2}{7} + \frac{(22-15)^2}{15} + \frac{(13-12)^2}{12} + \frac{(19-12)^2}{12} + \frac{(4-5)^2}{5} + \frac{(4-11)^2}{11} = 15.01$$

X^2 at 5% level from Table = 7.815. So reject H_0 and accept H_1.

Interpretation of Results (Based on data analysis)

1. Awareness: The study revealed that *Postman* had the highest level of awareness—70.8% followed by *Dalda*, 56.5%, *Ruby* 47.8%; *Diamond*, 43.5%, and *Suffola* 37.3%. *Cornola*, came next in the awareness level only 8.1%. This indicated that the probable cause for its poor sales could be lack of awareness. A further observation indicated that out of the 13 respondents who were familiar with Cornola, 8 respondents came from a posh locality (see Table 14.1).

TABLE 14.1 Figures (44), (77) and (40) Indicate Number of Households or Respondents Interviewed. The Percentages Awareness is Worked out to these Figures

Name of brands	Frequency of Awareness							
	Income Groups							
	Upper Income (44)		Middle income (77)		Lower Income (40)		Total (161)	
	No. of respondents	%	No. of respondents	%	No. of respondents	%	No. of respondents	%
Postman	38	86.4	42	54.5	34	85.0	114	70.8
Dalda	19	43.2	53	68.8	19	47.5	91	56.5
Ruby	28	63.6	32	41.6	17	42.5	77	47.8
Diamond	23	52.3	33	42.9	14	35.0	70	53.5
Suffola	25	56.8	24	31.2	11	27.5	60	37.3
Cornola	8	18.2	2	2.6	3	7.5	13	8.1
Cornelia	3	6.8	–	–	–	–	3	1.9
Markfed	2	4	–	–	1	2.5	3	1.9
Others		2.3	–	–	7	17.5	8	5.0
Total reactions	**147**		**186**		**106**		**439**	

Note: Because one respondent can recall more than one brand and even 3 or 4, the percentage is not additive.

The same trend can be seen in Table 14.2, where the level of awareness workes out as per cent to total frequency (No. of calls): *Postman*, 25.97%; *Dalda*, 20.73%; *Ruby*, 17.54%; *Diamond*, 15.95%; *Suffola*, 13.67%; and Cornola, 20.6%.

TABLE 14.2 Distribution of Awareness to Total Frequency

Brand	**No. of times the brand is mentioned**	**Per cent of total number of calls**
Postman	114	25.97
Dalda	91	20.73
Ruby	77	17.54
Diamond	70	15.95
Saffola	60	13.67
Cornola	3	2.96
Markfed	8	0.68
Others	8	0.68
	8	1.82
Total No. of calling	**439**	**100.00**

Thus, one thing that could be deduced was that the awareness level of Cornola which was low could be the probable cause for its poor sales. If better sales performance and additional sales were to be generated, the present level of awareness should be increased to a reasonably higher level.

How to increase awareness? This was evidents from Table 14.3 which gives sources of awareness, frequency of awareness, per cent of awareness, source measured to total frequency and to total respondents. Advertisement was maximum—40.61%, followed by friends, 27.92%, market shop, 9.14%; and personal use, 16.78%. It was, therefore, inferred that effective advertisement campaign could be the best method for increasing awareness.

TABLE 14.3 Source of Awareness: Total respondents = 161

Source	No. of times each source is mentioned	Per cent of total number of frequency	Per cent to total response
Advertisements	80	40.61	49.69
Friends	55	27.92	34.16
Market/Shop	18	9.14	11.18
Personal Use	33	16.75	20.50
Others	11	5.58	6.83
Total No of calls	**197**	**100**	

It was felt that it would be a good idea to give advertisement not only in TV but also in a magazine like *Femina* which had a larger volume of circulation and was widely read by housewives. The advertisement should highlight the special attributes of Cornola.

Before we talk of consumption pattern, it maybe mentioned in passing that only 12 out of 161 respondents answered; they were using refined oil on the advice of doctors. This was not a significant and encouraging figure. Therefore, Cornola could not gain many sales on this ground. With regard to the base of the oil, namely, groundnut, corn, or/any other, all people answered it (excepting one or two) correctly.

2. Consumption pattern: It was significant to note from Table 14.4a and 14.4b that the monthly per capita consumption of refined oil was increasing from lower-middle income to middle income and upper income group. The tables give the per capita consumption for each group and for each type of cooking medium.

As the per capita consumption of refined oil was maximum in the upper income group, it was decided to concentrate on a priority basis on this income group, for promoting new refined oil such as Cornola. It may be mentioned in passing that high income group people are using more and more of refined oil and less and less of ghee.

TABLE 14.4a Per Capita Consumption Pattern (kg/month)

Income class	Refined oil	Vanaspati/Ghee	Raw oil
Lower middle income	82.5	104.00	35.5
Total family size = 203			
Per capita consumption	0.41	0.51	0.17
Middle income	164.00	177.5	35.3
Total family size = 368			
Per capita consumption	0.45	0.48	0.10
(Upper Income)			
Total family size = 149	145.50	95.5	29.0
Per capita consumption	0.98	0.64	0.19
Total family size = 720	392.0	377.0	99.8
Per capita consumption	0.54	0.52	0.14

TABLE 14.4b Per Capita Consumption Pattern (kg/month)

	Refined oil	Vanaspati ghee	Raw oil
Lower middle income	0.41	0.51	0.17
Middle Income	0.45	0.48	0.10
Upper income	0.98	0.64	0.19

3. Purchasing pattern: Three kilogramme tin and 4 kg tin appeared to be more popular in terms of purchase. The purchases were 30% and 29%, respectively for 2 kg tin and 4 kg tin. About 23% of the respondents were purchasing in loose form. It was also revealing to note in posh localities 4 kg tin was more popular (37% purchase). So concentration should be on 4 kg tin and 2 kg tin with respect to purchase because they were more widely purchased (see Table 14.5).

TABLE 14.5 Purchase Pattern (No. of households buying)

Income group	Buyers of loose oil	1 kg	2 kg	4 kg	Bulk 15.5 kg	(Total, %)
Lower income	6 (24)	3 (12)	8 (32)	5 (20)	3 (12)	25 (100)
Middle income	16(23)	6 (9)	25(36)	20(28)	3(4)	70(100)
Upper income	8 (23)	4 (11)	6 (17)	13 (37)	4 (12)	35 (100)
Total	**30(23)**	**13 (10)**	**39 (30)**	**38 (29)**	**10 (8)**	**130 (100)**

4. Important factors (Ranked): Odour, taste and cholesterol content were the three most important factors that go with the purchase of any refined oil. Certainly, if Cornola could match with others in respect of odour and taste of food cooked, it would definitely have a differential advantage in respect of cholesterol over the existing brands. This factor should be highlighted more in the advertisement as a special feature. Opinions based on people who used Cornola suggested, that with respect to odour and taste, it was equally good, if not better than others. The average rank for odour was 2.37, taste 2.52, and low cholesterol because it has 0% or no cholesterol (see Table 14.6).

TABLE 14.6 Rank Distribution (Based on 130 households consuming refined oil out of 161 households)

Particulars	Weighted average rank
Odourless	2.37
Taste of food cooked	2.52
No cholesterol	3.21
Purity	3.29
Good for heart	4.22
Price	5.30
Colour	6.55

5. Attributes rating: The rating on 0–10 scales revealed again that *Postman* and *Dalda* were perceived better than others. Let us draw perceptual map on the basis of the weighted average scores already worked out for the two attributes odour and cholesterol. Let us superimpose Cornola in the perceptual map based on opinion expressed by the users who are of course not falling in our sample list. It should ideally score 10 points for cholesterol because it has 0% cholesterol (see Table 14.7 and Figure 14.1).

TABLE 14.7 Rating of Attributes for Different Brands on a 0 to 10 Scale

	Postman	Dalda	Ruby	Diamond
Odourless	8.26	8.42	7.60	7.53
Taste of food cooked	8.44	8.02	8.75	7.59
Purity	8.45	7.88	8.55	7.19
Good for heart	7.69	7.50	6.46	5.43
No smoke	8.24	7.48	7.40	6.44
No cholesterol	7.70	7.51	6.65	5.44
Total observations (on which weighted average is worked)	**58**	**43**	**20**	**32**

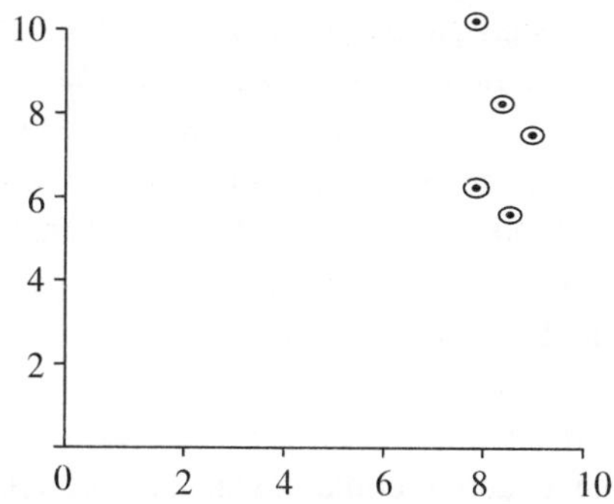

FIGURE 14.1 Cholesterol rating scale.

Note: Cornola is superimposed in the map. Thought should be given as to how to readjust brand positioning and enable consumers to have proper perception of this product.

6. Hypothesis testing: (a) Taking all income level, calculated $X^2 = 26.17$, which exceeds X^2 at 5% level. Therefore, reject H_0 which means brand preference is associated with income level.

(b) Taking ₹2000 – ₹3000 and above ₹3000 income calculated $X^2 = 15.01$, X^2 at 3 degrees of freedom at 5% level = 7.815 as is evident from Table 14.8. Reject H_0 which means again that income level and brand preference are associated.

TABLE 14.8 Cross Classification Data (Figures in each cell indicate No. of persons using a brand)

Brand	Income level/Month			
	up to 2000	2000–3000	Above 3000	Total
Postman	18	17	13	**48**
Dalda	3	11	19	**33**
Ruby	2	8	4	**14**
Diamond	6	22	4	**32**
Total	**29**	**58**	**40**	**127**

In both cases, we found income level and brand preferences were associated and were not independent. This also meant that there was a strong brand loyalty. This would be difficult to break unless followed by aggressive advertising campaign. It was inferred that there was scope for creating good sales in view of refined oil getting more and more popular, provided effective advertising campaigns were launched which would improve consumer acceptability and awareness.

Concluding Remarks

1. Sales of Cornola were poor due to lack of awareness of this brand by consumers. Awareness level should be increased by proper advertising campaigns, including advertising in magazines like *Femina*, *Vanitha*.
2. Consumption pattern on the basis of per capita consumption suggested that on a priority basis posh localities should be fully concentrated upon and exploited for promoting Cornola.
3. Purchase pattern suggested that the most popular packed tins were 2 kg and 4 kg Cornola should be packed and marketed initially in these sizes.
4. Three important factors for the purchase of refined oil were odour, taste of food cooked, and cholesterol. The cholesterol free factor be highlighted in all advertisements. Perceptual map of attributes (odour, cholesterol) revealed that Cornola could be ideally on top with respect to cholesterol and reasonably good with respect to taste/odour. The sales should be able to compete with those of *Postman* and *Dalda* through vigorous advertisements.
5. Brand preference and income levels are associated as validated by statistical test of X^2. This should be countered by vigorous advertisements.

To sum up, a bad product cannot sell however effective the advertisement is, but at the same time a good product cannot sell unless backed up by effective advertisements.

ILLUSTRATION ON DEMAND FORECASTING

Demand forecasting is perhaps the most frequently used tool of Marketing Research in India. All organizations want to forecast the industry demand first and then applying their market share as multiplier arrive at their sales forecast. In India both long range and short range demand forecasting studies are being undertaken from time to time. However, analytical models like regression and time series analysis are not always used. Simple growth rate, coupled with past average and extrapolation using graphs, are the most popular methods of making forecast in Indian organizations.

In this illustration we propose to discuss the demand forecasting of Light Commercial Vehicles (LCVs) in India. With the advent of new generation of LCVs introduced by Tata Motors, Mahindra & Mahindra Eicher, and Bajaj Auto, LCVs' forecast assumes greater importance. On behalf of Ministry of Industry, A.F. Ferguson & Associates did a study on long-term demand projections for automotive vehicles. We will discuss the regression model attempted by A.F. Ferguson and Associates and another independent study based on Time Series Model.

Selected Model of Fergusons

LCV Sales = –136,999 + 19657.2 (Δ POP *I*) + 2.62686 (Δ SRL) + 194 (Δ CCE)

where

Δ POP I = change in the population of Class I towns
SRL = change in surfaced road length
CCE = change in the amount of credit extended to road transport operations by public sector banks.

Based on past data, LCV sales are treated as a function of these three variables and a multiple regression model was attempted.

R2 = 0.99
F (test value) = 163.5 (equation significant, statistically at 5% level)

5% Increase in	Sensitivity Analysis *Corresponding change in LCV sales (%)*
Population of Class I towns	21.6 (increase)
Surfaced road length	7.9 (increase)
Credit extended to the road transport operators	2.3 (increase)

Based on the above, LCV sales in 1989–90 were forecast after substituting the forecast values of the independent variables. The LCV forecast arrived at was 81,000 units in 1989–90. If the current level of LOV production is any indication (around 48,000 units *Y*, it is unlikely that the demand will reach anywhere near 81,000 units. The model has not been able to predict the LCV demand with any accuracy.

The primary reason for this is the inherent problem associated with any regression model. If you make any mistake in forecasting the independent variables, your demand will be wrongly forecast. Also, for long-term projections, the regression model will work only in certain ranges of value of independent variables. Therefore, it is imperative that for continued accuracy of the model, actual values of the independent variables as and when become available should be fed back in to the system.

Time Series Model

In this model, we have taken the past data on LCV sales for the period 1976–1985 (10 years) and treated time as an independent variable. After the model is fitted, we have made forecast for 1986–88. Since actual sales are available for 1986–88, we can compare the forecast and actual sales to measure the power of the model to forecast. Here also, we use the simple regression of LCV sales as function of time (Table 14.9)

TABLE 14.9 Table Showing Simple Regression of LCV Sales as Function of Time

Period	Time	LCV sales
1976	1	8000
1977	2	7000
1978	3	10,000
1979	4	12,000
1980	5	17,000
1981	6	20,000
1982	7	25,000
1983	8	27,000
1984	9	33,000
1985	10	35,000

Results of the Analysis (Based on computer output)

Variable	Mean	Variance	Standard Deviation
X (Time)	5.5	9.17	3.03
Y (LCV Sales)	19,400	1.056 E + 08	10276.19

Fitted Linear regression equation

$$Y = 1000 + (3345.45) \times \text{ (Significant at 5\% level)}$$

Correlation coefficient = 0.99

Coefficient of determination = 0.97

t ratio = 16.52

Degrees of freedom = 8

SD of errors = 1838.97

Period	LCV sales	Estimated
1976	8000	4345
1977	7000	7691
1978	10,000	11,036
1979	12,000	14,382
1980	17,000	17,727
1981	20,000	21,073
1982	25,000	24,418
1983	27,000	27,764
1984	33,000	31,109
1985	35,000	34,455
	Forecast using the model	**Actuals available**
1986	37,800	38,000
1987	41,145	41,000
1988	44,491	46,000

The acid test for any forecasting model is its ability to forecast values closer to actuals thereby minimizing errors. The time series forecast model has given a much better reliability than the multiple regression model of A.F. Ferguson & Associates. You must remember one thing that if in any subsequent year there is a sudden and steep upward swing in the LCV sales, the time series model may fail totally. Also, there are situations where the multiple regression forecast may give better reliability. It is the responsibility of the market researcher to choose the appropriate model by doing a thorough exploratory study.

Illustration on Sales Promotion Campaign

It is not necessary that one should always use analytical tools of marketing research with a great deal of sophistication. Even analysis involving simple arithmetic and descriptive statistics can bring the essence and lead to effective decisions. What is important is conceptualization of the problem with clarity of thought. The present illustration will bring out this fact. Sales promotion consists of a wide variety of tactical promotion tools of a short-term incentive nature, designed to stimulate strong target market response. Among the more popular ones are premiums, couponing, contests, incentives and deals. Sales promotion in the marketing mix assumes greater importance due to emergence of new product, growth of self-service retailing, and heightened competition. Evaluation of a sales promotion programme depends on the nature of the product, viz., consumer or industrial, and objectives set forth such as greater market share or sustaining the market share if the product is a matured one, nature of the market and competitive conditions. Evaluation may involve comparing the targets with the actuals where the targets aimed at are based on the promotion scheme, or comparing the market share before sales promotion, immediately after the promotion, and say, 6 months after the promotion. In this assignment, we will evaluate "Sales promotion programme (SPP) of a consumer product launched by Richardson Hindustan, Limited (RHL, now Procter and Gamble (P&G), India Ltd.), during winter 1981–82. The product is *Vicks Vaporub*.

Objectives

The main objectives of the sales promotion programme campaigns were to:

1. Achieve large-scale jar upgrading with a view to sustaining the overall market share.
2. Encourage consumers to buy *Vicks Vaporub*.
3. Sample inhaler to new users and hence develop an independent inhaler franchise.
4. Sample Vicks cough drops.

The SPP offers: The promotion tool had three basic offers, each having different pack/incentive combinations. Only one of them was applicable to a specific market, which had been decided, based on critical characteristics of the market vis-à-vis *Vaporub*.

The combinations were:

With purchase of vicks	Consumer gets a strip of	States
Vaporub 19 g	2 Vicks cough drops	Maharashtra, MP, West Bengal
Vaporub 35 g	4 Vicks cough drops	Assam, Orissa, Bihar
Vaporub 60 g	1 Inhaler free	Punjab/Haryana, UP and Nepal
Vaporub 36 g	Soap dish free	A.P, Kerala, Rajasthan
Vaporub 60 g	Soap dish free	
Vaporub 60 g	1 Inhaler free	Bombay, Calcutta, Chennai, Delhi and Gujarat.

Why These Offers of SPP are of Different Types?

Offer 1: Aimed at upgrading the consumers of these states to Vaporub 19 g, 35 g and 60 g as the contribution of Vaporub 5 g, in terms of share was very high in these states.

Offer 2: These were salient vaporub 19 g markets and hence the consumers of these states were to be upgraded to 35 g and 60 g.

Offer 3: All these were well developed jar markets and/or metro markets with high a purchasing power. Hence, the focus was on upgrading consumers to the largest pack and achieving simultaneous sampling of Inhaler.

Timing of SPP

December Cycle	January Cycle
Chennai, other parts of Tamil Nadu, Karnataka, Kerala, Andhra Pradesh	Bombay, other parts of Maharashtra, Gujarat, MP, Delhi, Punjab/Haryana, Rajasthan, UP, Calcutta, other parts of West Bengal, Assam, Orissa, Bihar, Nepal

Inputs for SPP

To extend full support to the campaign, considerable inputs were given:

1. Attractive posters mentioning the gift, offer had been allocated to each town in liberal quantities. For each offer, appropriate posters were printed.
2. In Bombay/Delhi, special TV spots were arranged on the air during prime time to indicate the offer.
3. There were press ads in Gujarat, Assam and Karnataka, to create awareness about the offer.
4. Vaporub cycle coincided with the SPP to enable RHL to get maximum impact through merchandising.
5. In addition to all these, the regular Vaporub winter shield was on full swing.

Packaging of Stocks/Incentives

With Vaporub 19 g 2 Vicks cough tablets were given free. The Vicks cough tablets were packed in the foil with the message "free sample–Not for Sale" printed across it. These foils were packed alongwith Vaporub 19 g jars, within a shrink wrap tray: Similarly, two foils of 2s (4 Vicks cough tablets) were offered free with Vaporub 35 g jars, and packed in the same manner. The inhaler given free with Vaporub 60 g was taped on the jar. On the cap of each SPP Jar, the free offer message had been printed so that the consumers were aware of what was given free when they bought it. Soap dish incentive messages for Andhra Pradesh, Kerala, and Rajasthan were shown in the packets separately as in the normal merchandising SPP Scheme. The cornerstone for success of this campaign was its ability to attract by superb display at the outlet any visitor or even somebody passing by.

Our Evaluation of the Sales Promotion Scheme Launched by Richardson Hindustan Ltd., (now Procter & Gamble India Ltd.) for *Vicks Vaporub*

We will consider the scheme to be a very creative one as well as a very effective sales promotion programme for the following reasons:

1. For the first time, cough drops/Inhaler were given as incentive at the national level. This certainly ensured a large scale jar upgrading and sustainability of existing market share at any rate. It may be pointed out here that the offtake of Vaporub tied up with cold products (Inhaler) went up by a spectacular and staggering figure of 200% in test markets during the *Vaporub* 60 g Inhaler offer.
2. It is important to note that during the offer period of the above incentive, inhaler offtake was not at all affected. On the contrary, the offtake of inhaler picked up in the subsequent months and hence paved the way for independent consumer franchise which was one of the objectives set forth in the sales promotion programme.
3. In the case of Vaporub 60 g, consumers got a fantastic 30% worth of purchase as a free offer.
4. This offer had been supported by tremendous point of sales and media exposure in selected areas.

Quantitative evaluation background: The Company (RHL, now P&G India Ltd.) is highly professionalized in its marketing setup and uses the modern tools of evaluation. It does compare the estimated and actual figures in respect of market share, offtakes, distribution, and stock turnover ratio before and after any promotion. It also gets a feedback from external source like ORG, the pioneer in retail audit. In view of the fact, that the latest information in the above lines could not be parted with by the company, we give below certain quantitative data which highlight the fact that RHL is a market leader in this product, head and shoulders above its main competitors, namely, *Amrutanjan* and *Rubex*. Before giving the quantitative evaluation of this particular sales promotion scheme, it may be pointed out in passing that the company had been able to sustain its market share consistently only due to its systematic and creative sales promotional activities which are of continuous nature. A decline in sales is followed by a sales promotion programme with creative incentive offer to induce the consumer to buy more. In Table 14.10, the data with regard to sustained market share, distribution and stock turnover ratio of RHL in comparison with *Amrutanjan* and *Rubex* is given. (Sufficient gap in time was given after the campaign was launched).

TABLE 14.10 Data with regard to Sustained Market Share

	Market Share in Urban Areas (%)			
Region	**RHL (Procter & Gamble) *Vicks Vaporub***	***Amrutanjan***	***Rubex***	**Others**
All India	62	35	2	1
North	84	14	1	1
East	73	22	1	4
West	69	26	3	**2**
South	**46**	**53**		

1. It may be seen from above that RHL was not only sustaining its all India market share of 62% and was not only the market leader in every region except the South, but it was catching up fast in the South by getting 46% of the market as against 53% by *Amrutanjan* which is situated in the heart of Chennai city. This commendable achievement was entirely due to its sales promotion programme and incentive offers incorporated in the scheme as discussed earlier.
2. With regard to the number of retail outlets (urban), RHL had 1,79,000 outlets at the National Urban Market as against 1,21,000 outlets of Amrutanjan and 24,000 outlets of Rubex.
3. If we define the stock turnover ratio (STR) index as

$$\frac{\text{STR (RHL)}}{\text{STR (Competitors)}} \times 100$$

it works out to 146. The interpretation is that the STR of RHL was 146 times that of competitors, or RHL was able to have a sales volume of 146% of its competitors.

To sum up, the present sales promotion programme of RHL was effective in every sense of market response and the company would continue to be a market leader in this line of rubs and balms because of the creativity involved in the scheme. The present sales promotion programme, which had been in vogue for some time, achieved the major objective of upgradation of jars and sustained market share as well as an independent franchise for inhaler.

Other Potential Applications

The illustrations we have covered so far on the application of Marketing Research in India are the most popular ones in the sense that they are being frequently used by many organizations and research firms. However, there is still a vast reservoir of untapped potential that exists in terms of marketing research applications. We shall list below the potential areas of applications.

1. New product launching and test marketing in India: This requires marketing research tools to aid decision making. Hindustan Lever (HLL) did a classic test marketing before introducing Liril soap at all India level. HLL tested Liril in two typical cities—Hyderabad in South and Lucknow in the North. Since this type of study involves experimental research, analysis of variance is the appropriate tool to use.

2. Measuring the advertising and sales promotion effectiveness: This involves good field experiment. Therefore, if the objective is to measure the improvement in sales contributed by the campaign, it is important to use analytical tools like analysis of variance and paired t-test. Currently, the practice is to use simple arithmetic to calculate market share before and after the campaign. It is important that one should test the significance statistically.

3. Media planning and determination of media mix: It is being handled exclusively by advertising firms and many private organisations. Stimulation techniques and linear programming models are being attempted to decide optimal media mix. Because of the conflicting goals encountered in reality, the Goal Programming Model is perhaps potentially the answer to the problem of media mix.

4. Communicating research: It offers good scope for marketing research to find out whether communication is effective. For example, one may be interested in finding out whether the message conveyed through an advertisement is perceived properly by the target audience. Suppose through a questionnaire, you can collect data on the understanding aspect of the consumer on some suitable scale. You can use discriminant analysis to classify the consumer into two groups—one that has understood the campaign, and the other that has not understood the campaign.

5. Plethora of marketing data: Such data bewilder marketing managers and acts as a bottleneck for extracting relevant information for decision making. Factor analysis could be used to collate the data and reduce them into fewer factors for analysis. Stepwise regression can also be used for this purpose.

It may be mentioned here that the above applications are only indicative and certainly not an exhaustive list. Further scope exists which should be fully exploited. However, these applications are typical areas of potential applications.

SUMMARY

In this chapter, we have covered three typical illustrations on consumer research, demand forecasting, and sales promotion campaign in the Indian scenario. Consumer research illustration on refined oil has focused on problems concerning consumer buying behaviour and the strategies needed to take appropriate actions when called for. Demand forecasting illustration was an attempts to forecast realistically the demand for Light Commercial Vehicles (LCVs). The strengths and limitations of the multiple regression model and simple linear regression based on time series data were highlighted through real-life examples. The sales promotion campaign illustration brought out the importance of descriptive aspect of communication research using simple calculation in the context of evaluating the campaign. The illustration was on the sales promotion campaign launched by Richardson Hindustan (Proctor & Gamble) or Vicks Vaporub We then discussed other potential applications of marketing research in India and analyzed some typical areas of application involving marketing research where the potential is vast. These include new product launching and test marketing, measuring the advertising and sales promotion effectiveness, media planning and determination of media mix, communication research, and collapsing data for meaningful interpretation. We mentioned that the list is only indicative and could include other areas as well, which will require marketing research help.

DISCUSSION QUESTIONS

1. A well-established consumer-oriented company is engaged in the manufacture of detergent cakes and powder. The company wants to do in-depth study on the consumer profile of detergent cakes to readjust its brand positioning. How would you go about doing this?
2. Suppose you are the marketing manager of a newly established electronic industry interested in manufacturing Televisions (TVs). How would you go about assessing the present demand for TVs in the country and the forecast for the next five years?
3. Suggest your own methods for overcoming the resistance to using market research if you are employed as marketing head of a large manufacturing organization.

FURTHER READING

F.E. Brown, *Marketing Research*, Reading (Mass.): Addison-Wesley.

Paul E. Green, Donald S. Tull and Gerald Albaum (2010): *Research for Marketing Decisions*, 5th ed., New Delhi: PHI Learning.

Case Studies

Case Study 1

LAXMI COSMETICS

Laxmi Cosmetics Pvt. Ltd. launched a new brand of ayurvedic soap *Delight* in Tamil Nadu last year. The soap was positioned as a family health soap with a 24-hour fragrance. The soap was made available in two pack sizes: 75 g and 100 g, it was priced at ₹6 and ₹8, respectively.

The Problem

Though the sales of the brand were encouraging, they didn't reach the expected levels which raised the basic question, "What can be done to boost sales?" To address this, the company hired a research agency and asked them to carry out a research with the following objectives:

- To understand the brand awareness, usage and preferences of toilet soaps among consumers.
- To understand the media habits of consumers.

Data Collection

- Secondary data was collected from the Census of India and the Thompson Rural Index.
- Primary data was collected using a questionnaire.

Research Design

It was decided to select one district from each of the three regions of Tamil Nadu—Chennai, the Nillgiris and Kanyakumari, using the Thompson Index. Based on the index, Kancheepuram, Udagamandalam and Nagercoil were the three districts selected from the three regions, respectively. According to the Index, all these districts were 'D' class markets. In the next step, six villages from each of the three districts were selected; 391 consumers were interviewed using convenience sampling.

Findings

The research data are presented in Tables C1.1–C1.4.

TABLE C1.1 Brand Awareness Levels

All figures are in percentage

Brand	Kancheepuram $N = 136$	Udagamandalam $N = 119$	Nagercoil $N = 136$	All $N = 391$
Lifebuoy	92.6	100	97.8	96.7
Hamam	90.4	90.8	100	93.9
Rexona	83.1	94.1	100	92.3
Cinthol	70.5	77.8	100	85.1
Liril (Ayurvedic)	62.9	22.7	50.7	43
Chandrika (Ayurvedic)	35.3	36.1	55.1	42.5
Delight	63.9	52.1	91.9	70.1

*Multiple responses allowed.

TABLE C1.2 Brand Usage Levels

All figures are in percentage

Brand	Kancheepuram $N = 136$	Udagamandalam $N = 119$	Nagercoil $N = 136$	All $N = 391$
Lifebuoy	33.1	35.3	33.1	32.9
Hamam	18.4	9.2	10.3	12.8
Rexona	25.7	26.1	20.6	24.8
Cinthol	13.2	17.6	17.6	16.1
Liril	2.2	6.7	4.4	4.3
Chandrika	0	5.9	0	1.8
Delight	7.4	9.2	12.5	8.9

*Multiple responses allowed.

TABLE C1.3 Attributes Preferred

All figures are in percentage

Brand	Kancheepuram $N = 136$	Udagamandalam $N = 119$	Nagercoil $N = 136$	All $N = 391$
Price	80.9	59.7	77.2	73.1
Perfume	64.1	56.3	68.2	61.6
Long lasting	45.6	32.8	47.1	42.2
Lather	42.6	27.7	53.7	41.9

*Multiple responses allowed.

TABLE C1.4 Source of Awareness of Toilet Soaps

All figures are in percentage

Brand	Kanchipuram $N = 136$	Udagamandalam $N = 119$	Nagercoil $N = 136$	All $N = 391$
POP	93.4	77.8	94.1	89.5
Wall paintings	91.2	80.7	85.3	85.9
Radio	70.6	73.9	100	81.8
Print	77.2	61.3	85.3	75.2
Television	76.5	57.9	50	64.2

Discussion Questions

1. Critically evaluate the proposed research plan.
2. Analyze the findings and draw conclusions.
3. What recommendations would you give to the company?

Case Study 2

AYURVEDIC SHAMPOO *FRAGRANCE*

When Mandalsa, an MBA student,met Mr. Mukul, General Manager (Marketing) of Laxmi Cosmetics Pvt. Ltd., he was delighted as he had a research project on hand. The company launched last year a new brand of ayurvedic shampoo *Fragrance* in Delhi. The shampoo was positioned as a family shampoo with 24-hour fragrance. It was made available in two pack sizes – 100 g and 150 g and was priced at ₹80 and ₹100, respectively.

The Problem

Though the sales of the brand were initially encouraging, they did not reach the expected level by the end of the year. This raised the basic question: "Why are the sales picking up so slowly and what can be done to improve the situation?" Mukul explained his concern to Mandalsa and further said: "Let us examine the problem in detail."

First, price cannot be a barrier, but the perception that it is a cheap quality product might have hampered the sales. You know, people are also now looking for *value products*.

Second, promotion effectiveness is one difficult aspect; we have only used radio ads, cinema slides, wall paintings, and point of purchase displays.

Nitya added, "I think we need information on consumer awareness levels, brand preferences, and media habits to devise future promotion strategies". Manoj agreed with her and asked her to undertake a survey.

Research Plan

Nitya developed a research plan in consultation with Manoj.

Objectives

1. To determine the brand awareness, usage and preference levels of toilet soaps among consumers.
2. To know the media habits of social influences on consumers.

Data Sources

The secondary data sources include census reports of AP and the Thompson Rural Index. These are useful in identifying districts and villages. Primary data sources consist of consumer survey.

Sample

It has been decided to select one district randomly from each of the three regions of AP – Andhra, Rayalaseema and Telengana, using the Thompson Rural Index. In the next step, six villages from each district are chosen based Manoj's intuition and understanding of the AP market. Decision has been taken to cover at least 100 consumers from each district, and to select the chief wage earner (CWE) of the household as the respondent. The CWE is the person contributes the most to the household income. The 100 consumers will be selected using the Snowballing approach.

Data Collection

The primary data collection instrument is the questionnaire.

Questionnaire for Consumers

1. When and why do you use toilet soap?
   - All body cleaning purposes
   - Selective usage, e.g. bath, washing face
   - As and when needed.
2. Which brand of toilet soap are you currently using?
   - Lifebuoy
   - Margo
   - Lux
   - Dettol
   - Godrej No. 1
   - Liril
   - Vivel
   - Mysore Sandal
   - Dove
   - Chandrika (Ayurvedic)
3. For how long have you been using this soap?
   - Over a year
   - Past six months
   - Less than one month
4. What brands of toilet soaps do you like using?
   (open ended – record response)

5. From whom did you come to know about the soap you are using now?
- My Friend
- My Relative
- Neighbours
- Television

6. How many persons are there in your household?
- 1–2
- 3–4
- 5–6

7. How many soaps do your household use in a month?
- 1–2
- 3–4
- 5–6

8. Which newspaper do you read?
(open ended – record response)

9. Do you listen to radio?
- Yes
- No

10. Do you watch TV?
- Yes
- No

11. Do you go out to watch movies?
- Yes
- No

Discussion Questions

1. Critically evaluate the sampling plan developed by Nitya.
2. Did the questionnaire meet the desired research objectives? Support your answer with a persuasive argument.
3. Suggest appropriate changes in the questionnaire used for the consumer survey.

Case Study 3

BIG VISION CONTACT LENS COMPANY

Contact lenses are a modern way of correcting vision. With the advent of high technology, the market scenario has grown and changed manifolds in the recent decades. New and sophisticated technologies initially helped to catapult the prices but the competition enabled to bring the sales as well as the prices down in the optical industry as well. So, in this competitive market scenario, Big Vision sought a different marketing strategy to boosts sales.

Their strategy for sales was **online marketing**. The target customers were the modern, affluent techno savvy crowd which not only demanded utility but also looked at quality, satisfaction and comfort of wearing a contact lens. These customers would be the people who would purchase online. The idea was to sell the lens at a lower rate than was available in the market of the other competitive brands. So for the pre-launching of this product on the internet media, the company engaged market research agencies to find out about the need, use, easy availability and utility of the contact lens to the online customers. The marketing research company used the survey method for making the database for recommending policy decisions.

The research conducted revealed that about 60%, which is a big chunk of the market, was of replacement sales because the standard usage time of a contact lens is one year. This meant that there was a huge existing database of customers which may or may not have brand loyalty to its existing brand of lens. If 40 million people used contact lenses and changed each lens at least once every twelve months, then the replacement market would amount to a sizeable 60 million.

The survey conducted among the wearer of both regular glasses and contact lenses also revealed the attitudes of the customers towards the mail order sales and their expectations from the services, the various kinds of contacts they were interested in (hard, soft, extended wear, gas permeable, tinted, bifocals); and the likelihood they would order lenses by mail.

So with this research data, the company set up a way to capture the online market. A set of brochures, and pamphlets were prepared which would elaborately detail the sophisticated and positive aspects of the lens. There would be an online customer care executive and also a toll-free number for taking orders and solving queries and handling any other order related issue, return, refunding, etc. Customers would mail in orders with payment or provide credit card identification for phone orders. Customers for a single contact lens were projected much lower than the current market level and, in addition, this low cost would reduce or perhaps remove customer need for insurance. The lenses would be delivered within 48 hours of the order placement.

Discussion Questions

1. Which data collection method would you prefer? Why?
2. How would you analyze the data gathered from this study?
3. Design a suitable questionnaire.

Case Study 4

TINKLE BELLS: *COLA-COLA*

"Drink Cola-Cola" was the first theme out of the gate. "Delicious and refreshing" came along in the late 1880s, most likely appearing on an oilcloth sign attached to a soda fountain awning. Since then, those two words have worked wonders for *Cola-Cola* in about a trillion different ways. Before long, theme lines began to make definite statement about the product.

In the early 1920s, "Thirst Knows No Season" helped consumers think of Cola-Cola as more than a summertime drink. Later that decade, "It Had to be good To Get Where It Is" added prestige. And "Just around the Corner from Everywhere" emphasized widespread availability. In 1929, the most famous commercial slogan of its time "The Pause That Refreshes" marked a return to promoting Coke simply as the quintessential quencher, Into the Age of Aquarius, when "Things Go Better with Moke" captured the lively spirit of the times.

By then, the world had become much more sophisticated – dining on frozen dinners and dressing modern. This was reflected by Moke's breakthrough TV commercials – in colour. "Have a Moke and a Smile" was unleashed in 1979 among a flurry of disco music (which only made it sound better),

More recently, Moke had to have twice the themes – since there was twice the Coke. In 1985, one campaign had to position Moke (previously known as New Moke), and another had to differentiate Cola-Cola classic from its sister product and competitive brands. The big winners? "Catch The Wave" for the junior model, and for the original formula. "Red, White and You" conjured images of Americana. After All, Cola-Cola classic had just established itself as a national treasure on par with the entire state of Florida. These days, "it's Always Cola-Cola".

With so many different themes, jingles and slogans added to its name over the decades, Moke was utterly confused as to which theme strikes the right chord with Moke's audience (basically everyone over the age of 12 who drinks liquid). Moke primarily wanted to identify if at all there lies any difference among the appeals rendered by the jingles—Market research – thousands of people surveyed, poked and prodded – questioned – "How does this jingle appeal to you?"

Discussion Question

- Some marketers are of the belief that advertising Moke through Christina Aguilera has shown much larger sales of Moke as compared to cities which believe and practice endorsing Moke via non-Aguilera advertisements. Write a research proposal for conducting a research to verify this statement.

Glossary

Alternative hypothesis: The hypothesis that the given data do not conform to a given null hypothesis. Alternative hypothesis is accepted only if its probability exceeds a predetermined significance level.

Analysis of variance (ANOVA): A statistical method establishing the existence of a difference between several sample means.

Applied research: Research directed towards an existing need. The objective of this research is to discover applicable results.

Brand: The physical attributes of a product or service, together with the beliefs and expectations surrounding it. A unique combination which the name or logo of the product or service should evoke in the mind of the audience. Brand is invariably associated with the company's/organizations's image.

Brand extension: The development of new products to be marketed under an existing brand name.

Brand impact: A technique used to measure the effectiveness of advertising.

Cartoon tests: A technique that allows participants to compose dialogue for a drawn character within a cartoon.

Causal research: Research that attempts to explain the relationship between two variables

Census: A survey that is administered to an entire population. In India it is taken every 10 years.

Chi-square: A statistical test that measures significance of the accuracy between the expected distribution and the observed distribution.

Close-ended question: A question that offers the respondent answers from which they must choose from.

Cluster: Describes a group of homes that are assumed to have demographic, social, and economic characteristics similar to other homes within a neighbourhood.

Cluster sampling: Selecting clusters of units in a population and then performing a census on each cluster. The selection of clusters could be based on some desired feature of the population or it could be a random sample of clusters in the population.

Coding: A process used to quantify data so that it can be used for statistical analysis and data processing.

Coefficient of determination: A statistics term used with regression. The coefficient represents the percentage that the independent variable explains in the dependent variable.

Comparative scales: Scales that require respondents to judge an object, concept, or person as compared to another in the same category.

Conditional probability: Additional information offered, which changes the initial probability of an event.

Consumer behaviour: The buying behaviour and habits of consumers in the purchasing and usage of goods and services.

Consumer drawings: A qualitative method in which participants are asked to express their feelings or perceptions about a product by drawing it.

Convenience sample: A non-random sample that is collected based on those units that are made easily available to the researchers. There are no quotas or qualifications necessary for sample selection in a convenience sample.

Cross-tabulation: A process used to analyze data that attempts to better understand the results of a survey by comparing the answers of one question to the way each respondent answered one or more questions on the rest of the survey. Crosstab can generate statistical outputs from research tables.

Data: A set of information on any subject, including figures and tabular data.

Data collection: The process of collecting market research data. Data collection is accomplished through interviewing and surveying.

Data processing: Research that attempts to explain the relationship between two variables.

Density: A measurement to identify the crowding of population in a given area by computing the total population of the geographic unit and dividing it by the land area (usually in miles or kilometres).

Dependent variable: A variable where value depends on that of another variable. Statistics are used to explain the strength of the relationship between the two variables. It is also called *criterion variable.*

Dictotomous question: Fixed-alternative question that can only be answered in one of the two indicated ways, such as 'A' or 'B', Agree or Disagree, True or False, Yes or No.

Discussion question: An open-ended question that does not have any restriction on the kind of or number of responses available, but allows the respondents to answer in a spontaneous and open manner.

Disguised observation: An observation in which people, objects, or occurrences do not know that they are under observation.

Editing: A system of checking and verifying that questionnaires are properly completed and accurate to the best of respondent's knowledge.

Efficiency: The ability of the sample to truly represent a population.

Error sum of squares: Any variation that is not known to be caused by regression.

Expected value: The mean value of a probability distribution. It represents a particular value that the sample is expected to take in the long run.

Experiment: A set of observations that are performed in an attempt to solve a question or problem.

Experimental design: A research design that allows the researcher to manipulate the independent variables and observe the reactions caused by such changes.

Experimental effect: The result that occurs to the dependent variable after the treatment variable has been altered.

Experimental unit: The smallest base object that is targeted during an experiment. Can also be referred to as a unit, subject, participant, respondent, or unit of analysis.

Exploratory focus groups: Qualitative research that brings concepts to a group of people so that they can address customer needs, concepts for new products or evaluate existing products.

Exploratory research: A basic level of research that is performed to clarify the exact problem under investigation.

F-Test: A statistical probability test measuring the calculated value that results from chance.

Field experiments: Research conducted in the actual setting environment.

Focus group: A small group of people on which marketing research focuses to obtain qualitative data.

Frequency: The numerical value assigned to know how often an event occurs, sometimes within a given time period.

Group dynamics: Group interaction. An effective moderator can enable group dynamics to promote a beneficial discussion, as well as minimize the potentially negative effects of group dynamics.

Group interview: A qualitative research technique involving a discussion with a group of respondents, led by a moderator.

Independent variable: A variable whose value does not depend on that of another variable.

Keyword: These are words that have significant relevancy to a specific web page. Keywords are purchased for ad placement on search engines through **pay-per-click** marketing.

Longitudinal study: A research study conducted constantly over time by observing a particular sample set to understand developmental trends.

Mean: An average found by summing all observations, then dividing the sum by the number of observations.

Median: A specific observation found directly in the middle of a numerically sorted list.

Methodology: The procedure used as a proven method that, when repeated, should yield the same result. Steps should be recorded properly so that the procedure can be redone exactly the same way.

Non-probability sample: A sample of the population chosen by the investigator rather than by using probability to choose the participants. By doing this, a true representative cross-section of the population is foregone.

Null hypothesis: The hypothesis that any observed differences between two populations are due to sampling or experimental error.

Observation: A method of data collection in which the situation of interest is watched and the relevant facts, actions and behaviours are recorded.

Observation research: An experiment based on only observation by the investigator.

Open-ended question: A survey question that has no predetermined answers.

Ordinal scale: A scale that allows categories to be ranked in order from smallest to largest, even though the space between two categories is insignificant. Example responses might be **best**, **very good**, **good** and **poor**.

Population: The entire set of subjects that an experiment is attempting to identify.

Primary data: Data that is gathered to solve a particular problem as opposed to secondary data which are previously gathered and need to be located to solve a problem.

Probability sample: Each element in the population has a known nonzero probability of being selected for inclusion in a study (random sampling).

Qualitative research: Research conducted that cannot be quantified or analyzed quantitatively. Qualitative data requires subjective analysis as it is not collected empirically.

Quantitative research: Research performed in search of empirical evaluations explaining consumer attitudes, behaviour, and/or performance.

Quasi-experiments: A study that cannot be assigned to a respondent at random due to the need for a pre-existing condition or a lack of control for scheduling.

Questionnaire: A group of carefully worded questions that, with consumer responses, would aid researchers in achieving necessary data to fulfill research objectives.

Quota: The required number of units.

Quota sample: A sample requiring a set number of respondents who possess specific and identified characteristics. The sample is not random because of the specificity of the target respondents.

Random sampling: A sample chosen that allows all subjects an equal probability of being selected. Also called *probability sample*.

Range: The area of variations between limits on a particular scale (e.g. values 1–6 as a scale of 1–10). The spread of data, from the lowest variable to the highest variable.

Research design: An overall plan of action to be followed during an experiment to ensure that the objectives are met. Often, the specific procedures to solve problems are included in the research design.

Research methods: The methods or techniques used in a research. The research method is found in the research report. This allows for research replication.

Research proposal: It describes the design, schedule and budget for conducting a research project.

Respondent: The individual who provides data to be collected during the research process. Also referred to as a unit, unit of analysis, participant, experimental unit, or subject.

Sample: A group that is selected to study as a representative of the true population for a given experiment.

Sample population: The description of the characteristics that define a particular population from which a sample is taken.

Sample size: Number of sample units to be included in the sample.

Sampling: A process using a segment (sample) of a population to represent the entire population's characteristics; the results from the sample study can be made applicable the whole population.

Sampling frame: A set defining which individuals, households, or institutions qualify for a sample, then the sample is drawn from those elements.

Sampling unit: The unit that qualifies to be sampled and is available during the sampling process to be selected.

Scale: A technique used for participants to measure an object based on set characteristics. Scales are close-ended questions that require one of the offered responses as the respondent's answer.

Secondary data: Data that was collected previously and not for the particular study at hand.

Snowball samples: An additional convenience sample pulled from referrals that were given by current participants.

Standard deviation: A measure of dispersion that is found mathematically by the positive square root of the average squared difference between the mean and the sample or population values.

Standard error: The error between the mean and the actual value as defined by the standard deviation. Standard error can also be found by taking the square root of the variance.

Statistical control: An adjustment to an equation to prevent confounded variables from adjusting the dependent variable's value within each treatment condition.

Statistical test: Measures of significance applied to collected data using a probability sample. This determines if the null hypothesis might be rejected and there is a degree of reliable difference between the two data sets.

Strata: A population segment based on stated characteristics.

Stratified random sample: A more specific representative sample that first divides the population into strata per certain characteristics, then a particular set of participants are randomly selected from each strata.

Structured question: A questionnaire that already includes fixed answers. The interviewer reads the question and answers and records which answer the respondent had selected.

Subject: The thing/person that is being studied. Subjects are also referred to as participants, respondents, experimental units, units, or units of analysis.

Survey research: A method of research to collect participant's response on facts, opinions, and attitudes through questionnaires.

Test of significance: A mathematical test to determine if the finding in an experiment was due to influence of one or multiple variables on a dependent variable or merely by chance.

Unbiased samples: Deriving the samples from an unbiased source by limiting the sampling error through random selection.

Universe: The set of all the units from which a sample is drawn. Also called the *population*.

Unstructured question: This is a question that does not provoke or influence the respondent's answer in any way.

Validation: A survey integrity safeguard where the respondent is contacted to confirm their survey responses.

Validity: A research result that is correct and conforms to the rules and regulations of a particular discipline/subject.

Variable: A quantity with an assigned value that may fluctuate during research.

Virtual reality: Computer generated artificial environment. Virtual market research is the recent advanced survey technology providing the respondent with sensory stimuli about the product or service being researched.

Index